World Heritage Monuments

and

Related Edifices

in India

World Heritage Monuments

and

Related Edifices

in India

Volume I

Ali Javid
Tabassum Javeed

Algora Publishing
New York

ISBN-13: 978-0-87586-482-8 (trade paper)
ISBN-13: 978-0-87586-483-9 (hard cover)
ISBN-13: 978-0-87586-484-6 (ebook)

Library of Congress Cataloging-in-Publication Data —

Javid, Ali.
  World heritage monuments and related edifices in India / Ali Javid, Tabassum Javeed.
     p. cm.
  Includes bibliographical references and index.
   ISBN 978-0-87586-482-2 (trade paper: alk. paper) — ISBN 978-0-87586-483-9 (hard cover:
alk. paper) — ISBN 978-0-87586-484-6 (ebook) 1. Temples, Hindu--India. 2. Mosques—India.
3. Monuments—India. 4. Cultural property—India. 5. World Heritage areas—India. I. Javeed,
Tabassum. II. Title.

   NA6001.J28 2008
   709.54—dc22
                        2007052806

Front Cover: Bhubanesvara. Lingaraja temple. Decorations on Tower, 11-12th century,
sandstone (photo by the Author).

Printed in the United States

To my grandchildren
Saher, Jasmine, Samir, Nadim, Alma, Nihad and Navid,
who asked every day when I would finish my writing —
especially Samir, who wanted to know
where he could purchase the book when published.

Table of Contents

PREFACE

This book is the result of my visits to World Heritage sites in India and the monuments associated with them, to enjoy the depiction of human beauty in decorative sculpture and architecture and the narration of mythology therein.

I have included a synopsis of India's religions and religious monuments for readers unfamiliar with Indian cultures. I have limited vernacular terminology but included many photographs to illuminate the evolution of the monuments presented. The location of these monuments is shown in the map of India.

To denote the time, the following abbreviations are used. Prehistoric period is "BP" (Before Present). The era before Christ is "BCE" (Before Common Era). The era after the death of Christ is denoted as "CE" (Common Era). To avoid repetition, for the period after the fifth century, CE abbreviations are omitted.

My primary guides in this study were *The Art of Ancient India* by Susan Huntington and *The Art of Indian Asia: Its Mythology and Transformation* by Heinrich Zimmer. I also have leaned heavily on other publications listed in the Bibliography.

The person who helped me the most with my writing is Dr. Tabassum Javeed, Department of Philosophy and Religion, Bangalore University.

The late Dr. C. B. Kurdikeri also assisted me tremendously by insisting I pursue my writing and by withstanding the hardship of travel with me in south India. I miss him very much. Dr. Shanta Ratnayaka, Professor of Religions, University of Georgia at Athens was kind enough to review my manuscript and suggest improvements. His input on Buddhism was invaluable. I am indebted to Mrs. Irshad Javid for proofreading the manuscript and for as-

sistance in presenting the Hindu mythology. I am much indebted to Ms. Janice Levie, a technical writer who assisted in formatting the manuscript and helped in preparing the index.

My children Fiaz financed my travels to South-East Asia and Central America and allowed me the use of his office facilities and equipment, while Parviz and Samina led me through the computer programs for preparing the transcript and photographs. My friend Sagheer Akif traveled with me on most of my journeys. I am indebted to my wife Anser for traveling with me in India and allowing me uninterrupted extended periods of time to complete the manuscript.

Ali Javid
Sterling, VA

1

Locations of the World Heritage Monuments are highlighted in bold script

INTRODUCTION

In July of every year UNESCO (the United Nations Educational Scientific and Cultural Organization) designates a number of manmade monuments and natural wonders as World Heritage Monuments, selected under the advice of experts and critics from a list proposed by each member nation. The selection is based on both the cultural value and the universal appeal of the monuments, which are open to all humanity. UNESCO provides technical advice for monument maintenance and upkeep.

Solitary monuments may be selected or a group of monuments in a given location. As of 2003, there were twenty-three such monuments in India, including six natural wonders, one prehistoric site at Bhimbetka, and three Buddhist groups of monuments at Bodh Gaya, Sanchi and Ajanta. Others include Ellora, with a group of monuments constructed by Buddhists, Hindus and Jains, and seven Hindu sites with one monument each at Elephanta, Tanjur, Konark and four groups of monuments at Patadkal, Mamalapurum, Khajuraho and Vijayanagara. Delhi and Agra have two Muslim monuments each and a group of monuments are found at Fatahpursikiri. A group of Christian monuments is located at Goa. Some noteworthy monuments have not yet made the list, possibly due to restricted public entry which makes their study difficult for non-Hindu specialists.

There is an enormous wealth of sculpture in India, and the selected monuments present the best of Indian sculpture, art and architecture over a period of time. A comparative study of these monuments reveals the developmental history of India's religious monuments. This book presents all the manmade World Heritage Monuments (selected up to 2003) and related edifices in surrounding areas. It should be noted that since then, two Cola temples in south India, Victoria Railway Terminus at Mumbai and an archeological site in Rajasthan were added to the list. These monuments are not included in the book.

In order to highlight the major changes that have taken place, the monuments are classified in this book as early, early medieval, middle medieval, late medieval and recent. An outstanding monument in a group at one place typically incorporates attractive features of the surrounding buildings, all of which have evolved over a period of time causing some overlap of classification period between groups at different locations.

Early monuments constructed from the sixth to the third century BCE include Buddhist caves excavated in the hills and protected monuments at Sanchi and Bodh Gaya. The prehistoric site of Bhimbetka is included in the early group. All other structural monasteries and stupas that were constructed of perishable materials and not protected during the early period have perished. The protected monuments and remains of stupas that have survived bear the finest sculpture and paintings. Early medieval monuments were constructed from the sixth century to the end of the eighth century BCE. Hindus started construction of caves during this period. Buddhists constructed caves up to three stories high. After the construction of a few caves, Hindus constructed a huge monolithic temple that sits in a pit. Sculpture started showing signs of a decline in quality. The development of free-standing structural stone temples began, and structural decorations for temple beautification were developed. Free-standing structural stone monuments spread all over India, bringing an end to the era of cave excavation and monolithic stone structures in hilly regions. Although the quality of sculpture began to decline, most sculpture remained vibrant. Tantrism flourished and spread its roots. Construction of Buddhist monuments ceased except for a few temples at Sanchi.

In the middle medieval period, from the seventh to the tenth century, a race began between the Hindu monarchs to construct the grandest temple with the tallest towers. Jain sculpture and decorative art still retained their beauty. The era of painting came to an end and the quality of sculpture further declined. Monuments constructed in the late medieval period, between the eleventh and the thirteenth century, displayed religious fervor with structural decoration on temple replacing what had been "feminine" beauty. Temple construction ceased.

Recent monuments, constructed between the thirteenth and the nineteenth century, were built on imported architectural and decorative designs. Muslims developed a distinctive Indo-Islamic architecture and decorative designs while Christians primarily copied Roman churches, and Sikhs constructed a marble temple at Amritsar based on Hindu and Muslim architectural styles.

1. Religions of India

The four indigenous religions of India are Hinduism, Buddhism, Jainism and Sikhism. Two more religions entered India to stay: Christianity, in the third century CE and Islam, in the seventh century. Akbar, the Mughal Emperor (1542-1605), tried to develop a new religion, Dean-e-elahe, by synthesizing Hinduism and Islam; but it died in its infancy. His successor Shah-e-Jahan and orthodox Muslims did not favor it.

Mankind has inhabited India for over half a million years. The natural barriers that kept India in comparative isolation, allowing it to develop its own civilization, were not impermeable. There was always some migration through Himalayan passes. People of the proto-historic Indus River Valley civilization were not the first to enter India, but not much is known about previous immigrants. The cultural remains of the Indus River Valley civilization that flourished from 2500-1500 BCE (with a peak period between 2250-1750 BCE) indicate worship of procreative forces. The phallus, representing the procreative aspect of the universe by which the endless cycle of birth, rebirth and death occurs, and ring stones representing vulvae — the door through which one is born and reborn, dating to the third millennium BCE, have been unearthed here. A life-size Neolithic statue of a man carved in 9500-7200 BCE, excavated in Turkey, shows a prominent erect phallus, indicating the importance accorded to procreative forces long before the Indus River Valley civilization.

Aryans, coming in small groups, completely displaced the Indus River Valley civilization by 1600 BCE.

Hinduism

Hinduism, the oldest religion of India, has its roots in the Indus River Valley civilization and possibly beyond. Aryans migrating from Iran and surrounding regions brought gods of Iranian origin. Hinduism is not based on the idea of the revelation of a god conveyed by a messiah. Worship of natural forces was at the root of religions in the Indus River Valley civilization. Lacking any clear explanation of the origins of the universe, Aryans believed that there were two separate primordial worlds. One was a sacred world with the germ of life, characterized by a complete and undifferentiated unity inhabited by a group of gods called *asuras*. A god Indra was born outside this primeval world and he created the world we know by rearranging the existing matter. He caused the separation of sky and earth by propping up the sky with a pillar, and he released the cosmic ocean between the sky and the earth by slaying the demon guarding the imprisoned cosmic ocean. He acted as catalyst for the creation of all the identifiable individuals and distinct categories of objects and beings within the world. Along with Indra came *devas*, the gods of the Vedic pantheon. The constant struggle between the asuras and devas resulted in a constant menace to the existence and coherence of the ordered world. Some asuras joined the ranks of the devas. Others, personifying negative characteristics such as ignorance, in *Puranas* or ancient tales, were vanquished by the devas.

Vedas, Hindu sacred texts, were developed between 1500 and 800 BCE. They present a pantheon of 33 gods representing various forces of nature and personification of the sky, thunder, sun, fire, and rivers. Indra became the head of the council of gods, and was god of rain and of war — two of the most important factors affecting life. Agni became the god of fire; Surya became the sun god and Vayu the god of wind, amongst a multitude of minor gods. Some of these gods are prototypes or aspects of gods known in later Hinduism.

The function of these gods was to provide material blessing, and to focus worshipers on a desire for gain, reward or gain, rather than penitence and asceticism. Ceremonies that took place in the altar area developed into worship in the Hindu temple which included sacrifice of humans, animals and offerings of grain, milk and flesh through Agni, the god of fire. During sacrifice a grand ritual feast was arranged to which gods were invited and hymns of praise were sung. This developed into the present day Puja, which is a hospitality ritual offering food, water and flowers to the deity. Final codification of the rituals and ceremonies is found in the Brahmans, a group of texts written later. Priests (Brahmanas) became influential as sole authentic authorities to transmit sacrifices and some more so by their expertise in effecting transmittals. The basic religious beliefs set in the Vedas were possibly different from the prevalent ideas. These ideas were not fixed but developed over centuries. The Harappans, part of the Dasa tribe, were mentioned as worshipping the phallus with strange vows but no specific rites; they were inhabitants of the Indus River Valley.

The multiplicity of gods increased with time. During the early Vedic age, starting perhaps in the second millennium BCE, when various kingdoms emerged in the valleys of the Indus and Ganges Rivers, three gods that affected human lives most were said to govern the universe. The concept of a triad of gods is rooted deep in the Indian mind and with the ebb and rise of the popularity of various gods, four successive triads of gods ruled the universe during Vedic era. There is no evidence of the existence of temples, any religious buildings or facsimiles of Vedic gods in Indus River Valley civilization or the Vedic age before the Christian era. The worshippers wrote hymns in Sanskrit to the gods and sang them in religious ceremonies.

Buddhists developed facsimiles of Buddha under the influence of Kusanas who had migrated from Central Asia and settled in India. Under the influence of Buddhist sculpture idols of Vedic gods were carved after the first century CE, and nature worship assumed the form of idol worship.

During the Vedic age a minor god, Vishnu, distinguished himself by taking three steps to conquer the universe, reflecting his sovereignty over the universe. By the advent of Brahmanism, especially in the Upanishad period, the most important Vedic god was Vishnu, not Indra (the head of the council of the last Vedic triad). Siva, early identified with fire, and a pre-Vedic Indus River Valley deity, became popular. An attempt was made to synthesize a single god by combining Vishnu and Siva as Harihara during the Brahmin era. This went against the concept of triad of gods and Harihara did not become popular.

Around 300 BCE, near the end of the Vedic era, the multiplicity of gods and myths and the absence of a detailed explanation of the creation of the universe gave way to a search for some creator, a supreme god amongst the existing gods. A deity Brahma emerged from the confusion as a manifestation of all the old gods. It was an uphill battle to establish him as a new god. To settle various concerns a myth similar to the present day "Big Bang" scientific theory evolved. According to the myth, universal time is a never-ending cycle of creation and destruction, each cycle lasting for one hundred years in the scale of Brahma's life. At the end of a creation cycle everything — including Brahma, the other gods, sages, demons, mankind, animals and matter are dissolved into a great cataclysm, the Mahapralaya. This is followed by a hundred years of chaos. Before the beginning of another creative cycle a golden cosmic egg, symbolic of fire, floats for a thousand years on the water of the cataclysmic flood that covers the universe. At the end of this time, the cosmic egg bursts opens and the Lord of the Universe emerges. He takes the form of the first eternal man and destroys all sins by fire. He was called Purusha. According to myths developed later he is Narayana, who appears to be an aspect of Brahma, and in other myths he is an aspect of Vishnu. According to another myth the Lord of the Universe lay brooding over the cosmic sea on Ananta, the sea serpent, for a thousand years. At the end a lotus as bright as a thousand suns rose from his navel and grew as big as the world. On this lotus Brahma sprang, self created but imbued with the powers of the Lord of the Universe (believed to be Vishnu). He started the work of creation but he was not omniscient — and he made several mistakes.

Brahma lost his earlier position as All-god to Vishnu or Siva and remained only as creator. For the creation cycle to occur, a mythical world was created which changes little. Seven concentric rings of continents surround the earth like a wheel. In the center of the earth is Mount Meru, the Heaven of Brahma, circled by the River Ganges and surrounded by the cities of Indra and other deities. Benevolent spirits like Gandharvas inhabit the foothills of Mount Meru, and demons live in the valleys.

By the end of the Vedic era, the first triad of the Brahmin era took shape. A philosophical and abstract concept, the world spirit became a personalized deity and took up a position in the triad of gods as Brahma the Creator. Vishnu became the second member of the triad as sustainer of the universe and supreme god. As a self-existing and all pervading power, he became preserver and maintainer of the universe and of the cosmic order. As preserver he embodied the quality of mercy and goodness and became an object of devotion rather than fear. To acquire and retain more prosperity and happiness he fought demons and supervised procreation.

Siva, earlier identified with fire, and who was an Indus River Valley deity, became the third member of the triad. At the beginning of the Vedic era Aryans took delight in persecuting Dravidians as worshippers of the phallus. But by the end of Vedic era Hinduism absorbed Siva, as it had absorbed Buddha as the seventh incarnation of Vishnu. Many other Vedic gods became minor gods. To balance the popularity of Buddhism, Hindus pushed the idea of intense loyalty to one chosen god and Vishnu and Siva became the most popular.

The Upanishads, a set of scriptures, largely philosophical, spiritual meditations on the nature of god(s), were developed between 800 and 400 BCE in reaction to the priestly Brahmins who were ruining the laity with their excessive demands for sacrifices. The reaction emphasized philosophical and speculative questions. The main concerned was the relationship between individual and the universal being. Atma, the Brahman principal, was equated with individual being, and in the second phase by practicing yoga the individual becomes the universe, assuming the undifferentiated and non-dualistic world that existed before Indra. Jains call this Mokasa (release) and in Buddhism it is called Nirvana (extinguishing the self). Two other concepts in the Upanishads are *Karma*, which is "as he acted, as he lived, so he becomes: he who has done good is born again as a good man and who has done evil will born as an evil man"; and *Samsara*, earthly existence with cycles of birth and rebirths. The Upanishads came to be considered the philosophical portion of the Vedas and formed the textual basis of the Hindu religion.

The early Puranas, Mahabharata and Ramayana, possibly finalized in the fourth or fifth century CE, are records of events that took place centuries ago. They are imperfect as historical records but provide a great deal of information from a non-Brahmin point of view. The early Puranas record information about a prehistoric flood, and King Manu who alone saved the world from inundation and became the progenitor of the human race. Ramayana, the story of Rama, possibly occurred between 900 and 650 BCE. No archeological record of these events has been found. Starting in the late Upanishad period historical information has become comparatively specific. Puranas place the Vedic gods in position subordinated to other gods.

JAINISM, BUDDHISM AND SIKHISM

Jainism and Buddhism were developed as a reaction to what was seen as an excessive number of Hindu priests during sixth century BCE. Sikhism developed in the eighteenth century as reaction to communal strife in India. These religions downplayed the role of gods and laid more emphasis on the actions of man. Jainism does not deny the existence of the superhuman but in Jainism there is no creator of the universe and the universe is not guided by a divine will or mind. The laws of nature are considered sufficient explanation. The transmigration of souls is taken for granted. The religious philosophy of Jain is also based on an undifferentiated and non-dualistic world. Jain explains time and the creation of the universe as an eternally revolving wheel with upward and downward cycles but without the great cataclysm, the Mahapralaya. In every cycle twenty-four Tirthankara are born; the last of them is Mahavir. Most of the Tirthankara have some connection with Hindu mythology, attaining Nirvana on Mount Kailas the abode of Siva. Tirthankara are individuals who have attained perfect knowledge and have give up attachment to the vices of life. They are not ultimate gods and cannot intercede on behalf of the faithful. Their value is as objects of meditation. The Jain universe resemble a headless man. The right leg has seven hells where lesser gods torture souls before they are reborn. The left leg is inhabited by minor deities and demons. The middle portion, the waist, is our world with eight concentric rings of continents separated by eight ring-shaped oceans surrounding Mount Meru. Gods of various ranks and other spirits inhabit the upper region, the trunk, sub-divided into many regions with Indra as their king. Jain gods and demons are largely of Hindu inspiration. Demons can eventually work for their salvation but gods cannot attain liberation without becoming human.

Jains by their religious beliefs are restricted to the professional trades; they are the richest and most literate community in India. Possibly due to the lack of political base they took back seat to Buddhist and Hindus in the construction of religious monuments.

The female attendants with their special features and mounts identify the Tirthankaras, the twenty-four Jains who have attained perfect knowledge. Bahubali is presented with vines trailing from his limbs and an anthill beside him. Parshvanath is carved with long hands standing under the *naga* hood (the cobra-like hood of a mythical serpent). Icons of only few Tirthankaras are popular.

Buddhism does not reject the existence of gods but believes that the world goes through periods of evolution and decline, without any significant influence of gods on the cosmic process. Buddhism rejects the existence of a permanent soul but accepts the transmigration of souls; this doctrine which appeared in the late Vedic age (1000 to 600 BCE) is assumed.

All things in the universe, according to Buddhism, are made up of form and matter, sensation, perception, psychic constructions and consciousness and conscious thought, which are in a state of constant flux. Each act, word or thought in life leaves its traces on the constituents that make up an individual and his character. At the end of an individual's life, the material and immaterial separate, and the immaterial, called soul, obtains another body befitting his deeds in the previous life. No permanent entity transmigrates from body to body. In the end the individual becomes an undifferentiated and non-dualistic entity.

The Buddhist universe that evolved later has three planes: above, around and below Mount Meru. The lower plane has one hundred thirty-six hells, the plane around Mount Meru contains the world of animals, ghosts, demons and men, and above the peak of Mount Meru are the heavens, arranged one above the other, occupied by various gods and spirits of higher order.

In early *jatakas* (tales of the former lives of the Buddha) Sakyamuni (the sage of Sakyas) was presented as an incarnation of various animals. Later he was presented as various symbols, mostly the pipal tree (*Ficus religiosa*) with its characteristic long-pointed leaves, under which he attained enlightenment. Buddhas born before the birth of the historical Buddha are identified with the species of Ficus and other trees under which they were enlightened. The image of Buddha was carved in the last quarter of the first century CE with characteristic features like a knot on the top of head (*usnisa*) and an elongated earlobe. The image took time to spread in India as it was considered improper to present Buddha in the human body which he discarded after 550 rebirths. He was presented as a human engaged in human activities to reach Buddha-hood and as *mahasattva*, the perfect being awaiting his birth in *Tusita* heaven. The final stage of Buddha's life, depicting his demise, is carved as *Parinirvana*. Images of Buddha might have been created on perishable materials after his demise. It is reported that a Chinese ware made in 36 BCE bears a clear figure of Buddha with a few characteristic features. Chinese Buddhists generally followed Indian initiatives, so that facsimiles of Buddha may have existed in India earlier than 36 BCE. In earlier carvings, Buddha is depicted as an ascetic but from the tenth–eleventh century he has been carved as a regal person wearing a crown and ornaments.

A statue of Buddha dating to early first century CE, carved during the Saka-Parthian period, was discovered in the Swat Valley of Pakistan. The statue depicts Buddha sitting crossed legged (*Vijraparyankasana*) and holding his hand in a protection gesture (*abhaya mudra*), introducing yoga postures in Buddhist art.

A devotee, by taking a vow, becomes a *Bodhisattva*. One who has fulfilled the vow and has attained the stage of Bodhisattva-hood is *mahasattva*. A few mahasattva seek nirvana

and attain Buddha-hood. Others forsake nirvana to stay on earth to help laymen, to guide them on the right path. They are carved standing or seated in regal attire, wearing jewelry, and are recognized by symbols on their headdresses or attributes held in their hands. Bodhisattvas are usually carved similar in height but smaller than Buddha. Carvings much larger than Bodhisattvas also depict Amitabha (Amitayus), the Buddha who presides over his paradise, Sukhavati (Full of joy). The aim of the residents of this paradise is to be born again and again in the paradise till they attain Buddha-hood. He holds his hand in a variant of the preaching gesture.

The most important Bodhisattva is Maitreya Buddha. Because of his imminent Buddha-hood he is carved as Buddha. In early carvings he is shown standing in a regal pose wearing a long lower garment, jewelry, and a lock of hair falling around his shoulder or a curl on his head resembling snail shell. He holds a vase in his left hand.

The most popular Bodhisattva, recognized by the lotus held in his hand, is Avalokiteshvara (Padmapani). His consort Tara is also identified with the lotus. He is the personification of compassion and a guide to lost travelers. Vajrapani, the personification of wisdom, holds a Vajra (thunderbolt scepter) in his hand. Sometimes he carries a broken piece of a bell in the other hand. Some Bodhisattvas carry flags of different shapes, a lotus stalk, or book. The accompanying peacock or peacock feather in the hair identifies Mahamayuri, the goddess of learning.

Other individuals depicted are Pancika and Hariti. Pancika is carved with a full body, wearing princely garb and jewelry representing wealth and abundance. Hariti is carved with five small children representing her five hundred children. Pancika and Hariti are also depicted as keepers of wealth or treasurers of enlightenment. Hariti sometimes is considered as the embodiment of the mother of Buddhas. Angry Hariti has been carved with fangs protruding as tusks from her mouth and trident.

Sikhism

The founder of the youngest religion of India, Guru Nanak (1469-1539), was born in Punjab to a Hindu family. The details of his life are not known. The Sikh scripture Adi Granth, recorded during the time of the fourth guru, Arjan, gives little information on his life.

By the fifteenth century Indian society was torn by intolerance of Muslims and the injustices of the caste system in Hindu society. Guru Nanak taught that the almighty creator and sustainer of the Universe is timeless, without form and beyond human reason. True religion is inward meditation and outward observance, like worship and mere reading of scripture, is futile. Liberation can be obtained only by inward meditation. His message was to love god, remember him all the time, follow the work ethic, share the fruit of your work with others and lead a proper family life.

As in Buddhism and Jainism, the role of god was pushed to the background and emphasis was laid on the actions of man. The concept of rebirths (*Samsara*) and karma (the accumulation of good and bad deeds) and the final merging of the soul with god are the foundation of the Sikh religion.

The guru as the mediator of the divine voice is eternal. He lives in direct consciousness of god, experiencing no separation.

Before his death, Guru Nanak selected a guru to take his place, and a succession of ten gurus followed. Babar established the Mughal emperor in India during the life time of Guru Nanak.

Very soon the Mughals' apprehension in relation to the Sikhs grew. A few skirmishes with Mughals occurred during the lifetime of the third guru, Arjan. Guru Arjan died while in the custody of Punjab Mughal rulers. Relative peace followed in the sixteenth century. Under the rule of Aurangzeb, the ninth guru was executed in Delhi. During the time of the tenth guru, Gobind Singh, Sikhs were required to identify themselves visibly.

Guru Gobind Singh created Khalsa, the spiritual brother and sisterhood devoted to purity of thought and action. He prescribed a distinct dress code known as the five Ks to install self-identity and militant spirit to face the persecution by neighbors and Mughals.

The most sacred book of the Sikhs is *Guru Granth*, compiled by Guru Arjan and updated by the last guru, Gobind Singh. It includes hymns sung by Guru Nanak, the teachings of nine gurus, texts by Muslim and Hindu saints, and many independent statements of beliefs and practices.

Guru Gobind Singh declared that all the guidance required by Sikhs in temporal matters is complete and there will be no more gurus. At this time the functions of the guru passed to the holy book and the custodians of the book, abolishing the need for priests. Guru Gobind Singh died in 1708.

Religious Monuments

The early religious monuments constructed by Buddhist, Jains and Hindus that have survived the destructive forces of nature are the caves temples excavated in sandstone, basaltic hills and granite outcrops.

These caves are the product of sculpture on a grand scale, not rock-cut architecture. Few or no architectural principles are involved. To excavate a cave like those at Ajanta and Ellora, the face of the rock with its perpendicular drop was burrowed into horizontally; the space marked for doors and windows was hewn in the solid rock mass. Rock splitting was accomplished by inserting wooden pegs into holes cut close along the proposed line of split. When soaked with water, the wooden pegs would expand and exert pressure, and when the temperature fell at night this would fracture the rock along the intended line. After the passage into the rock was cut, the roof was designed by removing the rock above. By cutting the rock below, the floor was created. Large masses of rocks for columns and other structures were left attached to the roof and mother rock for later finishing. Rock cutters using pickaxes separated the split rock and removed the debris. Masons executed more precise cutting. Sculptors carved, and fine finishing was done by polishers using iron chisels and hammers. The absence of faults and deposits of sedimentary rocks in the basaltic lava flow was a great bonus. Caves in sandstone hills were excavated using the same technique.

The caves and monuments in large granite boulders as seen at Mamalapurum were excavated by a different technique, presumably because of the hardness of rock. The surface was first delineated by cutting square-inch wedge-shaped holes at close intervals using a hammer and chisel. Flat-edged iron wedges of the same thickness were inserted into the holes and driven with a heavy hammer and the broken pieces of rock removed. Then deeper work was done by cutting grooves in a two-feet-square area to the depth of two or three inches and chiseling out the projected square blocks. The process was repeated, keeping the excavated surface at uniform depth. Rock for structures like pillars and walls were left in place for later chiseling. While the work went on in one direction, often another excavation was started down from above. Because of the hardness of the rock, the depth of the cave was kept to bare minimum. This technique can be seen on the unfinished surface of a boulder in front of the Mahisasuramardini cave and on the unfinished surface of the sculptured cliff at the left bottom corner at Mamalapurum.

Hindu Temples

There is no evidence of the existence of any type of religious buildings during the Indus River Valley civilization or the Vedic era in India. Destructive forces of nature and the passage of time obliterated any temples built with perishable materials in the early part of the first millennium. Sculptures, created from clay since pre-historic times, were also lost except for a few terra-cotta figurines.

The few brick temples built in the early fourth century CE that survived weathering show a fairly developed stage in temple construction. In the early fifth century stones were introduced to the construction of temples and the present-day freestanding stone structural temple was evolved over next two hundred years, starting as a simple structure.

The earliest stone temple, developed in the fifth century, had a sanctum enshrined with the deity and an open, pillared hall called a *mandapa* to accommodate visitors (but not large gatherings). Later the open hall was enclosed, a front porch was added, and a tower was developed on the center of the temple roof. The tower was soon moved over the sanctum. A small cell (vestibule) between the sanctum and hall, called the *antralia*, was added to allow the few visitors to wait while the Brahmin and a worshipper (alone or with his family) occupied the sanctum. Still later the front hall was divided into a small hall (*ardha-mandapa*) and a relative large hall (*maha-mandapa*).

By the seventh century the basic design of the present freestanding stone temple was complete and was adopted in the plain regions. By the eight century the race was on for the construction of grand temples with the tallest towers under the patronage of Hindu monarchs. The basic units of temple building have remained the same except for the number of individual units and regional diversification of units.

Hindus started excavating cave temples in mountain terrains in the fifth century at Ellora on the model of Buddhist caves, but without the funeral mound in the cave. Almost simultaneously the development of freestanding stone structural temples started. The caves are decorated with sculptures of Hindu gods and some decorative elements developed on freestanding Hindu temples. The structural temples had tall towers — which could not be accommodated in a cave. To maintain the tall tower and to free the temple from the confinement of the cave, very soon Hindus opened the roof of the cave at Ellora, ending the era of caves in the seventh-eighth century.

Regional developments modified the temple complex. The small hall (*ardha-mandapa*) and front porch were modified into a comparatively large hall for the offering of food (*bhoga-mandapa* — dining hall) and hall of pleasure (*nata-mandir* — dance hall) in some Orissa temples. The large hall, Maha-mandapa, was retained as the *Jagamohana*. The roofs of the front units of the temple remained flat, in the south, but in the north roofs were built in a pyramidal shape. Further developments added a large court, subsidiary shrines for spouses and children of the god, saints, and a holy basin in large temple complexes.

The external decorations on Hindu monuments are unique in different regions. Although most of the decorations and shapes of the units were developed in the south, the north and west adopted specific shapes and decorations for different units. The temple gateway towers (*gopuram*) remained simple and inconspicuous in the north and west of India. The high gateway towers of south Indian temples with the wagon-shaped roof became the most prominent structures of the temple gateways, with more than one gateway in some temples. In later-built temples, gateways taller than temple towers apparently assumed the role of a secondary sanctum.

The decorations used on gateway towers and temple towers in the south are similar. These decorations were adopted from the tower of Ganesha Ratha at Mamalapurum, which became the prototype of gateway towers. The most commonly used decorations are chaitya windows — the circular or semi-circular arched blind windows with carvings inside. Miniature shrines were carved on the tower with the wagon-shaped roof called a *sala*, with the bulbous-shaped roof called *kuta* and a bulbous decoration with a pointed tip called *stupi*. The small circular decoration with carvings (mostly of human heads) inside is called *kudu* and the overhanging cornice with kudu is called *kaputa*. On gateway towers females, particularly *mithuna* (embracing) couples, became prominent but females were rarely carved on the temple towers. Representing the mountain of gods, the tall towers with many stories were constructed to provide dwellings for the gods.

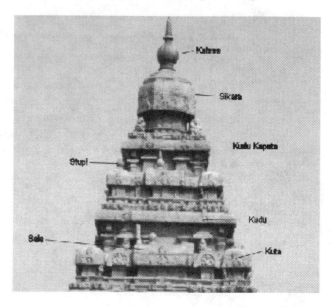

Fig. A. Shape and Decorations of south Indian towers. Shore temple. Mamalapuram. 7th Century.

The pyramidal tower in south Indian temples bears a square or octagonal but mostly dome-shaped *sikara* on the top, surmounted by a water pot called *kalasa* (Fig. A). In a later development a *sukanasa*, an elongated structure with a wagon-shaped roof, was added at the base of tower with a chaitya window on front façade. The decorations on the south Indian temple towers are similar to the decorations on gateway towers.

The towers on north and west Indian temples differ radically from south Indian temple towers in both shape and decorations. The curvilinear tower developed in the south was also used in the north and west, but there were changes in height, shape and embellishment with locally developed decorations (Fig. B). The crowning element of these towers is a flat stone with ribbed margin called *amalaka*; it bears a finial (*kalasa*).

The structural decorations on the north and west India temple towers include full or half interlocking circles called *gavaska* that give a mesh appearance to the tower. The corners of the tower are imbedded with small ribbed pieces of amalaka. Temple towers are generally decorated with a few gods and goddesses.

The decorations on the walls of north and west India temples generally differ from the decoration on south Indian temple walls. The base of south Indian temples is molded, and the wall above bears niches with flanking pilasters enclosing carvings and foliated decorations above pilasters. The top of the wall is decorated with an overhanging cornice with kudu decorations (called a kaputa cornice) (Fig. C). The walls of the sanctum are usually carved with images of gods and goddesses.

In north and west Indian temples the base is generally not molded. The plinth is decorated with females, in bands, with mythological creatures interposed. The walls above bear sculptured panels between pilasters decorated with full or half interlocking gavaska above and below. The walls of sanctum are carved with a sprinkling of female forms.

Fig. C. Patadkal. Virupaksha Temple. Carvings on exterior wall. Ca. 8th Century. Sandstone.

Gods and Goddesses

Most of the gods and goddesses in the Hindu pantheon have multiple hands, two legs and some have multiple heads, but only the seated Siva in a carving at Khajuraho has four legs. The emblems they carry or the mounts they ride identify major gods and their spouses. Siva is mostly depicted as a phallus (lingam), sometimes with a beautiful female face carved near the tip. In human form he carries a three-pronged trident, and a begging bowl made of a half skull, or a noose held in his hand. His mount is Nandi (the bull). The spouse of Siva, Parvati, is mostly identified with a rosary, ladle or water pot she carries and sometimes she is accompanied by Nandi.

Vishnu carries a conch shell and a wheel-disc. The conch shell represents eternal peace. The wheel disc represents eternal time and the power to destroy all things. The conch shell and wheel disc in combination with gestures made by his other two hands identified some of his form. Animals such as the fish, boar and lion identify some of his incarnations. His mount is Garuda, mostly carved as a man with wings. His spouse Lakshmi is identified with the lotus, in Buddhism, and sometimes by the emblems of Vishnu.

Brahma is identified by having four faces and by his swan mount, and Indra with his elephant mount (later replaced by a horse). Varuna carries a noose in his hand but he is not stern

Fig. B. Shape and decoration of North Indian temple tower and temple walls. Visva-Brahma Temple. Alampur. 8th Century. Sandstone.

looking and travels on a *makara* (quasi-crocodile). Yama, the god of death, is identified with his mount, the buffalo.

Goddesses also have emblems representing their nature and power. The river goddess Ganga travels on Crocodile and Yamuna on Tortoise. Goddess Ganga has three heads, as three rivers join to make the Ganges River. Durga, the mother goddess, carries a multitude of weapons including a trident. Sarasvati, the goddess of music and learning, is identified by a musical instrument.

Temple Sculpture

Hindu temple is a place to worship the facsimile of a god and offer him gifts. The social and religious lives of Hindus revolve around the temple.

The canons of temple building ordained that temples should be attractive and beautiful to induce frequent visits. Sex is sacred and females are more attractive than any flower or sunset that can be carved in gray stones. Thus there were no better assets than the female to decorate the temple.

Indian artists idealized feminine beauty with large almond eyes, chiseled nose, sensual lips, a full firm breast, narrow waist, bulging hips, and long cylindrical thighs with shapely legs. Serving as places to worship the gods and glorify their accomplishments, temples blossomed with feminine beauty, emphasizing her charms and reproductive servitude.

Gods were carved in the image of mortals with features like special hairdos, often with multiple faces, hands, and in one instance multiple legs, or an erect lingam to emphasize their superior nature. They look stern, evoking respect and submission and in few cases fear. Gods were given the position of honor in the sanctum.

Goddesses were carved in the image of idealized females with all the feminine charms. The Goddess Durga was created, possibly as a revolt against male dominance, by combining the attributes of all the gods. She fought with many demons but could not stay on top because she was female, and later became associated with Siva.

Yoga, a graded path leading to final salvation through body control and meditation, was introduced in the Buddhist and Hindu religion. Yoga is an attempt to yoke or unify oneself to the divine, or the universe, eliminating the duality of the individual and the greater being. Meditation and use of *asana* (sitting position of legs) and *madura* (hand gestures) are associated with yoga.

The use of yoga as a religious practice appeared in Harappa civilization (Indus Valley Civilization) but was not necessarily connected to a particular sect. Hindus, Buddhists and Jains adopted yoga in historic times. It led to organized

Tantrism in Buddhism by the seventh century and reached a peak in Hinduism in the tenth century, exploiting sex on temple walls.

The artists at Sanchi in the first century carved the most beautiful female torso and gave her a three body-bend pose imbued with sensuality. The Pallava dynasty of the Andhra region in the fifth century made her tall, slim, delicate and radiantly beautiful. Her body started to become more voluptuous but still she remained radiantly beauty by the sixth century under the Kalacuri of central India. The Cola in the tenth century started changing her stature. The Candella dynasty of Khajuraho started modifying her proportions by giving her longer legs. The Ganga of Kalinga in the eleventh century made her tall, more graceful and poetic.

In the thirteenth century the Hoysala of Karnataka gave her an attractive face and compressed her height, making her shorter and bulkier, and buried her naked body in ornaments. The emphasis on the beautification of temples shifted from female beauty to decorative sculpture. With the destruction of temples by the Muslim sultans in the thirteenth century, temple building came to a halt and the sublime female creation vanished into thin air.

Female nudity is common in temple sculpture. To the Indian mind every thing exists at three levels: the physical, the subtle level of senses and emotions; and the spiritual. Artists depict the world of senses and emotions. The human body is the wrapping worn by the subtle level, and to put dress on the body was considered to bury the subtle further down. Therefore in temples the image was mostly left disrobed. The designs or folds of fine textiles cleaving to her body were considered dress enough. She was pure, sweet and tender. The artists presented her with all her attributes as seen by her lover, but she was not carved nude entertaining groups of males.

Even by the eleventh century her upper body was visible through translucent drapery and the lower body showed the contours of her thighs and hips. She remained radiantly beautiful through the thirteenth century — and then vanished.

As in most cultures, woman was not elevated to the status of men in Indian society though the female was considered auspicious. Because of her fertility she was associated with growth, abundance and prosperity. The mango tree was believed to blossom at the sound of the goddess' laughter and unlike Eve she was not associated with the fall of man.

The view of female procreative servitude changed with different ascending gods. When the Vedic god Indra, controlling the rain clouds, ruled the agrarian society, she was a fertility deity who provided sons to till the soil. With the attainment of some prosperity the obscure god of thunderbolts, Rudra, appeared as Siva, representing the male reproductive nature with an erect phallus; he became a popular god in south India, eclipsing Agni of the Vedic triad.

Though Siva is associated in Indian thought with the female active principle (*prakrti*, nature) that makes possible the manifestation of the inactive male principle, it was the lingam that dominated. The *yoni* was given the shape of the spout on a pedestal to drain the gift of milk poured on the lingam standing in the pedestal pit.

Like the erect lingam, the yoni did not become a major symbol. The yoni was presented as a simple slit, except in a few early carvings of a squatting mother goddess in Karnataka and in Konarak it was carved with a few anatomical details. In the Preah khan temple of Cambodia, the spout of lingam pedestal is carved like lips of yoni.

On the main gateway of Virupaksha temple at Vijayanagara an *apsara* with a beautiful body and firm breasts is standing flanked by attendants with her shapely long legs spread apart. With the fingers of both hands inserted in her yoni, she pulls it open, exposing the erect clitoris, resembling a phallus, possibly to indicate that lingam resides even in yoni.

A couple of circular yogini temples constructed in west India have the main shrine in the center of a circular space representing the womb of the female installed with the lingam. In rectangular temples the projected entrance represented the lingam.

The development of the female spirit Shakti was snubbed and she was installed in the subsidiary Devi shrine of the temple complex, subordinating her to the male god. Most Shaktis of Siva took cruel aspects.

Depiction of sexual acts is not rare in temple sculpture. It started with *yaksis*, the fertility deities with bulging breasts and apsaras, courtesans bursting with sex appeal. Loving couples holding hands and in the act of disrobing the female appeared on a carved railing of Bodh-Gaya temple, erected in around 150 CE. The first large carving of a couple engaged in sex appeared in the fifth century in south India at Aihole. In north India this started proliferating from the ninth century, leading to larger-than-life carvings of copulating pairs on the walls of Konarak temple. In later Puranas it is reported as mentioned that the gods are interested in a variety of sexual poses for the sake of novelty as well as for the satisfaction of their female partners.

Possibly this trend was started to stimulate the sexual urge of devotees to increase the population, to meet the needs of agrarian society. Meanwhile Tantrism emerged, leading to sexual orgies. Sucking of the phallus by a female squatting between an embracing couple is explained in Tantrism as freeing the self of desire by excessive indulgence on the part

of souls who have attained some merit. Sexual orgies of three females with one male and one female with three males, female masturbation with inanimate objects, fingers, licking of the yoni by dogs and men were carved on temple walls.

The apsaras' dignity is often violated by devotees rubbing their hands, resulting in blackening of breasts, thighs, yoni and even anal region. Philip Rawson has suggested that such rubbing for good luck by devotees has caused pits in the vulva of some apsaras. The pit in the yoni of Durga in Mamalapurum Varaha cave has deepened considerably in just three years. However, except at Khajuraho and Konarak, the sexual act is carved on temple gateways or in corners and in generally unnoticed part of the temple.

The hands of sculptors fulfilled the canons of temple construction and made the temple an attractive, beautiful and romantic place. Even with an excess of Tantrism it is a beautiful, sweet and poetic world to live in, full of life exuberance, sensory delights and tender emotions. Even with stern-looking gods it is a world of beauty and delight. The blessings of the gods and the engrossing myths and fables carved on the walls are an added bonus.

BUDDHIST AND JAIN TEMPLES

Buddhists built monasteries, *stupas*, caves and freestanding stone temples for devotional and residential purpose. Most of the early monasteries are in ruins. The earliest extant temples are stupas and caves. Stupas are funeral mounds to incarnate the sacred relics. There are many ruins of stupas all over the country. Some stupas have beautifully decorated gateways and a railing around. Buddhists visit stupas to feel the proximity of Buddha's relics.

The best and most famous stupa is located at Sanchi. The brick stupa at Bahurath, with square base and beautiful sculpture on stone railing posts, has become a victim of time, although parts of the railing are saved. Another stupa at Amaravati leaves its trace only in bits and pieces of sculpture in various museums.

In the mid fifth century, Buddhists built a simple and eminently logical freestanding structural temple at Sanchi but did not improve on it. The later built Buddhist temples resemble Hindu temples.

Buddhists were the first to excavate caves during the regime of Maurya dynasty in the second century BCE. The early Buddhist cave temple complex with a hall and a shrine in the shape of funeral mound are called chaitya. Most of the chaitya are carved in imitation of thatched-roofed huts of central India with non-functional accessories like beams, imitating wooden beams on the ceiling, and pillars supporting the roof.

A few caves have arched windows, imitating the wood window of the time, above the entrance façade. The windows were covered with wooden screens to filter sunlight into the caves. Chaitya evolved into *vihara* caves with pillared verandahs, a hall without funeral mound, a shrine in the back wall with vestibule and residential cells on the sidewalls for the monks. In further developments the shrine was moved to the center of the hall and circumambulatory passage around the shrine was added. Hindu and Jain caves were modeled on Buddhist Vihara but without funeral mound. Jain cave complexes to a large degree resemble Hindu caves.

The Jain started constructing caves in first century CE. The early built caves and shelters were used by monks as residences. The caves built later were on the model of Buddhist caves without funeral mound and facilities for residence of monks. The freestanding structural temples of Jain are similar to Hindu temples.

The sculpture in Buddhist, Jain and Hindu monuments is similar. The Jains have excelled in decorative sculpture, particularly on pillars. Sexual love is implied in Jain sculpture, but not sexuality. Buddhist sculpture set new standards for carvings of female figures by introducing three-body-bend poses, an idealized female torso, and sensuality in the carving. It exhibits sexuality but not the excesses of Tantrism.

SIKH MONUMENTS

The third guru, Ram Das, excavated a pool in 1577 at Amritsar, built a temple in the center of the pool, and made it a place of pilgrimage. The fifth guru, Arjan, enshrined the holy book in the temple. The city was sacked and the Mughal Emperor demolished the temple in 1761. But the temple was rebuilt in 1764 and the roof was topped with copper plate in 1802. The two-story high marble temple built in a Hindu and Muslim architectural style sits in the large pool and is reached by the marble causeway known as Guru Bridge.

Sikhs in the early stage assembled in halls for congregational singing of hymns. These halls developed into *gurdwara*, the Sikh temples in India. A common kitchen to feed the people is an essential part of the gurdwara.

CHRISTIANITY AND ISLAM

The triad of gods of ancient West Asian religions was gradually replaced by belief in a supreme god. Christianity replaced the triads of gods with their own trinity, in which there is one god with three distinct co-equal and co-eternal entities who are equal gods, the father, the son and holy spirit. The son, like the Hindu gods appeared as a human, to guide humanity. Islam replaced the trinity by one omni-present and omnipotent god who created the universe by his personal will.

CHRISTIAN ARCHITECTURE AND SCULPTURE

Christian churches constructed in India show the strong influence of the western world. No composite Indo-Christian architecture was developed, possibly because the colonial powers, in spite of their long stay in India, remained alien for political expediency.

Syrian Christians were living in Cochin, south India, as early as the Gupta period (300-500 CE), but organized Churches in the western style appeared only in the fifteenth century with the arrival of colonial powers. Well-known churches built on the model of European churches are located at Goa in India. Local craftsman and artists decorated the interior of the churches. The alien rulers exerted no effort to synthesize Indo-Christian architecture, although some see a hint of Khajuraho curvilinear towers in the retable of some churches. The intricate and beautiful woodwork of the retables by local craftsmen has no equal. The wooden statues that adorned the altars are beautiful imitation of western art. The paintings, done in the Italian style under the supervision of Italians, on wooden boards, are a poor imitation, but Indian artists excelled in painting frescoes with floral designs.

INDO-ISLAMIC ARCHITECTURE

Islamic sculpture is primarily ornamental with calligraphic, geometric and floral designs combined in endless ways with inlay of semiprecious stones in marble.

Reproduction of real animals (much less humans) in two- or three-dimensional form is not permitted in Islam.

In Islamic art, primacy is given to calligraphy. Architecture is important because it leaves the stamp of Islam on the land. The most numerous and important structures in the Muslim world are mosques and tombs with their long cylindrical minarets and round domes with pointed tips staring at the sky. The mosque, a place for congregation of devotees to pray, is a large, open, lighted court with arcades or galleries or cloisters, the *mihrab* — a niche in the wall indicating the direction to Mecca, a pulpit (a raised platform from which to deliver the sermon) and a tower from which to call the devotees to prayer.

Temples are large, closed structures with a small, dim, mysterious cell in the center or rear of the temple to accommodate the image of deity and couple of devotees, a narrow passage around the cell to circumambulate the cell, and a comparatively large hall (not for the congregation of devotees, but for devotees waiting to enter the cell).

The Muslim Mohamed Qasim conquered the lower Indus Valley in 711-712. In the late tenth century Turkish slaves and nomads settled and established an empire in what is now Afghanistan. Mahmud (998-1030), a fierce fanatic from Afghanistan, invaded India seventeen times to loot and destroy temples. Qutabuddin Aibak, a Turkish slave, led another Turkish clan from Afghanistan and settled in India. He demolished Hindu and Jain temples, and re-used the stones (some even retaining Hindu sculpture) for the construction of Islamic monuments. In 1193, to construct the tall colonnade of the first mosque built at Delhi, pillars of uneven height from a demolished Jain temple were placed on top of each other to obtain the required even height. Muslims designed the façade of the mosque but Hindu masons built it, giving the sculpture and Arabic inscription friezes a purely Hindu background.

In 1200, Qutabuddin did not demolish a Sanskrit college in Ajmir but built a beautiful stone screen in front of the mosque (called Adhai-din-ka-jhonpra) using stones from demolished temples.

The first Islamic monument in India, Qutab Minar, considered a perfect tower, owes much to the skilled native masons with their centuries-old tradition of working with stone and other spoils from Hindu temples.

In all, Qutabuddin destroyed twenty-seven temples and re-used the building materials. His choice of design was limited by the shape and size of the looted stones. In addition, the dearth of experienced Muslim craftsmen meant that others had to be brought in, and this led to the meeting of alien minds and changes in the traditional training of Muslim craftsmen. Thus the influences of Central Asia (Turkey, Persia and Afghanistan) on the architecture of India combined to create a synthesis: Indo-Islamic architecture. Indo-Islamic art reached its glorious culmination in the golden age of the Mughal Empire. It is neither imitative nor hybrid art but distinct in itself.

In the Lower Sindh Valley, excavation has revealed the ruins of a small Samara-style mosque with thick brick pilasters. This mosque was possibly constructed during the late eighth century after the invasion of Mohamed Qasim in 711.

At Banbhore, 67 km (40 miles) south of Karachi, Pakistan, the foundation of a mosque approximately 128m (397 ft.) square has been discovered. A doubtful inscription dates the mosque to 727. There is a definite record of repairs to this mosque in 907. If the construction date is truly 727, this mosque is as old as any in the world.

Before appearing in India, tombs were common in the Muslim world. Mosques and tombs did not change much when introduced in India. But the shape of the base of the dome was changed from square to octagonal to round, and the dome itself from semicircular to bulbous. Central Asian architectural features, arcades and galleries were modified; the true arch and its variations and vaults were introduced. Perforated stone screens and inlay work covered the monuments. A little pillared dome pavilion without walls, called the *chatri*, of Hindu origin, appeared around the drum of the central dome. Indigenous features were added to the Islamic monuments: *jalis*, or pierced stone screens, *jharoka*, a projecting balcony with a small vaulted roof, and *chajja*, the angled eave. The gateway to the courtyard of Muslim monuments, with the dome and interior bays, remained different from temple gateways.

Mughals were nomadic and their buildings resemble tents built of stone. Jami Masjid in Delhi is an example. After the nomadic influence, the Persian cultural influence was strongest. Humayun's tomb, with a circular dome resting on the high circular neck of the supporting drum, brilliant glazed tiles, and six-pointed stars, is in the Persian style, but Akbar's Fatahpursikiri is almost Hindu in construction. The architects added temple bells to the arches and the lotus to the Islamic geometric designs. Ribbed fruits and pot-like finials, the traditional Indian temple motifs, crowned the apexes of vaults. Brackets were sometimes fashioned as animals and birds in full relief. The curved roof with its downward-slopping cornice imitating the thatched-hut roofs of Bengal were introduced. The hallmark of Mughal architecture is the multi-cusped arch. Columns were multifaceted or had fluted sides with vase-shaped bases.

By the seventeenth century, pure Persian art disappeared. Under Jahangir and Shahjahan, semi-precious stones like jade, lapis lazuli, and carnelian were set in white marble panels to create delicately-tinted flowers and leafy arabesques. Different colored sandstones and limited use of glazed tiles added to the color effect.

Orthodox Muslims gained influence during the regime of Shahjahan and the preference shifted to the Persian style again. The twelve-door pavilion with triple entrances on all four sides and vaulted halls called "Baradari" were introduced.

Taj Mahal is thoroughly Indian in spirit but some critics offer qualifications. At its peak, Indo-Islamic architecture started showing significant elements of Persian style and a sort of decadence set in. Before the end of the Mughal dynasty, the development of Indo-Islamic architecture had ceased and with the end of the dynasty it became a real orphan.

2. The Rock Shelters of Bhimbetka

(Prehistoric–18ᵗʰ Century)

Bhimbetka in Madhya Pradesh, central India, is one of the three richest sites of painted rock art in the world. This is the largest group of pre-historic painted shelters and perhaps the oldest paintings in India.

Bhimbetka, meaning the seat of Bhima, a hero of the Mahabharata epic, is located 47 km (28 miles) from Bhopal in central India in the Vindhyan Mountains — one of the oldest geological formations in central India. Transportation facilities are scarce and no facilities of any kind are available at Bhimbetka. Bhopal is the convenient center for boarding, lodging and transport to visit Bhimbetka. UNESCO declared the rock shelters a World Heritage site in June 2003.

Bhimbetka represents a group of seven small hills, designated as areas 1 to 7, extending over 10 km (6 miles). There are 754 natural rock shelters with cave paintings on these hills. The hills are designated A through F and on each hill the shelters are in numbered groups. Area 7 at Bhimbetka has only 10 shelters grouped under A. Area 3 has 291 shelters grouped in six groups, A, B, C, E, F, & G. The shelters are painted with scenes from the life and times of Stone Age nomadic hunters that occupied the shelters from 1.5 million years up to about CE 1700, representing the earliest human cultures in India.

V. S. Wakankar discovered more than 500 of these shelters in 1970. The surrounding area, covered with dense deciduous trees and abundant wild life, offered plenty of food and three perennial water springs; it was an ideal habitat for prehistoric men. As the shelters are spread over a wide area (currently uninhabited) in locations difficult to access without guides, the Archeological Survey of India has selected a few representative shelters for visitors on Bhimbetka and has provided a guide facility. The photos presented here are from these caves, numbered 1 to 10 by the Archeological Survey.

The Bhimbetka hills, formed of sedimentary rock, are six hundred meters (1860 ft.) above sea level and 100 meters (600 ft.) above the valley floor, and crest at a 25-meter (75 ft.) high flat-topped ridge. The ridge has broken into large boulders of various shapes due to weathering (Fig. 1.1). Mechanical and chemical weathering of the base of boulders by water and wind carrying sand and debris has eroded the lower layers of the boulders, thus naturally creating the shelters. Some large boulders dislodged due to the erosion of the base have formed shallow caves (Fig. 1.2). Weathering has carved the boulders into various shapes and sizes.

The shelters vary in size and height, but most are large enough to provide shelter and high enough to serve as a look out for the game animals that once visited the water holes in the area.

Fig. 1.1. Bhimbetka. Ridge of the hill. Sandstone.

A few shelters are so small that they are suitable only for small animals. The shelters provide some protection from rain, tropical sun and predators. Weathering has exposed metamorphosed crystalline rocks, in some places, containing quartzite as outcrops through the sedimentary strata. Early inhabitants used this crystalline material to make tools.

Fig. 1.2. Bhimbetka. A large detached boulder. Sandstone.

The northern slope of Bhimbetka Hill, due to considerable tree felling in recent times, shows much erosion. A road suitable for vehicular traffic has been built up to the base of the ridge. There are considerable Hindu and Buddhist archaeological remains in the region. A temple dedicated to the mother goddess is located very near to the shelters.

The rock art includes petroglyphs (engraving), geoglyphs (large figures drawn on the ground by arranging stones), rock bruising (chipping off the weathered rock surface to create a two-dimensional picture by changing the surface color) and pictographs (paintings on stone). The major art form of India, rock-cut architecture and sculpture, is possibly the outgrowth of early practices as evidenced here.

The earliest rock paintings in Europe were discovered at Altamira in Spain in 1879. Twelve years earlier, in 1867–1868, Archibald Carlleyle discovered rock paintings in Uttar Pradesh, a neighboring state of Madhya Pradesh. He described the paintings as "Illustration in a very stiff and archaic manner, scenes in the life of the ancient stone chippers; others represent animals or hunts of animals by men armed with bows and arrows, spears and hatchets." Carlleyle had no doubt about the prehistoric vintage of the paintings. But he did not publish his finding and left his notes with a friend. In 1906, V.A. Smith published the notes. In 1883, J. Cockburn discovered a well-preserved painting of a rhinoceros in the region. But he believed the painting to be only 300 years old, as the Mughal Emperor Babar had reported rhinoceros in the region in 1529. V.S. Wakankar, who had discovered painted shelters earlier in the adjacent region, noticed the broken

cliff of Bhimbetka Hill in 1970, while traveling by train, and suspecting there might be something there he arranged to visit the hill.

Rock art is pure art as it reflects the infancy of painting without the complex influence of the mainstream of civilization, and there are many masterpieces. In rock art we see the history of man presenting his rituals, myths, beliefs, customs and way of life through the ages. In addition the art reveals evidence of early tools used by man. Microliths are small stone projectiles attached on the tip of wooden handles for use in hunting. It would have been difficult to understand the use of microliths in the absence of these paintings.

A few scientific techniques can be applied to date the rock paintings. The most often used technique is radiocarbon dating. This method is not reliable for dates going back more than 40,000 years as the amount of radiocarbon remaining in the residue is too small to provide a reliable test.

In colored paintings where bird droppings are used for white, or colored pigments are mixed with binding agents containing organic compounds like blood, plant gum or sap, the age of the painting can be determined. Regrettably, to obtain sufficient quantity of sample for analysis a large chunk of painting need to be scraped.

Other analytical techniques are the potassium-argon and thermo luminescence (TL) methods. Rocks that are 100,000 years old can be dated by the potassium-argon method, but not embedded objects.

The TL technique is based on radioactive elements in pottery (soil). When heated to 500 C, pottery releases electrons in the form of light energy. This method is suitable for measuring the age of objects up to 80,000 years old.

The stratified deposits in refuse dumps also provide a rough way to estimate the age of manmade artifacts. Most of the Middle Paleolithic habitation deposits ranging from 140,000 to 70,000 years BP are well preserved at Bhimbetka, but remains of human skeletons pertaining to this period have not been found. The few human burial sites and skeletons unearth at Bhimbetka belong to the historic age. It is difficult to ascertain the type of human who occupied the cave during this period.

In one cave excavated at Bhimbetka the lowest layer was found to contain pebble tools similar to pebble tools found in East Africa, where they have been dated to 1,500,000 years BP. Based on this evidence, R.R.R. Brooks suggest habitation of some of the shelters by predecessors of modern man (Homo sapiens) who entered Asia between 150,000 and 120,000 BP. There was one major glaciation during this period.

As noted above, Wakankar discovered the Bhimbetka shelters in 1970. The first attempt to date the paintings was made on the basis of stylistic drawing, but none of the paintings were considered more than a thousand years old. Wakankar had discovered paintings in shelters in the surrounding area and in 1955 proposed another method to date the painting by studying the style used in each superimposed layer of painting. By this method he dated some paintings in Madhya Pradesh to the Mesolithic period.

Man has been living in India for more than 500,000 years and has left his material wealth, mostly tools, in the habitation deposits. The general sequence of prehistoric and historic cultures in India, some based on C14 carbon dating, has been determined. The top most Iron Age covers 2300 to 3000 years BP, followed by Copper-Bronze Age 3000 to 5500, Mesolithic 7000 to 10,000, Paleolithic 10,000 to 1000,000, Acheulian 4000 to 500,000 and pebble-tool culture 500,000 to 1,500,000 BP.

To study the times and life of the Stone age man through various ages and find artifacts in habitation deposits that may relate to the paintings, archaeologists started excavating shelter floors in 1972. It was noticed that some shelters were used for habitation only once or twice, some shelters were used intermittently, and some were in continuous use. The excavation of the largest rock shelter (IIIF-23) in 1973–76 by V.N. Misra, revealed habitation deposits ranging over all the archeological periods, starting from pebble-tool culture.

The earliest culture recognized in habitat deposit above the bedrock in Bhimbetka shelter III F 23 and 24 is pebble-tool culture (500,000 to 1,500,000 BP), characterized by tools made from river pebbles. A clear evolution of Acheulian culture from pebble-tool culture was not seen in Bhimbetka excavations. But study of the open campsites in areas near Bhimbetka showed a change from pebble tools to Acheulian bifacial tools. Early man had started fashioning simple tools by breaking one side of an oblong stones small enough to hold in hand by striking it with another stone to get a sharp edge on one side (choppers) and by breaking both sides of the same stone to create bifacial chopping tools. The bifacials made at Bhimbetka are 22 centimeters (9 inches) long.

Chalcedony, agate and chert, hard stones widely distributed in the area, were used to make tools in the Acheulian period but sandstone tools were also widely used. The evolution of upper Acheulian from Lower Acheulian is also marked at Bhimbetka. In the lower Acheulian thick bifacial tools were in use. In the upper Acheulian, flakes and thin tools were manufactured.

Possibly the oldest wall in the world was built at Bhimbetka during Acheulian era.

There is a habitation gap after the Upper Acheulian period. Thick deposits of Acheulian cultures were left by Homo

erectus, the nomadic hunter-gatherer using the shelters. They had migrated throughout the world except the Americas and Oceania. They discovered methods to make fire about 500,000 years ago, which helped them survive the Ice Age.

A form of art has been ascribed to the Homo erectus occupying the shelters during Acheulian era. On the floor of the Auditorium shelter at Bhimbetka and in various sites in Africa, Home erectus made shallow circular cavities a few centimeters (inches) in diameter and in depth. An unknown tool was used to make and polish the inside of these "cupules". It has been proposed that these cupules were used over 100,000 years ago, in the Acheulian age, as the depository of human placentae to assure long life. Engravings around cupules have been made, making them appear like vulva, a link to fertility. Cupules between the legs of human engravings were made to indicate female sex.

No other forms of art are attributed to Homo erectus.

The Ice Age (Pleistocene) was a long period between 1.8 million and about 12,000 years BP. Glaciers intermittently advanced from the north and retreated eight times in the northern hemisphere, followed by shorter interglacial periods. (The interglacial period we enjoy today started around 12,000 years BP.) There were three glaciations during the early Paleolithic period. The effect of climatic changes on habitation deposit is seen at Bhimbetka. To study the climate of Bhimbetka, trenches were excavated in few shelters to observe soil profile characteristics, weathering of tools, presence of highly cemented breccias and conglomerate and encrustation with $CaCo_3$, etc.

It was concluded that during the Middle Paleolithic the climate had become comparatively drier. Late summer had heavy rains but not as much as in the Acheulian. During the Upper Paleolithic and Mesolithic period rainfall decreased and drier conditions prevailed. The Mesolithic period was extremely dry. During the Mesolithic age profound changes took place in fauna and flora. New species of plants appeared. Swift and agile animals requiring light tools to hunt like bow and arrow dominated the fauna. The climate was similar to today's. The detailed correlation of climate with glaciations and inter-glacial periods has not been worked out.

The next culture represented at Bhimbetka is Middle Paleolithic (30,000 to 100,000). In India the Middle Paleolithic culture is outgrowth of Acheulian culture. The traditional development of Upper Acheulian into Lower Paleolithic (540,000 to 140,000) did not take place at Bhimbetka. Evolution of Middle Paleolithic from Acheulian is distinct at Bhimbetka. In the middle Paleolithic Period tools made from chert and jasper as well as from fine sandstone were used. It is natural that early hunter-gatherer occupying sandstone hills would manufacture scrapers, blades and points from sandstone and as he moved back and forth to the plains at the foot of the hills in the Malwa region he used chert and jasper, available in the trap region, to make tools. The color and transparent appearance of these minerals are attractive, besides.

Such movement has also been recorded in other regions. A shift in tool manufacturing also took place resulting in manufacture of composite tools. Cleavers and hand axes disappeared. Smaller tools were made of flat natural slabs. There was increased use of tools made of organic materials, like bone. Scrapers were used for woodwork and to insert bones on other tools or clubs, using natural resins. Other tools made during this era included side-scrapers with many subtypes; and points with circular cross-sections and borers. Early Stone Age tools were also still in use. There was a major shift in raw materials used for tool-making in Europe, but at Bhimbetka quartzite remained in use.

The evolution of the Upper Paleolithic (10,000 to 20,000) from the Middle Paleolithic might have taken place in the Deccan Trap region. The Upper Paleolithic tools obtained from the top red silt layers of the south campsite in Bhimbetka have longer blades with fluted cores. Burins are extremely common.

The tools were characterized by the introduction of true blade technology along with the use of flake tools. The tools were mostly non-geometric microliths. Bone tools were also in use. Evidence of fireplaces and animal remains is seen. Worship of the mother goddess and fire, and painting of shelters at Bhimbetka and other shelters in Vindhyan hills in central India began. At Bhimbetka thick blades with burin and several types of scrapers are found just below the deposits of next period.

The next cultural period, the Mesolithic or Middle Stone Age, extended from 20,000 to 9500 years BP. Small "pigmy" tools were in use. Pottery did not yet exist. The last glaciations occurred near the end of the Mesolithic period, when the present climate appeared, with new flora and fauna. Big game became extinct, giving place to smaller and faster animals that required light, small and thin tools to hunt. Geometric microliths were mostly fitted into wood and bone and used as compound tools. There was marked increase in use of triangles and trapeze-shaped microliths.

Decoration on bones and bone ornaments was evident. In Bhimbetka the preferred raw material for tool manufacturing changed to chert and chalcedony, available in the vicinity. Rich deposits of such tools are found at Bhimbetka.

Intentional human burial occurred during this period for the first time. An appreciable increase in population is indicated by occupation of the maximum number of shelters and an increase in habitation deposits. Construction of fireplaces, artificial stone slab floors, and walls have been detected. This was the golden age of rock painting at Bhimbetka.

The chronology of the Mesolithic period is not securely established for all shelters. For some Bhimbetka caves the oldest date is 7790 +/- 220 years.

It is suggested that man in the Middle and New Stone Age gave aesthetic consideration in the making of stone tools by selection of color and the process of carving facets. Carvings on shell and bones also suggest that early man was concerned with more than the utility of the tools.

The New Stone Age (Neolithic), from 9500 to 4500 BP in India, refers to the era with settled life, animal husbandry and cultivation, but primarily man still depended on stone tools. In the plains below Bhimbetka Hills a Neolithic transition from food gathering to food production, requiring some control of the environment, gradual took place between 8000–6000 BP in Baluchistan. In northern, eastern and southern India the change appeared during the second millennium BCE.

The Chalcolithic (Heliolithic), from 4500 to 3500 BP, refers to the age when copper and bronze tools were used along with stone tools. Microliths were used along with metal tools. Earthen pots replaced basketry. Beads were used for decoration. The tribal lifestyle was not much different from that of the Mesolithic period but contact with people living in the plains made possible the exchange of copper objects, pottery and other objects for jungle products. The basic tools of hunting remained the same.

During the Iron Age, from 3500 BCE, iron tools were in use. Domestication of animals was another accomplishment. In the upper most layers the presence of iron tools, historic pottery and punch-marked coins suggest persistence of the Mesolithic way of life in the shelters well into the Iron Age. Increased contact with agricultural communities finally brought the inhabitants of these shelters to the plains.

The excavation work at Bhimbetka shows that the shelters were in use for more than 100,000 years. However, the human bones found in habitat deposits were from no earlier than 10,000 BP and no direct evidence of earlier habitation was unearthed. Indirect evidence suggests occupation of shelters by Homo erectus, Homo sapiens and true man in progressive sequence.

The presence of many-faceted hematite pebbles used for red coloring of paintings was first found in the Upper Paleolithic layers (70,000–20,000 BP) in close proximity to the paintings. Nodules and rubbed cakes of mineral colors, mainly hematite red, were found in early Mesolithic caves. Green colored pieces found in Upper Paleolithic shelters were not found in any Mesolithic deposits. It was concluded that some of the art is prehistoric, dating to about 10,000 years BP. Man has inhabited some of the shelters for well over 100,000 years and some of the paintings could be much older. Further research is required.

The paintings are broadly classified into prehistoric and historic. Prehistory refers broadly to the period before which writing was developed. Proto-history refers to the period when early writing had been developed, which remains undeciphered today.

Many paintings in Bhimbetka are very faint or obliterated. Due to calcification many paintings are obliterated in part, and imagination in many cases takes over as we strive to interpret the images.

In Bhimbetka paintings were done without any preparation of the shelter wall. A rock surface was used or re-used, without rubbing off the old paintings, resulting in as many as fifteen layers of figures superimposed — even though a large blank area remained available in the shelter. In most cases two or three superimposition layers are noticed. This preference for a particular location may be due to the availability of light in these areas that are easily observed from outside. Super-imposition of paintings has provided further clues as to the relative age of the paintings.

Pigments used for coloring were obtained in the surrounding hills. Ochre, hydrated oxide of iron, was used mixed with clay for red color. When burnt it yields a wide spectrum of colors: yellow, brown and orange. Copper compound produces green. Kaolin, gypsum, bird droppings or plant latex was used for white. Pigments were mixed with water. White and green were diluted greatly with water to give transparent colors. Solid or powder colors were used rarely. Wet opaque colors were achieved by application of pigments in oils. In historic paintings dark crimson and dark red were applied as non-transparent colors.

Pigments were applied to the rock wall by fingers, stick, chewed palmetto stick washed to remove broken fibers and dried. Most paintings were possibly drawn by brushes made from the hair of animals living in the vicinity. Handprints on the walls are an important element. A few handprints appear to be those of infants and children.

The medium to carry pigments varied from water to blood, oils, plant sap and white of egg. Fat is reportedly not used in Indian paintings.

The inhabited shelters have no paintings or have paintings of poor quality. Those shelters that show no signs of habitation have superb quality paintings, drawn by skilled artists who were keen observers of nature and life. Some

paintings are done on high locations, probably using scaffolds or branches of trees. In some cases projection platforms were constructed (which have since collapsed). These artists seem to have been provided with facilities to paint and freedom from the daily routine of life in order to develop their skills.

Shelter IIIE-9 is richly painted with the oldest and finest paintings. There are fifteen horses and fifteen buffalo, six chital deer, six langur or leaf monkeys, five elephants, two cows and an ox. One boar and one unidentified animal are also painted in this shelter. Eleven of these drawings are from prehistoric times. It is difficult to ascertain if the bulls and cows were drawn to record life as it existed or had any religious significance to the occupants.

The paintings depict all the activities of primitive life, like hunting, dancing, religion, domestic, recreation, copulation, picnics, collection and transportation of foods.

The trees are very natural (Fig. 1.3).

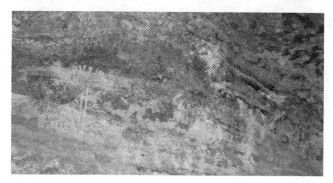

Fig. 1.3. Bhimbetka. A tree. Prehistoric.

Natural scenery is almost non-existent. Different kinds of birds in groups are depicted. One painting depicts men trying to steal eggs from a huge bird and the bird attacking them (Fig. 1.4). A feline beside them is awaiting her chance.

In another painting, a large predatory type of bird with large claws is seen (Fig. 1.5). One man is throwing a spear at the bird while another man, camouflaged as a bird, is aiming an arrow at a chital deer.

Fig. 1.4. Bhimbetka. Bird attacking men stealing eggs. Prehistoric.

The characteristics of paintings differ in the prehistoric and the historic periods. Most historic paintings were drawn from 600 BCE to as recent as 1700. Most of the historic period scenes depict battles between the rulers governing the valley below with swords, shields, spears, bows and arrows. One painting realistically depicts a cavalry charge with men carrying spears in raised hands on galloping horses (Fig. 1.6).

Fig. 1.5. Bhimbetka. Camouflaged men hunting bird and chital. Prehistoric.

A panoramic scene in shelter III A-30 depicts a march of cavalry through a pass. The cavalry has taken all the precautions to avoid surprise attack. Some men on foot are leading the horses by holding the reins and some are marching holding drawn bow and arrows. Many birds and a scorpion are interposed in the marching cavalry to make the scene authentic. Near the end of the painting a large drawing depicts a blooming lotus, possibly on a flag, which is the quest of the marching cavalry (Fig. 1.7).

Fig. 1.6. Bhimbetka. Marching cavalry. Historic.

Fig. 1.7. Bhimbetka. Cavalry passing through Mountain pass. Historic.

Another painting in shelter III A-30 depicts men riding horses and carrying iron weapons; they have breached a circular enclosure, possibly a fort. Tame elephants with men carrying spears are also part of these scenes.

Fig. 1.8. Bhimbetka. Colored flowers and stallion. Prehistoric.

Decorative paintings and flowers appeared in the historic age. Flowers and leaves are mostly drawn in color. A stallion is standing near a bunch of colored flower in valley in Fig. 1.8. Above, on the ridge, a man is standing with weapon near a tree. A man driving a domesticated animal with a thick stick in his hand suggests the settled way of the life of the people living in the valley (Fig. 1.9). Most of these paintings lack naturalism and show marked decline in artistic quality.

Fig. 1.10. Bhimbetka. Multi-armed Ganesha. Historic.

Fig. 1.9. Bhimbetka. Man leading a domesticated animal. Historic.

The earliest historic period paintings do not contain fighting scenes, pre-Vedic gods, or the proto-historic fertility symbols of the phallus and vulva. The historic symbols and gods that are drawn in the shelters include the trident (the three-pronged emblem of Siva); Nandi, the carrier of Siva, the elephant-headed and multi-armed Ganesha carrying the trident in one hand (Fig. 1.10), and a multi-armed Siva dancing with an inverted trident in one hand (Fig. 1.11). All other Vedic gods including Vishnu (he was a Vedic god till the advent of the Brahmin era) are absent.

Other celestial figures are *yaksa* or nature spirits, and a multi-armed being drawn in shelter IIIF-35. In shelter IIIC-19 a boar is drawn using a technique which makes him appear gigantic: the boar has large, broad face, and the men standing beside it are drawn in stick style, so that the boar dominates the entire scene. In the foreground a stick-figure man is running, possibly in fear. This could possibly be the germ for the creation of the boar incarnation of Vishnu.

The inscriptions found in some of the shelters were not written by the early inhabitants. Visitors during historic times introduced wrote in a few shelters.

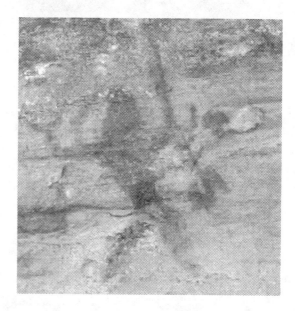

Fig. 1.11. Bhimbetka. Multi-armed Siva. Historic.

Animals are the most common subjects of the paintings. In the Upper Paleolithic paintings realistic outlines of animals are drawn. Sometimes a sense of the modern art styles of impressionism, cubism and symbolism can be imagined. Chalcolithic drawings are less realistic and dynamic. The animal body infilling is generally accomplished by cross hatching or different geometrical designs. Humped bull was introduced during this period.

The most common animals in the paintings are chital, both stags and does; the most beautiful scene is of a fawn looking back. The majority of paintings, especially of the early prehistoric age, depict closely-packed large mixed herds of herbivores and carnivores. The animals are full of vitality, always drawn in motion or grazing. Men carrying spears are interposed in herds, walking, running or galloping behind the animals. In later paintings hunting tools depicted include bows, arrows, traps, nets and snares. Animals drawn smaller in size also show remarkable realism. Most animals are drawn in a side pose but their horns are painted in front profile (Fig. 1.12).

Fig. 1.12. *Animals in side pose with large horns facing front. Prehistoric.*

Some animals are drawn in what we might call an x-ray style to show a fetus (sometimes two), or the vegetation that has been eaten in the stomach. Stomachs are decorated with lines or geometric designs (Fig. 1.13). Large animals like boar and buffalo are interposed in herds of other animals or drawn alone on ceilings. Few of the large animals are drawn in life size.

Small lizards and scorpions are also seen in the paintings. A large scorpion is drawn with a hair-like structure on the back — probably the mother is carrying the newly hatched baby scorpions on her back (Fig. 1.14). In addition to the scorpion the drawing shows a rabbit, goats, a donkey and a bird.

There are no scenes of animal copulation, although some animals are drawn with an erect penis. In a few drawings an animal is painted with an erect penis standing behind an animal with slightly raised tail (III-E-9). Animals with udders, like cows and buffalo, are rare, possibly due to the inhabitants' lack of pastoral background.

Fig. 1.13. *Bhimbetka. Animals in X-ray style and with geometric designs. Prehistoric.*

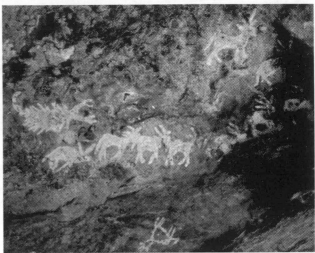

Fig. 1.14. *Bhimbetka. Scorpion and other animals. Prehistoric.*

Carnivorous animals include the tiger, leopard, cheetah and hyena. One sketch of a tiger crouching, muscles tensed to jump on a stag in the foreground, indicate the keen observation of the artist (Fig. 1.15). In the background a leopard is drawn with white outlines, the white dots applied on the body by the fingertip.

The predatory instinct of man in some cases is accompanied with sympathy for the injured animal. The wounded animals are generally depicted standing majestically, surrounded by hunters, and very rarely shown fallen down.

Fig. 1.15. *Bhimbetka. Tiger posed to attack stage. Leopard in background. Prehistoric.*

The artists were also capable of depicting emotion. In the neighboring state one painting in a shelter depicts a deer standing with a large spears thrust in her chest by a man standing in the foreground. Blood is gushing out of the wound and milk is spilling from the udder. Her entrails have dropped out of the abdomen. Two hunters are running away, in shame or fear.

Artists have also portrayed the expression of fear and bewilderment in animals. In shelter IIIA-21 a boar is shown chased by two dogs. The galloping boar shows the signs of fear; open mouth, ears turned back and erect tail. The bewilderment of animals upon the appearance of hunters is visible in most scenes.

Economic activities include depictions of a group of men carrying loads, or collecting honey (Fig. 1.16). One man appears to be running away, possibly because of the bees' attack.

The depiction of cultural life in shelter IIIC-9 shows a family on a picnic: a pregnant woman, two old women, and three children of various ages playing around. Boys are always depicted playing or running. A painting on Shelter IIIA-21 gives a panoramic view of community life similar to the depiction of morning activities of village life on the wall of the Krishna *mandapa* (pavilion) at Mamallapuram. Animals of various sizes move about, running and galloping. Hunters carrying bows move slowly towards an animal. A group of men carrying spears are driving a large buffalo with huge horns, possibly into a trap. The huge buffalo appears to be charging the people standing near the trap gate. In the center of the painting some men carrying weapons are climbing, possibly on a high lookout. In one corner bushes are drawn in a semicircle, with men standing, surrounding a beautiful female wearing a pigtail. Her lovely body possibly coincides with the start of the development of the idealized feminine body as drawn at Ajanta. A very faint figure appears to be prostrated before her, indicating her status.

Fig. 1.16. Bhimbetka. Men collecting honey and carrying loads. Prehistoric.

Drawing of humans are always stylized and schematic but full of dynamic spirit. In early paintings men are drawn as stick figures, later as geometric figure with triangles, circles and straight lines. In late drawings humans are drawn more naturally.

Fig. 1.17. Bhimbetka. Group and solo dancing. Prehistoric.

These artists had good knowledge of animal anatomy and animals are drawn with more naturalism than humans. The artists were keen observers and could hardly have missed the detailed observation of human anatomy. A superstitious belief that has survived to the present is that painting a figure (never mind taking a photograph) seizes the soul of the object. It is likely these artists drew the animals to seize them and thus facilitate the hunt. It is interesting to speculate whether these Stone Age hunters were wary of drawing a human too realistically in case that would make him easy prey.

Women, even when drawn with stick bodies, are rhythmic, and those drawn in abstract and natural styles are shapely. Facial features are omitted in all human renderings and people are always shown in motion. In early paintings both men and women are drawn naked. Occasionally a naked man with erect or pendulant penis was drawn but not decorated as in African paintings. By the Mesolithic period, leaves or loincloths were worn. Men wear long hair and females tie back their hair. Some women are shown wearing ornaments such as armlets and knee bands. Wall and ceiling paintings of the Mesolithic phase depict scenes of hunting, food gathering and fishing. The hunters carried long harpoons (lances), bows and arrows.

Dance and rituals seem to have been important cultural features in a life full of fear and struggle with nature. There are many scenes of men and women dancing together, arm in arm, in rows or in circles. Rarely, solo dancers are also depicted (Fig. 1.17). The drum is the only musical instrument depicted.

Man, armed with bow and arrow, was the most powerful entity in the jungle during the Mesolithic period. This kind of hunting was comparatively safe and easy, leaving a little leisure in which to ponder life and the changes in nature. At this stage some sort of primitive spiritualism or religion seems to emerge. Fantastical large and composite animals appear in the art work; ceremonial dances are created. Superstitious fears are warded off by masked and animalized representations in the person of the sorcerer, who protects man from harm. In Shelter IIIE-3 two sorcerers wearing elaborate masks and grass skirts are drawn. One of the sorcerers is hitting a lizard on the head with the end of a long stick. A scorpion is shown advancing toward the sorcerer. Possibly the drawing depicts some superstition associated with lizards, or hunting lizards for food.

In shelter III C-12, an infant is shown lying on the ground below between the outstretched thighs of a spider-shaped women, indicating birth. Possibly she represents the mother goddess. The death of a child is depicted by the excavation of a circular pit with the body of a child placed at one end and three same size-bodies placed at a right angle to the first body. Possibly it was a mass burial. In this painting there is only one man, who is digging the grave, and a pair of mourning figures sitting beside the grave. The children must be from a single family and one can only suppose the deaths were due to an epidemic or accident.

There are only a couple of human copulation scenes. On the ceiling in shelter III B-20 a painting depicts a woman drawn in white, in stick style, lying on the ground with her legs wide open. The outstretched erect penis of the man standing in front is touching the junction of the woman's thighs. In shelter IIIF-1 a naked woman with outstretched legs is sitting on the ground and a man is moving away in a hurry, with his loincloth floating behind.

Men and women in erotic postures are seen in four caves. Y. Methpal (1984) has attributed the scarcity of erotic scenes to the indifference of the artists to sex. It could as well reflect a low level of sexual activity on the part of the inhabitants. The census of humans in the paintings given by Methpal indicates a monumental scarcity of females. There are 2076 figures of men compared to 67 of women, a ratio of 31 men to 1 woman. Some of the women are also shown engaged in hunting along with men. The indifference to sex in the face of a monumental scarcity of females is possibly due to the daily constant struggle with harsh environmental factors. The most revealing census is the drawing of only 7 pregnant women. In addition only 24 boys, 2 girls and 6 infants are found in the paintings. Rarely is the death of an adult or child depicted. The artists were keen observers and unless there were other considerations that remain unknown, these numbers indicate that in a total population of 2175 there were only 32 children, representing stagnant population growth. The abundance of erotic sculpture in temples of recent (historic) times possibly suggests that efforts were made to draw the attention of man to procreation, which in combination with other factors has led to the present overpopulation of India.

Rock art has been described as the first conscious effort of prehistoric man in the abstraction of reality, to communicate, to create and to influence the course of life. It is said to portray the origins of human the conception of reality and to perpetuate the cultural precedent of a society. It throws light on the contemporary life. The development of rock art is intertwined with the emergence of abstract concepts, the ability to symbolize and to communicate at an advanced level, to develop the notion of the self.

With or without a sufficient number of women, the most important force for society was fertility, the ability to reproduce its own kind. As a result figurines of Venus were carved; the earliest known is dated between 28,000–23,000 BCE, followed by other deities. The first life-size statue of Neolithic man unearthed in Turkey was carved between 9500–7200 BCE, and he has a prominent, erect phallus. The most common figurines from this era are of women. Terracotta female figurines associated with fertility, procreation and continuity may not have had divine status but they were a popular motif.

Whether these painting were intended as a kind of food magic to establish control over game and insure success in hunting, as an effort to propitiate the spirits that live in dark places to obtain their help in bringing rain, to provide some kind of totemic protection or merely to document and illustrate life, the paintings reached a glorious height of beauty and perfection at Ajanta, after which the era of rock paintings in India came to an end.

Some of the people who still live in the valley below could be descendents of the Stone Age hunters that occupied these shelters. Their ancestors have not passed on any information about the paintings; or the descendants, thinking the paintings an unworthy inheritance, have discarded the knowledge. They believe witches and goblins did the paintings on moonless nights. In a way, this is fortunate as it has kept the caressing human hand at a distance and helped the pictures survive so far.

3. Bodh Gaya

(260 BCE–11ᵀᴴ CENTURY)

The most sacred Buddhist religious center in India is located at Bodh Gaya, which is 13 km (8 miles) from Gaya railway station on the Delhi–Calcutta railways, with direct trains from Delhi, Calcutta, Varanasi, and Panta. Crowded public transport buses and auto-rickshaws are available for transportation from Gaya to Bodh Gaya. Monasteries and residential facilities are available at Bodh Gaya. UNESCO declared the monuments at Bodh Gaya World Heritage Monuments in 2002.

Buddha, the founder of one of the largest religions of world, was born at Lumbini in 562 BCE (according to Nepalese tradition, in 624 BCE). His father Shudhodana was chief of the Shakya tribe, ruling Kapilavastu, in Uttar Pradesh, on the present-day border with Nepal. All the places associated with Buddha's life and travels are shown in the map of western India below. Except Lumbini (now in Nepal), they are all in the Uttar Pradesh and Bihar states of India.

While Buddha's mother was pregnant she dreamed of a white elephant entering her body. Shudhodana invited astrologers to interpret the dream and was told that the child to be born would become a universal monarch or universal teacher. The mother of Buddha delivered him while standing under the Shala tree (*Shorea robusta*) in the garden of his grandfather's palace. At birth, the prince Sidharta was given the family name, Gautama. He was well educated, and sheltered from the needs and suffering of men in the palace of his father at Kapilavastu. He was married to his lovely cousin Yashodhara of the Kolia tribe, and had a son, Rahula. He was pampered with the luxuries and pleasures of the palace. But during his

visits to the town he spied an old, debilitated person, a sick person, and a dead body. Even more affecting was the sight of an ascetic who was peaceful and happy without the luxuries of life or any possessions. That started him on a quest to find the cause of sorrow in life and a way to escape its miseries.

Map of West India showing places associated with Buddha.

One night at the age of twenty-three, when everyone was asleep, he left the palace, with his personal attendant Chandaka. When they reached the outskirts of the city he sent Chandaka back with his belongings, cut off his hair, turned mendicant and walked 650 km (300 miles) to Rajagraha (modern Rajgir) in Bihar, the capital of Magadha and a great center of learning with many resident philosophers and teachers. When the king of Magadha, Bimbisara, learnt that son of his friend King Shudhodana was begging in the city, he went to meet him — and learned that Sidharta had renounced the luxuries of world. Bimbisara begged Sidharta to return to the kingdom of his father, as the life of a mendicant was not befitting to him; or to accept half of his kingdom to rule if he did not wish to go back.

Sidharta gracefully declined the offer. Then Bimbisara begged Sidharta to visit him first, after he attained enlightenment; Sidharta agreed. But he was not satisfied with what he learnt at Rajagraha and left for the forest at Uruvela, near Gaya, where he mediated on Gayasirsa hill for some time. Then he moved to the outskirts of Uruvela and settled at Bodh Gaya, on the banks of the river Neranjana, to meditate under a Bodhi tree (*Ficus religiosa*), after a grass cutter spread some grass for him. The five ascetics he had met at Rajagraha joined him.

During the first six years of his search for enlightenment Sidharta by practicing self-mortification, and was reduced to skin and bones. One day he fell unconscious and a shepherd give him milk, and took him into his care. After the incident Sidharta concentrated more on meditation than on austerities, realizing the futility of bodily mortification. At this time Sujata, the daughter of the Senani village chief, who was expecting a baby, had vowed that if a son were born she would make a special offering of food to the deity of a nearby banyan tree (*Ficus indica*). When a son was born to her, she prepared rice pudding and sent her maid to the banyan tree to clean the area and arrange the offering of food to the god. Meanwhile, Sidharta arrived at the banyan tree and sat down to mediate. When the maid saw Sidharta seated under the tree, she reported to her mistress that the god himself had appeared. Sujata excitedly hurried to the tree and offered the food to Sidharta in a golden bowl, saluted him with respect, and withdrew in consideration and modesty, leaving the golden bowl. It was the first solid meal Sidharta had in years. After accepting the food, Sidharta went to the Neranjara River, nearby. He put the bowl in the river, thinking that if the bowl floated it was a sign that he would achieve enlightenment; if it sank, he would not. The bowl floated against the water current, and then sank. Those who had joined him in his ascetic meditations now left him, disgusted at his taking solid food.

Determined to attain enlightenment, he continued to mediate deeply on the mysteries of life. After a few years of meditation, one evening Mara, the god of evils and death, sent his beautiful daughters to break Sidharta's concentration. When they failed, he sent his army of demons, the personification of human desires. But Sidharta remained steadfast. Mara sent storms, with thunder, lightening and blasts of cold air. Buddha pointed his hand toward earth and said, "Let the earth be my witness that I will attain enlightenment and put an end to the sorrows of mankind". Then the earth shook with a roaring noise and a thunderbolt flashed in the air; the army of ugly demons ran away. Sidharta entered into deeper meditation.

He learnt about his previous lives, acquired divine vision and understood the law of cause and effect; by morning he was enlightened. It was the year 528 BCE. For one week he sat under the Bodhi tree, enjoying the bliss of enlightenment. The second week he spent walking to and fro near the tree, the third week he stood staring at the tree and the fourth week he meditated under the tree. The next three weeks he spent under the banyan tree where Sujata had offered him sweet rice pudding, near Muchalinda Lake where the Naga serpent had protected him from rain and a freezing gale; and the final week under Rajyatana tree where two traveling merchants had offered him honey and cake. By this time he had possibly decided his future course of action. Seven weeks after enlightenment he returned to the Bodhi tree, bowed to the tree in reverence and left for Sarnath (also called Deer Park) near Varanasi in Uttar Pradesh. There, he gave his first sermon to an audience that included the five ascetics who were his first companions for some time at Rajagraha and Uruvela.

Prasenjit, King of Kosala, Bimbisara, King of Magadha, and his son Ajatashatru became his followers. Anathapindaka, a rich merchant of Sravasti in Uttar Pradesh donated the Jetavana garden and built a vihara for the use of Buddha and his disciples. Amrapali, a royal courtesan of Vaishali, gave the gift of a mango grove. King Bimbisara donated a bamboo grove near Rajagraha. His father invited him to Kapilavastu and donated a banyan tree grove. Buddha turned all these places into residences for monks. He converted his father, his father's wife Yashodhara and son Rahula to Buddhism.

He continued wandering in the Ganges River Valley for fifty years after his enlightenment and preached four holy truths based on psychological (not metaphysical or theological) foundations. These holy truths are that birth, age, sickness and death are the causes of sorrow in life. The second truth is desires and attachment to the pleasures of life cause suffering and result in the chain of rebirths. The third truth is that the extinction of desires is essential to break the chain of rebirths and escape from sorrow in life (nirvana). Lastly, that detachment from life can be achieved by following the Eightfold Path. The Eightfold path was explained as having the right view, right intention, right speech, right action, right living, right effort, right mindfulness, and right meditation on the mysteries of life. This doctrine is very different from the doctrine portrait as represented by the ninth incarnation of Vishnu born as Buddha.

Buddha died at the age of eighty on the outskirts of Kusinara (Kushinagar) on the boarders of Uttar Pradesh and Nepal. According to his wishes he was cremated, and his ashes and relics were buried in stupas at important crossroads. Ashoka reopened these stupas collected some relics, and distributed them all over his kingdom in hundreds of stupas he constructed.

Buddhism enjoyed royal patronage from Bimbisara and Ajatashatru in the sixth and fifth centuries BCE. He became well established in the region and survived the Jain dynasty regimes that followed. When Ashoka (272-232 BCE), the third Maurya emperor, became Buddhist, Buddhism spread all over India (except the deep south). Under the Kusanas, early in the Common Era, Buddhism spread to Central and Southeast Asia, the Far East, China, and many other countries of Asia. It finally started declining in India and was confined to eastern India in the seventh and eighth century. Buddhism as an organized force disappeared from India with the Muslim invasion of west India in the twelfth century.

The first image of Buddha was carved in India in the last quarter of the first century CE in north India and it displays some characteristic features. Carvings of Buddha usually show him seated cross-legged upon a lotus, with long earlobes, and a protrusion between his eyebrows and on top of his head. His hands depict four gestures (*mudras*). Both hands laid in the lap with upturned palms placed one on top of the other indicate meditation; one hand in the lap and the other pointing to the earth indicates a witness-calling gesture. In the teaching, gesture the thumb and forefinger of the left hand form a circle, recalling the wheel of law, while the palm of the right hand faces forward. Sometimes the fingers of both hands form a circle. In protection gestures, the right hand is held in front, palm facing out, with fingers pointing up.

Ten years after reincarnation Ashoka (272-232 BCE) visited Bodh Gaya. He is credited with erecting a shrine at Buddha-Gaya, although the present monument is of much later period and bears very little resemblance even to the shrine carved on the Sanchi Gateways. He also erected an Ashoka pillar. Two centuries later a female devotee built a railing around the Bodhi tree, carved with images of life at that time. The extant portions of the stone railing, the stump of the broken Ashoka pillar, and the diamond shaped vajrasana (the stone representing the seat of Buddha) installed by Ashoka are the only antique structures at Bodh Gaya.

Possibly in 120-160 CE, the shrine was dismantled and another shrine was built during the reign of the Kusana king Huviska (by generous donations of the king). The present Mahabodhi Temple with its pyramidal tower, 50m (150 ft.) tall, possibly built in the eleventh century, resemble somewhat the earlier structure. The shape of the tower is alien to India and possibly it was constructed under foreign influence. Contributions from Indian Buddhists and foreign Buddhist nations helped make repeated extensive repairs,

embellishments and renovations over following centuries. These works saved the brick built monument but modified the temple complex. Many new structures appear to have been added around the temple and the date of construction of these structures is not certain.

The 55m (170 ft.) high temple with its tall pyramidal tower, built of bluish brick and covered with plaster, is located in a valley; a long, steep stair descends to it (Fig. 1.20). There are many stupas of all sizes along the passage and a row of small shrines to Buddha and the Bodhisattvas on the left.

The temple itself consists of a two-storied square surmounted by a tall, steep, pyramidal tower. On the top of the tower is a circular bell resting on the neck of an elongated drum.

Fig. 1.20. Bodh Gaya. Mahabodhi Temple. Front view. Ca. 11ᵗʰ Century. Brick.

Above, a small, similar bell, pointed end upward, rests on the bell below. The rims of the bells are carved with deep vertical groves. The surface of the tower is divided into several tiers with a number of empty niches. Four 18m (58 ft.) tall pyramidal towers stand on the corners of the temple roof, surrounding the main tower.

The entrance to the temple features two pillars and pilasters supporting the upper storey.

The facade extends above the first story to form a multistoried pavilion. The lower portion of the façade above the first story is dominated by a large, round niche bearing a large statue of the seated Buddha, in the center, and a door is located above. The entire façade is covered with niches, empty except for a few bearing statues of Buddha. Niches carved on large bells decorated with the seated Buddha are the most common decorative elements (Fig. 1.21).

Fig. 1.21. Bodh Gaya. Mahabodhi Temple. Entrance. Ca. 11ᵗʰ Century. Brick.

The entrance passage is flanked by niches decorated with Buddha statues standing serenely on the lotus (Fig. 1.22), and standing Bodhisattvas Avalokiteshvara and Vijarapani. There is a delicate, beautifully decorated statue of Buddha wearing jewels and a crown (Fig. 1.23) in one niche.

Fig. 1. 23. Bodh Gaya. Mahabodhi Temple. Crowned and ornamented Buddha with flanking figures. Ca. 10ᵗʰ Century.

Fig. 1.22. Bodh Gaya. Mahabodhi Temple. Buddha statue in passage. Ca. 10ᵗʰ Century.

By the eleventh century, carved statues of Buddha were decorated with jewelry and a crown. The shrine in the center of the main hall has a 2m (6 ft.) high image of Buddha enclosed in a glass case, seated in the witness-calling posture on a cushion (Fig. 1.24). The original statue dates from tenth century CE. It was removed from the shrine by a Hindu priest who occupied the shrine in 1811, but was reinstalled by Sir Alexander Cunningham in 1880.

Fig. 1.24. Bodh Gaya. Mahabodhi Temple. Buddha statue in main hall. Ca. 10ᵗʰ Century.

Two steep staircases on each side of the entrance to the hall lead to the upper storey. D.C. Ahir (1994) reported that there is a fairly large shrine in the center of the hall with a wide passage around. Four small towers at each corner add beauty to the floor. There appear to be many changes and re-rearrangements of materials taking place and it may not have the same appearance in few decades. On the exterior walls the two stories are demarked by mythological lion heads. The walls have many large niches with statues of Buddha seated on a lotus throne with the wheel of law and two lions flanking the wheel on the base (Fig. 1.25).

Fig. 1.25. Bodh Gaya. Mahabodhi Temple. Statues of Buddha and Bodhisattvas on temple walls. Ca. 11ᵗʰ Century.

With his gleaming halo and his hands in a preaching gesture, Buddha looks serene. The statue of seated Tara is particularly beautiful. The statues of Bodhisattvas Avalokiteshvara and Vijarapani stand in separate niches. The niches are bordered with pilasters decorated with intricate designs, and below a band of delicate peacocks stand face to face holding a pearl necklace in their beaks, with their tails spread in delightful pattern.

Fig. 1.26. Bodh Gaya. Mahabodhi Temple. Bodhi tree behind the temple. Planted in 1876 CE.

The sacred Bodhi tree (*Ficus religiosa*) stands about one meter from the back of Mahabodhi Temple on the spot where the original tree stood in the third century BCE (Fig. 1.26). At that time Devanampiya Tissa, a king of Sri Lanka who had accepted Buddhism, asked Ashoka to send a branch of the tree to Sri Lanka. Sanghamitra, daughter of Ashoka, carried the branch to Sri Lanka where it flourished after planting.

Another purpose of her journey to Sri Lanka was to ordain women and girls as nuns in the Buddhist order. King Sasaka of the Hindu Sailodbhava dynasty that ruled Orissa in the seventh century cut down the tree but another tree sprouted from the stump. In 1876, the tree came down during a rainstorm; Sir Alexander Cunningham re-planted a cutting from the same tree on the original spot and it flourished.

Ashoka placed a diamond-shaped throne called the *vajrasana* between the temple and the tree on the spot where Buddha was enlightened. The red polished sandstone throne is about 2.3m (7 ft.) long, and 1.3m (4 ft.) wide and 0.2m (6 inch) thick, placed 1.3m (3 ft) above ground level. It is carved with a geometric design above and encircled in a frieze of geese. It was rediscovered in 1880 during renovations. Now it is covered with red velvet and is enclosed by a gilded railing.

Fig. 1.27. Bodh Gaya. Mahabodhi Temple. Shine marking spot where Buddha meditated during the third week after enlightenment. Ca. 11ᵗʰ Century. Sandstone.

Fig. 1.28. Bodh Gaya. Mahabodhi Temple. Ratanagraha marking spot where Buddha meditated the fourth week after enlightenment. Ca. 11th Century. Sandstone..

Outside the railing under the Bodhi tree a beautiful statue of Buddha is placed in a glass case. The spot near the Bodhi tree where Buddha walked to and fro during the second week after his enlightenment, the path of Buddha is marked with small stones carved in the shape of lotus flowers and arranged in a row on the north side of the temple. Ahir (1994) in his book has mentioned a masonry platform 17m (53 ft.) long 1.1m (3.5 ft.) wide and 1m (3 ft.) high in the vicinity of temple with images of lotus flowers to indicate walk of Buddha. It has disappeared. Possibly the stone lotus flower kept on the side of the temple are copies of the flowers on the missionary platform. Like the Muslims' sacred Mecca, the temple has undergone many renovations in a short period of time.

Fig. 1.29. Bodh Gaya. Mahabodhi Temple. Ashoka pillar near the Temple Lake. Ca. 2nd Century BCE. Sandstone.

A shrine in the courtyard marks the spot where Buddha stood gazing at the tree during the third week (Fig. 1.27).

Fig. 1.30. Bodh Gaya. Mahabodhi Temple. Statue of Buddha under Muchalinda hood in Temple Lake. Ca. 11ᵗʰ Century.

A small roofless shrine, known as *ratanaghara* or the jewel house, marks the spot where Buddha spent his fourth week

in meditation (Fig. 1.28). A small tenth-century shrine in the southeast corner of the temple with Buddha statues in witness-calling pose marks the spot where Brahma appeared before Buddha and asked him to teach Buddhism to the gods.

A section of Ashoka pillar is located near the entrance to the Temple tank (Fig. 1.29).

A large lotus lake in the temple complex holds a statue of Buddha in witness-calling pose in the center. Buddha is seated under the hood of Naga king Muchalinda. The lake represents the Muchalinda Lake (Fig. 1.30). The actual lake was supposed to be about 1.6 km (1 mile) from the temple in Mocharin village (said to have derived its name from Muchalinda Lake).

Fig. 1.31. Bodh Gaya. Naranjana River in knee-deep flood during heavy rains. November 2003.

The river Neranjana, now called Nilajan or Lilajan, near the temple, is a sandy, shallow creek most of the time, but floods knee-deep during rainstorms (Fig. 1.31). A spot on the premises of a Hindu temple on the eastern bank of the river is supposed to represent the spot where Sujata offered a meal to Buddha. Locals refer to a recently-excavated brick mound in the vicinity of Bodh Gaya as "Sujata place". The site of the Rajyatana tree where Buddha spent his seventh week and where two traveling merchants offered him honey and cake has not been identified. However, a Rajyatana tree is growing beside the temple. After his five companions left him, Buddha stayed for some time mediating in a cave called Dungeshwari in Pragbodhi hill (now called Dhongra hill). It is about 1 mile (1.6m) towards Rajgir.

Buddhist pilgrims have erected a large number of stupas in the complex at various times. The best are inside the railing on the eastern side. A pyramid is carved all over with figures of the seated and standing Buddha, and shrines (Fig. 1.32).

Fig. 1.32. Bodh Gaya. Mahabodhi Temple. Pyramidal tower carved with Buddha and shrines. Ca. 11th Century. Sandstone.

Fig. 1.33. Bodh Gaya. Mahabodhi Temple. Railing around temple. Ca. 2ⁿᵈ Century CE. Sandstone.

To the south of the temple are the foundations of a large stupa supposedly built by Emperor Ashoka. In the seventh century the last descendant of the Ashoka dynasty in Magadha enlarged and rearranged the railing erected around the Bodhi tree by a female devotee two centuries after construction of the temple. Of the sixty-four old sandstone posts only seven have survived. The carvings on the broken posts, kept in the local museum, have been copied on cement posts and installed in place of the broken posts. The railing posts added in the seventh century are of coarse granite. The posts are carved with three medallions, one in the center and two at the ends; most medallions are decorated with carvings. The railings between the posts are decorated with medallion carved

with lotus flower (Fig. 1.33). The carvings on the posts depict animals and life in the village. The animals include elephants and horses. A cow feeding her calf is a marvelous expression of motherly love, similar to the carving at Krishna mandapa at Mamalapurum (Fig. 1.34).

Fig. 1.34. Bodh Gaya. Mahabodhi Temple. Railing. Cow feeding calf. Ca. 2ⁿᵈ Century CE. Sandstone.

Fig. 1.35. Bodh Gaya. Mahabodhi Temple. Men toiling in field. Ca. 2ⁿᵈ Century CE. Sandstone.

Fig. 1.36. Bodh Gaya. Mahabodhi Temple. Railing. Worshipping tree. Ca. 2ⁿᵈ Century CE. Sandstone.

Village life is represented by men working in the field (Fig. 1.35) and a woman worshiping (Fig. 1.36).

A curvaceous female with slightly bulging belly standing under a tree with her hands spread wide (Fig. 1.37), a man and women with their hands arms around each other's waists (Fig. 1.38) and an embracing mithuna couple (Fig. 1.39) depict love.

Fig. 1.39. Mahabodhi temple. Railing. Mithuna couple. Ca. 2nd Century. Sandstone.

Fig. 1.37. Bodh Gaya. Mahabodhi Temple. Railing. Female standing under tree. Ca. 2nd Century CE. Sandstone..

Religious symbols include the stupa and wheel of law. Hindu gods assimilated in Buddhism are a standing Lakshmi carved in a medallion, flanked with two lotus buds, and elephants wedged in the upper corners pouring water on her (Fig. 1.40).

Surya is carved standing in chariot drawn by four energetic horses (Fig. 1.41). He bears a halo behind his head resembling the rays of sun and is flanked by two female attendants, each holding a bow and possibly bundle of arrows. The post on which Surya is carved appears to be coarse granite, indicating that the pillar was raised in the seventh century.

Carvings in a lighter vein present a horse with human torso and head pulling his own tail and a curvaceous female with a donkey's head pulling a reluctant man.

Fig. 1.38. Bodh Gaya. Mahabodhi Temple. Railing. Loving couple. Ca. 2nd Century CE. Sandstone.

Fig. 1.40. Mahabodhi temple. Railing. Lakshmi flanked by Elephants and lotus buds. Ca. 2nd Century CE. Sandstone..

Fig. 1.41. Bodh Gaya. Mahabodhi Temple. Railing. Surya driving chariot. Ca. 2nd Century CE. Sandstone.

beautiful structures at Bodh Gaya include Tibetan, Chinese, Thai, Bhutanese and Japanese monasteries.

A large statue of seated Buddha of recent origin stands on the outskirts of Bodh Gaya (Fig. 1.42)

Fig. 1.42. Bodh Gaya. Statue of Buddha in the town. 20th Century. Sandstone.

The Mahabodhi temple, one of the most attractive and colorful monuments in India, stands in pristine glory in spite of all the tribulations it had to undergo over the ages. After the slaughter of some Buddhist monks by Muslim invaders in the twelfth and thirteenth centuries, the temple was deserted by the monks and the temple was forgotten for two centuries. In 1590 a Hindu ascetic occupied the temple and made it his permanent abode.

Slowly the Mahabodhi temple was engulfed by thick jungle. In 1811 Hamilton Buchanan of the Indian Medical Service visited Bodh Gaya. He found the courtyard of the temple littered with broken pieces of sculpture. The first Director General of the Archaeological Survey of India, Alexander Cunningham, visited Bodh Gaya in 1861 and conducted studies of the temple in repeated visits. Attempts to convert the Mahabodhi temple into a temple to Siva started soon after 1811 and a long legal struggle ensued. In spite of the various acts passed by the state government, with loopholes, effective control of the temple has remained in the hands of Hindus.

Many foreign nations have built monasteries and rest houses at Bodh Gaya for the use of their nationals. King Devanampia Tissa (247–207 BCE) of Sri Lanka was the first foreign king to accept Buddhism. King Meghavana (362–398 CE) of Sri Lanka built the first monastery at Bodh Gaya.

Myanmar (Burma) was the second nation reached by Buddhist teaching, during the times of Ashoka. Myanmar helped with extensive repairs to Mahabodhi temple at various times and constructed a monastery at Bodh Gaya. Other

4. Jain Caves at Udayagiri & Khandagiri (100 BCE–100 CE)

The twin hills of Udayagiri and Khandagiri with Jain cave and shelters excavated in first century BCE are situated at a distance of 6 km (3.5 miles) from Bhubanesvara, Orissa in East India. A narrow defile separates the hills. The crests of Udayagiri and Khandagiri are 33.5m (102 ft.) and 37.5m (114 ft.) high. The hills are made of coarse-grained, porous, brittle sandstone outcrop in laterite terrain. The sandstone is easy to excavate but less suitable for fine carving. The color of the rocks is different shades of yellow, grey or mauve. The caves situated near the ancient capital of Kalinga (Orissa) were convenient for Jain monks to reside and make rounds of capital on missionary work or begging. Most of the caves were converted into Hindu sanctuaries.

Mahavir, the twenty-fourth Tirthankara and reformer of Jain faith, born in the latter half of the six century BCE, was contemporary to Buddha. His father was the chief of a warrior clan living around Vaishali in North Bihar. Mahavir was possibly born a few decades after Buddha and died fifteen years after Buddha, in 468 BCE, at the age of 72 years, at Pava, a village near Patna. After wandering and meditating for twelve years Mahavir achieved enlightenment at the age of 42. He gave up all his possessions including clothes, because like all possessions clothes are believed to impede the liberation of self by wrapping the body. A farmer was once strangling Mahavir, believing that he was trying to steal his bullocks. Indra intervened and saved him. Since then Indra became the bodyguard of Mahavir. It is felt now that Mahavir, the attendant of Matanga, whose vehicle is elephant was mistaken to be Indra.

Jainism became influential when Ajatashatru murdered his father Bimbisara, the supporter of Buddha, and became the ruler of Magadha. The Nanda and Maurya dynasties that followed Ajatashatru were followers of Jainism. Chandragupta, the first king of the Maurya dynasty, became disciple of Jain guru Bhadrabahu. It is said that in his old age Chandragupta moved to south India along with his guru and settled around Saravana Belgola, in Karnataka state. Chandragupta's move to the south encouraged many monks to migrate to south. Ashoka, the grandson of Chandragupta, became a Buddhist and North India became less hospitable to the Jains. The monks migrated southward to Karnataka, eastwards to Orissa and westwards to Saurashtra and Gujarat. Mathura in central India and Valabhi in Saurashtra became important Jainism centers between 100 BCE and 100 CE. The oral Jain traditions were written down in a council at Valabhi in 454 CE. In South, the Ganga dynasty patronized Jainism in third century and spread the religion in the Deccan.

The history of Kalinga (parts of Orissa) first came to light in third century BCE when Ashoka conquered Kalinga and Buddhism started flourishing in Kalinga. After conquest by Ashoka, Kalinga history was obscured till the first century BCE when the powerful Jain Chadi dynasty came to power. Jainism became the state religion. Names of only three rulers of this dynasty are known from inscriptions in Udayagiri caves. The third king, Kharavela, was contemporary to Satavahana, the king during whose regime the gateways of Sanchi were constructed. The similar dress style of both men and women and the deep carving of figures at Sanchi and Udayagiri support this view. It is probable that most of the monuments, particularly Cave 1 at Udayagiri, were completed during early first century CE, influencing the sculpture of some other caves. However the carvings of doorkeepers with long legs and broad feet are of Sunga origin. The Sunga, the successor of the Maurya dynasty, built a stupa at Sanchi before Satavahana from South replaced them. The carvings of doorkeepers on the stone fence of the stupa built by Sunga at Sanchi and on guard cells of Cave 1 are similar. The comparative inferiority of the carvings in other caves suggests the excavation of these caves from second or first century BCE. It is likely that before Chadi rule the hills were honeycombed with caves decorated with sculpture carved under influence of dynasties before Sunga and during the rule of Chadi more carvings under Satavahana influence were added. With the death of Kharavela the influence of Jainism started declining, but Jains retain regional influence around Udayagiri and Khandagiri for some time. In early fifth century Hindu gods were carved in few caves. In eleventh century few caves were converted into Hindu sanctuaries and Jain structural temples were constructed on Khandagiri hill. The only other well-known Jain caves are located at Ellora. Jain mostly built religious monuments at centers of Hindu religion.

The caves are non-homogenous group used by Jain monks for protection from natural elements. There are eighteen caves on Udayagiri hills most in dilapidated condition. Most of the caves on right side of the hill bear exterior columns (Fig. 1.45). Some of these caves are converted into Hindu sanctuaries. Some natural cavities were modified to serve as residences (Fig. 1.46). The Buddhist viharas were used for assembly, residence and had a sanctuary for worship and veranda. These cells lack all the facilities except residence. Some caves have open space in front instead of veranda. Original carvings in the caves depict worship of trees possibly reflecting Buddhist or Hindu influence. In Jainism Tirthankaras are not ultimate gods. Most of the caves are not high enough to stand or deep enough for sleeping.

Fig. 1.45. Udayagiri. Caves on right side of hill. Ca. 1st. Century BC. Sandstone.

In some caves the floor at the rear is raised to serve as pillow indicating a number of monks used the cave to sleep. Some shelves were cut on the walls of the verandah to keep articles of necessity. The cells are plain but in a few caves their façades and brackets are carved with crude images. In the two storied cave the upper storey is recessed a few me-

ters back. None of the caves have inside pillars, which in a cave are nonfunctional anyway. The doors are small and were probably fixed with single wooden shutter. The numbers of doors vary from one to four depending on the size of the cell and were the only source of light except in cave 1. The pillars of the verandah are square below and above and octagonal in the middle. As there is no river nearby reservoirs were cut on each hill to collect rainwater.

Fig. 1.46. Udayagiri. Natural cavities modified for residence on left side of hill. Ca. 1st. Century BC. Sandstone.

Due to nature of the substratum and direct exposure to natural elements by collapse of cave sections most carvings on the caves have disintegrated. Some caves still bear faint remains of the sculpture but their subject matter and beauty is not apparent. Sculpture that has survived on caves 1, 3, 6 and 10 is in tolerable condition in spite centuries of dirt, dust and encrustation of mineral deposits from leaching. Though most of the carvings are primitive exhibiting Sunga and earlier influence some carvings are distinct and decidedly advanced surpassing Satavahana carvings on Sanchi gateways in beauty and plasticity. The carving is deep as in Sanchi and few carvings are almost three-dimensional. Most carving depicts non-religious subjects. The female figures are suppler; exhibit more charm and beauty than the figures at Sanchi. The individual figures carved are relatively large in size than at Sanchi possibly thereby enhancing their appearance, but their beauty is marred by centuries of neglect. The emotions are well expressed. Both men and women wear similar dress, rarely covering the upper body, and similar ornaments except for the large and bulky ornaments on women's legs. Women are carved engaged in music, dancing, hunting and occasionally in violent sword fight.

Cave 1 Rani Gumpa is locally called Hati-Gumpa because of its location in a group of small caves carved with elephants on façade. It is two-storied with short right and left wings on both stories and open spacious quadrangle in front (Fig. 1.47).

Fig. 1.47. Udayagiri. Cave 1. Rani Gumpa. Ca. 1st. Century BC. Sandstone.

Fig. 1.48. Udayagiri. Cave 1. Front and right wings. Ca .1st. Century BC. Sandstone.

The central wing of the lower storey has lost roof of the veranda and all the six front pillars (Fig. 1.48). Guard cells are located on ground floor where the right and the left wings join the central wing. Each guard cell has two decorated entrances similar to the façade of the lower storey. The exterior wall of the guard cells façade are profusely decorated with trees, monkeys, birds, elephants frolicking in a lotus pond, hills and lovely maidens, one fondling a child (Fig. 1.49). The secular scene is somewhat similar to the sculptured cliff at Mamalapuram, without any religious theme.

Fig. 1.49. Udayagiri. Cave 1. Carving on façade of Guard cell. Ca. 1st. Century BC. Sandstone.

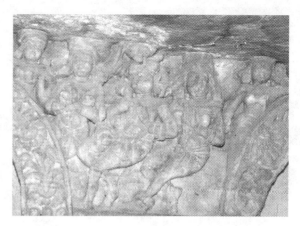

Fig. 1.50. Udayagiri. Cave 1. Court scene. Carving on façade of right wing.

Fig. 1.51. Udayagiri. Cave 1. Tree worship. Carving on façade of right wing. Ca. 1st. Century BC. Sandstone.

The central wing of the lower storey has lost the roof of the veranda and all the six front pillars.

The right wing of the lower storey consists of a single cell with open verandah with two pillars on front and benches in the verandah. Animals are carved on the capitals of pilasters. Entrance to the verandah is flanked with guards carved in distinct Sunga style. On the façade of the central wing, the space between decorated pilasters and arches is carved with friezes. Only four friezes have survived. The first depicts a court scene with king seated with queens (Fig. 1.50). The second carving depicts two lovely pairs flanking and possibly worshipping the tree. The females are holding tray full of flowers in raised hands (Fig. 1.51). A court scene depicts a curvaceous female dancer flanked by seated musicians seen from behind. The last carving depicts a man with folded hands going to worship accompanied with a boy and two females. The left wing has three cells one with a window in addition to doorways. All the pillars have collapsed.

The upper storey is recessed a few meters back on the lower storey. There is an open terrace in front of the upper story. Only three of the nine pillars supporting the verandah of the upper main wing are original. The central wing has four cells with two doors each. Auspicious Jain symbols like

snakes and lotus are carved on top of arches and doorways. The spaces between the arches have been carved with nine carvings each depicting different non-religious episodes.

Fig. 1.52. Udayagiri. Cave 1. Façade of upper main storey. Elephant attack. Ca. 1st. Century BC. Sandstone

Weathering has damaged most friezes. Some of the surviving friezes like gateways of Sanchi are the glories of Udayagiri.

Fig. 1.53. Udayagiri. Cave 1. Façade of front main story. Abduction. Ca. 1st. Century BC. Sandstone

The first frieze depicts a flying Vidyadhara in Sunga style with long legs and wide feet. He is elaborately dressed and is holding a big tray full of flowers and garlands in one hand and lotus buds in other hand. His face is expressive. The floating

Fig. 1.54. Udayagiri. Cave 1. Façade of front main storey. Shakuntala and Dushyanta. Ca. 1st Century BC. Sandstone

scarf and lower garment indicate flying motion but the feet resting on the ground belies it.

The second relief is carved with one man and ten women in a forest fighting to ward off an elephant attack (Fig. 1.52). The women carved are lovely and charming. The supple body of the female bent down to pickup fallen comrade resembles the body of a beautiful female bent at the feet of Buddha painted on ceiling of cave 2 in Ajanta. Other females also exhibit beauty in all their movement. The group while walking in the forest had come upon a lotus pond where elephants were bathing. One irritated elephant attacked the party. The consternation, panic and confusion caused by the elephant attack are realistically depicted with details. The female standing nearest to the elephants is aiming a round object, possibly a bulky anklet removed from her leg, at the elephant. Another anklet from her leg has hit the hindquarters of the elephant. Possibly the panic caused by the sudden attack of elephants did not give her time to search for other objects. One female is bent to lifting a fallen comrade on her shoulder in front of the elephant while another is dragging a fallen comrade. One female beside is holding a branch and another holding a club have their hands raised in threatening gestures. The man is swinging a large staff. Three frightened females in the rear have formed a group near a tree. The elephant, surprised by the fury of the group, is squatting on his hindquarter trying to pull back with his trunk withdrawn.

The third relief depicts the abduction of a female (Fig. 1.53). A cave with an arched entrance is located in a forest suggested by the carving of a snake beside the arch. A man sitting near the entrance of a cave is resting his head in the lap of the beautiful female sitting beside. The woman has one hand on the shoulder of the man and other hand resting in her lap. Next a woman is carved, advancing towards the couple, leading a man with drawn sword and shield. In the middle of the panel a violent sword fight between man and women is depicted. The lovely female warrior is shown with the sheath of the sword and a braid hanging on her back. The beauty of the female is apparent in all her actions and movements. Next the man is shown physically carrying the vanquished female in his hands.

The next relief depicts the love story of Shakuntala (Fig. 1.54). A king on a deer hunt in the forest has dismounted from his horse. A groom is attending the horse while three attendants are behind king. One is carrying a pot of water, tied to the back end of a staff resting on his shoulder. Another is carrying possibly a spare sword and a third is carrying a Chamara and parasol. After dismounting the king is shown holding bow in his outstretched hand and drawing an arrow with his other hand from the quiver on his back. A herd of deer is running in front, looking back with turned heads at the king. Next the king is shown standing in front of

a tree with his bow drawn near his body in his right hand. A deer is standing under the tree. A supple, curvaceous, lovely maiden is sitting perched on a fork of the tree with her arm extended in a gesture imploring the hunter not to shoot the deer. She appears agitated and, sliding from the tree, is ready to jump in front of the deer. This was the first meeting of Shakuntala with her lover Dushyanta. Kalidasa (ca. 400 CE) the Indian poet, made the rest of the love story renowned. Possibly this is the best carving of a romantic theme. The next panel depicts three women dancing in front of the king and the queen and three women musicians playing different musical instruments.

The wings of the upper story have one cell each. The right wing has a benched verandah with two restored pillars and two pilasters. The pilaster on the right is carved with a Sunga style guard in foreign costume and the left pilaster is carved with a guard in Indian costume with sheathed sword. On the left there is a disintegrated carving of, possibly, a rider on a tiger. An open verandah appears to have existed on the right. Only the stumps of a few pillars, verandah floor and a few disintegrated carving on one wall are remaining.

Cave 3 has carvings of six vigorous elephants and a statue of a guardian. Cave 5 has a carving of a female standing near the entrance. The charming, sparsely draped female is wearing heavy earrings, bands on her hands and beautifully decorated hair. A parrot is sitting at her right hand and her other hand is resting on her waist. By shifting her weight on one leg she has created a beautiful three-body-bend pose.

Cave 10 has a statue of an elephant in front of each corner holding mango-laden branches and lotus flowers in front of the cave. Ganesha is carved on the back wall of the right cell. The carving of Ganesha's image on the cave wall appears to be an assimilation of Ganesha in Jainism during medieval time as suggested by a few scholars. The carving between the arches of the doorways depicts the abduction episode carved in Cave 1, starting with a carving of a lovely maiden sitting by the side of a man lying in front of a cave. One of her hands is resting on the man's thigh, indicating a close relationship. Next an old woman is carved, leading by her hand a stooping man toward the resting couple. The rest of the frieze depicts the violent sword fight and physical carrying away of the vanquished female.

The second frieze depicts the story of the elopement of the Ujjayini princess with the king of Kausambi accompanied by a friend. The carving starts with the hot pursuit of an elephant carrying three riders by a group of soldiers armed with swords and shields. One of the riders is a woman, who is driving the elephant. The second rider shooting arrows at the pursuers is possibly the king and the third throwing coins at the pursuers from a bag held in his hand is possibly attempting to delay them by stopping to pick up the coins. One soldier is bent over; possibly he is looking for coins. In the middle of the frieze three riders are dismounting from a kneeling elephant. Next the princess is following the king, holding a bunch of mangoes in her right hand and her left hand on the king's shoulder. The carving ends with the king standing in front of the princess half reclined on a bed. The king is standing with folded hands, possibly trying to console the princess who is depressed by separation from her parents. The carvings are damaged by weathering; still they are delightful and artistically superb.

Fig. 1.55. Khandagiri. Caves. Ca. 1st. Century BC. Sandstone.

Cave 12 is shaped like tiger head and cave 14 is a large natural cavern enlarged to form shelter for assembly. The remaining caves are mostly dilapidated. An apsidal shaped foundation of a temple constructed of laterite blocks surrounded by stone pavement of recent origin is located on the crest of hill. It is the earliest apsidal structural temple in East India.

Fig. 1.56. Khandagiri. Jain temple on crest of the hill. Ca. 15th. Century AD. Sandstone.

Fifteen caves are located on Khandagiri hill. Most of them are decorated. Fragments collected have identified a collapsed Jain structural temple. Caves 7, 8, 9 and 10 were carved at later dates with images of gods for worship (Fig.

1.55). Cave 8 has sculpture of a twelve handed figure and 25 Tirthankaras. Tirthankara Parshvanath has been carved twice.

A structural temple was constructed about three centuries back on the crest of hill (Fig. 1.56). In the marble hall of the temple a colossal black marble statue of Mahavir is enshrined. The main shrine has a fifty-year-old marble statue of Mahavir. It also contains a large number of Jain statues. There is a small temple by the side with five statues of naked Jains. From the crest of the hill panoramic view of environ including temples of Bhubanesvara can be seen on a clear day.

5. Karli and Bhaja Caves
(Ca. 1ˢᵗ Century BCE–120 CE)

The largest Buddhist chaitya cave in South Asia is located at Karli, 168 km (105 miles) south of Mumbai. Convenient trains are available from Mumbai to Lonavala Station on Mumbai-Poona Railway line. The cave is located 12 km (7 miles) from Lonavala on a steep basalt cliff. Local transportation is available from Lonavala Railway station to the cave. A road suitable for vehicular traffic leads half way up the cliff, after which it is a hard climb on steep steps, rubbing shoulders with throngs of pilgrims going to a modern temporary Hindu temple occupying more than half the entrance to the cave.

The monuments built by Buddhist are stupas, caves and monasteries. Some monuments were constructed during Buddha's life time but none have survived. The Maurya emperor Ashoka (272-232 BCE) and Sunga dynasty that succeeded Maurya in 151 BCE and lasted up to 71 BCE built many stupas. Ashoka and his grandson Dasaratha excavated seven caves in the Barber and Nagarjuni hills near Gaya in Bihar to provide shelter to the wandering non-Vedic religious sect "as long as the sun and moon last." Ashoka is also credited with construction of a shrine at Bodh-Gaya, but the present monument at Bodh Gaya is of a later era.

During the Sunga reign a number of caves were excavated in the mountain chain of western India in the second and first century BCE, including the chaitya and vihara caves at Pitalkhora. Chaitya caves are apsidal shaped large halls with vaulted roof with a stupa near the apsidal end excavated to provide space for monks to meditate and pray. Residential facilities were not provided in chaitya caves. Viharas were excavated to provide shelter in the rainy season to monks with usually more than one cell arranged along the periphery. The cells had one or more raised stone beds and niches to keep a burning oil lamp, a shrine excavated in the rear wall for worship and open space in the center for meditation. In later developments the shrine was moved to the center of the cave to allow circumambulation of the shrine. The best preserved of the early caves are at Bhaja was possibly excavated in 100-70 BCE. The two caves at Bedsa in Western Deccan are ascribed to the Sunga period based on the carving style. One cave is a chaitya and the other a modified vihara with apsidal plan. In addition to Vidisha (modern Besnagar), their capital, Patliputra, Mathura, Ayodha, Kusambi and Ahicchattra became famous Buddhist art centers. Satavahana who invaded central India for a short period in the mid first century BCE, replacing the Sunga, excavated some Buddhist caves during their rule at Ajanta and Aurangabad.

The Sakas, a branch of the Scythians living in the area adjacent to the Black Sea, entered portions of modern Afghanistan and Pakistan in 135 BCE and extended their rule slowly to large parts of Bactria in Afghanistan and to Mathura. During this period the area called Gandhara or Bactro-Gandhara was split into small states. A statue of Buddha carved in the first century CE was discovered in the Swat Valley of Pakistan with Buddha sitting cross-legged (Vijraparyankasana) and holding his hand in the *abhaya mudra*, introducing the yoga posture in Buddhist sculpture. Bodhisattvas were also carved.

The Kusanas living in northwestern China entered Bactria in about 135 CE and extended their control over much of Afghanistan, Pakistan, and Bangladesh and the Indus River Valley in north India. The Kusanas excavated many stupas but only a few have survived. During this period Mathura became a major Buddhist art center. In addition to carvings of Buddha and Bodhisattvas statues, beautiful figures of females on the Bhutesvara stupa railing were carved at Mathura, in UP. Many Buddha statues from this time have survived. Pancika and Hariti, the two Buddhist divinities, were also carved. Pancika later became the keeper of wealth or treasurer of enlightenment and Hariti became mother of Buddha. The Kusanas lost control of the region to immigrants entering from the same corridor they entered.

Parallel with these developments by the Kusanas, caves of considerable complexity and grandeur were built in Western Deccan in the second and third century CE. A branch of the Sakas, the Ksaharatas (also called Satrapas), who entered India in 135 BCE, established their rule in Deccan subcontinent and constructed caves in central India. The excavation of Buddhist caves continued during the Satavahana and Vakataka Dynasty feudatories of the Gupta regime at Ajanta from the first century BCE to the end of the fifth century. Later during the Vakataka regime the last Buddhist caves were excavated, during the seventh century, at Ellora.

This largest and the most ambitious Buddhist chaitya cave in South Asia was constructed and dedicated by the Saka King Nahapana Satrapa in 120 CE Karli. An inscription carved on the façade of the cave refers to Nahapana and inscriptions on the inside pillars donated by various satraps corroborate 120 CE as the date of dedication. The cave consists of a front stone screen, large verandah and chaitya hall with three entrances. The cave is set deep into the hill. An enormous mass of hill was cut deep through the bedrock to open a wide passage and obtain the height required for excavation of a cave with such a high façade. The wide passage in front of the chaitya gives a full view of the façade, but a temporary modern Hindu shrine dedicated to a goddess, built in the passage, obstructs the full view of the facade (Fig. 1.60).

The screen wall with two openings to the chaitya verandah is partially collapsed on the left, leaving only the entrance on the right. The upper portion of the screen wall, cut with short pillars designed to admit light and air into the verandah hall, has also collapsed, leaving some upper pillar stubs hanging from top of the façade. Outside the screen wall a tall and heavy column is carved from the hill matrix resembling the Ashoka pillars. The lions carved on the top of the column are not as graceful as those on the Ashoka pillars. The holes visible on the screen wall indicate that considerable wooden structures were erected for the construction of façade.

The verandah behind the screen wall is large. Three life size elephants at the base of the sidewalls of the verandah appear to bear the sidewalls on their backs (Fig. 1.61). The elephants' trunks are gone. Above the elephants Buddha is carved, sitting cross-legged in meditation; he appears to be sitting on the elephants. The sidewalls of the verandah above

elephants are carved to appear like stories (Fig. 1.62). In the first storey loving couples are depicted beside huge blind doorways and balconies. The rest of the stories are carved with blind doorways and balconies. The back of the screen wall entrance is also carved with loving couples similar in stature to the Mamalapurum carvings. The carvings on the right side were lost when the right side of the screen wall collapsed.

Fig. 1.60. Karli. Chaitya. Front View of Chaitya. Ca. 120 CE. Basalt.

Fig. 1.61. Karli. Chaitya. Elephants carrying sidewall of Verandah hall. Ca. 120 CE. Basalt.

All three entrances to the chaitya hall are flanked with carvings of the most sensuous females carved on any religious monument (Fig. 1.63), along with their lovers, standing mostly with arms on each others' shoulders. Numerous Buddhas, Bodhisattvas and loving couples are carved all over the walls surrounding the chaitya verandah, but attention is immediately focused on the large carvings of the loving couples carved on the façade of the chaitya hall. These life size voluptuous females, each featuring different costumes and affectionate gestures, have smiling, lovely faces.

anklets on their legs, large earrings, and bands on hands. They are virtually nude and implicitly sexual. Jewelry on the hips and a sash running between the legs constitutes the main adornments of these females. The males are carved with proportional fleshy bodies with heavy folds of diaphanous lower garments between their legs and around their hips. They wear turban with a mushroom-like growth on top and large earrings similar to those of the females. The loving couples look full of life, with slight smiles on their faces and relaxed postures. They represent the concept of individual reintegration with the universal principle.

Both sides of the central entrance are flanked with Buddhas and Bodhisattvas and lovely couples. On one side Buddha is sitting on a throne, his legs hanging down and resting on a lotus flower with a long stalk, held by two naga accompanied with attendants (Fig. 1.64). He bears a sweet smile on his face and a halo behind his head. Above the Buddha are two Vidyadharas carrying what looks like a decorated crown. On his right, in the same panel, Avalokiteshvara is standing holding lotus bud with long stalk and chamara.

Fig. 1.62. Karli. Chaitya. Sidewall of Verandah hall above elephants. Ca. 120 CE. Basalt.

Fig. 1.64. Karli. Chaitya. Chaitya façade wall. Buddha flanked with loving couples. Ca. 120 CE. Basalt.

They have soft bodies, full, firm round breasts, narrow waists, and wide hips with soft, full thighs and shapely legs crossed in a different style in each carving. They wear thick

On the other side of Buddha another Bodhisattva, possibly Vijarapani, is standing, holding an unrecognizable object. Lovely couples flank the Buddha in niches. On the other side of the main entrance, Bodhisattva Avalokiteshvara is carved standing, holding a lotus bud with a long stalk in one hand and his other hand in a protection gesture. He is attended by

Fig. 1.65. Karli. Chaitya. Chaitya façade wall. Bodhisattva Avalokiteshvara flanked by Loving couples. Ca. 120 CE.

females on each side. Seated Buddhas with teaching gestures are carved in the upper corners (Fig. 1.65). Pairs of loving couples flank the carving of Avalokiteshvara.

A little distance to left of the chaitya a few caves have been hewn from the bedrock of the same hill. A panel in one of the caves is carved with Buddha seated on a throne with hands in a teaching gesture, a few devotees seated at his feet and Bodhisattvas standing beside them. The carving is similar to the carving of Buddha on the façade wall of the chaitya hall but with the addition of Tara, holding a lotus bud, and standing with Avalokiteshvara, indicating the slow integration of female deities into Buddhist sculpture.

Bhaja is located 10 km (6 miles) south of Karli on a road suitable for small vehicular traffic up to the village. Buddhists excavated 18 caves in the hill near the village, possibly during 100-70 BCE. The caves are situated in beautiful and serene surroundings but it is a hard and long climb to each of them. These caves contain interesting early Buddhist sculpture. Cave 12, a large chaitya standing in the center, is flanked by other caves (Fig. 1.70).

The space between the corners of the façade wall and the side entrances is carved with single pairs of loving couples (Fig. 1.66 and 1.67). All these images were carved in the fifth century when the iconographic program of the cave was modified. The large central entrance leads into the nave of the largest chaitya hall with a huge vaulted ceiling carved with rib like beams (Fig. 1.68). The chaitya hall is spectacular

but simple. A row of perpendicular pillars, unlike the slightly inward slanting pillars of earlier chaitya caves, follows the shape of the chaitya hall separating the nave and aisles. The roof of the aisles is flat. The large, thick, six-sided shaft of the pillars sits in a vase of plenty at the base resting on three flat thin square bases of decreasing size. The pillars on the top are carved with lotus bell capitals, a short box with four short pillars, and a round, short, stout pillar. The box supports a circular disc. On the disc, four square plates increasing in size are placed horizontally, one above another. On top of the last square, elephants are carved carrying a loving couple but most prominently a pair of beautiful females. A few elephants carry a single rider. The only animals carved in the cave are elephants. The pillars around the stupa are undecorated at top and bottom. The stupa located near the apsidal end has carvings of two railings on the body, possibly implying two circumambulatory passages around the stupa. The lower railing has niches carved at the base to keep burning oil lamps. On top of the stupa a square neck is mounted with horizontal squares of increasing size, and capped with a large, thick, elongated oval shaped umbrella. In the stupas carved in later chaityas, the superstructure was modified to carry three umbrellas, one above another, to represent three basic tenets of Buddhism: Buddha, the laws, and the monastic order. In the last stages the superstructure was eliminated and the shape of the stupa was modified to look like a dome.

Fig. 1.63. Karli. Chaitya. Chaitya façade wall. Apsara. Ca. 120 CE. Basalt.

The chaitya appears to have a small verandah in front, reached by a flight of a few steps (without a front screen). The façade of the chaitya has collapsed, destroying any carvings, leaving a large opening surrounded by the remaining arch of the chaitya window. The extant protruding façade wall on one side of the chaitya window has a carving of a partially destroyed and extremely voluptuous female. It is similar to the carving at Karli, though not as curvaceous (Fig. 1.71). It is possible the sculpture was carved when iconographic program at Karli was modified in the fifth century CE, but these carvings are not as sophisticated as those on the chaitya at Karli. Some carving of loving couples on the façade above the arch of the chaitya window have surveyed under small ogee-arches and windows. These carvings appear to be in Sunga style. The large hall of the chaitya has pillars along the periphery, leaning slightly inwards, indicating that the chaitya was excavated before the chaitya at Karli. The vaulted roof of the hall is carved with rib-like beams. A stupa stands near the apsidal end. There are no carvings inside the hall.

Fig. 1.67. Karli. Chaitya. Chaitya façade wall. Loving couple. Ca. 120 CE. Basalt.

Fig. 1.66. Karli. Chaitya. Chaitya façade wall. Loving couple. Ca. 120 CE. Basalt.

Fig. 1.69. Karli. Chaitya. Elephants on pillars carrying riders. Ca. 120 CE. Basalt.

The chaitya caves by this time had reached a fair degree of standardization but the use of viharas appears confused. The exterior of the viharas are plain but the interiors are decorated with varied sculpture. The capital of a pilaster in one cave is carved with two short and stocky couples (Fig. 1.72).

The females are loaded with heavy ornaments and their hair is decorated in huge fan-like masses on their heads. The viharas have small cells with raised stone beds for the monks

Fig. 1.68. Karli. Chaitya. Chaitya hall. Ca. 120 CE. Basalt.

to sleep on. There are carvings of chaitya windows and stupa railing on the lintel of the cells. Cave 19, raised on a small basement, has an open verandah with a very short parapet wall and five pillars and a pilaster on the façade. The tall and lean pillars without brackets are square at the base and top and eight-sided in the middle. The carvings on the top of the pillars have disintegrated. The entrance to the verandah is on the side, between the last two pillars (Fig. 1.73).

Fig. 1.70. Bhaja. Cave 12. Chaitya. Side view 2ⁿᵈ-1ˢᵗ Century BCE. Basalt.

Fig. 1.71. Bhaja. Cave 12. Carvings on Chaitya façade. 2ⁿᵈ-1ˢᵗ Century BCE. Basalt.

The verandah has a half-barrel vaulted roof with ribs attached to the central horizontal beam. In a longitudinal niche below the beam, seven stupas are carved. There is a bench in the right corner of the verandah.

There are two entrances and three carvings on the façade of the vihara. The carvings on the facade do not show the so-

phistication of Buddhist art of Sanchi carved in the later part of the first century BCE. These carvings represent early stages of Buddhist art. The first carving, starting from the right, is a male with a slightly oval face (Fig. 1.74). He is wearing a long coat; hair is piled high on his head like thick, twisted ropes. A few ornaments hang from his neck and beaded ornaments are on his hands. He is holding a long club.

Fig. 1.72. Bhaja. Vihara cave. Loving couples on top of pilaster. 2ⁿᵈ-1ˢᵗ Century BCE. Basalt.

Fig. 1.73. Bhaja. Cave 19. Front view of Vihara. 2ⁿᵈ-1ˢᵗ Century BCE. Basalt.

The figure in the center, with a narrow waist, has a smaller pile of hair on her head, a round face, large eyes, and flared lips. She is wearing attractive ornaments around her neck. The hands of the figure are broken but appear to have held a long stick. The male in a third carving, near the window, has a very tall arrangement of hair on his head and few ornaments. A large bow appears to be resting on the wall beside the figure (Fig. 1.175).

On the left side of the verandah a cell is excavated with a central entrance. Indra and Surya flank the entrance of the cell. Indra, wearing a large turban, earrings and large garland, is riding an elephant (Fig. 1.76). He is holding an artifact with a sharp tip in his right hand. The sharp end is resting on the head of the elephant. The elephant, in a rage, has uprooted a tree and is holding it by his trunk, with men hanging from the branches. He is trampling another tree under his right foot. Men and animals are running, scattered all around the elephant. A small figure wearing a long, twisted pigtail around his face and a short skirt with leaf-like margins is sitting behind Indra. He is holding a banner and two long sticks ending in what appears to be a head of wheat.

riding a chariot drawn by four highly decorated horses depicting the travel of Surya across the sky (Fig. 1.77). Two females with facial features similar to Surya's and coiffures resembling thick, twisted ropes, flank him. They are holding chamara and parasols instead of the traditional drawn bows and arrows to drive away the darkness. The horses are trampling a fat, ugly female, representing darkness, under their hoofs. A beautiful female on horseback follows the chariot, on the left.

Fig. 1.74. Bhaja. Cave 19. Carving on Vihara facade. 2ⁿᵈ-1ˢᵗ Century BCE. Basalt.

Fig. 1.76. Bhaja. Cave 19. Indra riding Elephant. 2ⁿᵈ-1ˢᵗ Century BCE. Basalt.

Fig. 1.75. Bhaja. Cave 19. Carving on Vihara facade. 2ⁿᵈ-1ˢᵗ Century BCE. Basalt.

Surya is carved as a handsome male wearing an ornate head-dress on a slightly oval face with large eyes and flared lips. He is

Fig. 1.77. Bhaja. Cave 19. Surya riding chariot. 2ⁿᵈ-1ˢᵗ Century BCE. Basalt.

6. THE GREAT STUPA AT SANCHI
(250 BCE–11TH CENTURY)

Sanchi boasts a Buddhist monastery that has been in existence for more than 2300 years, since the golden age of early Indian art.

A small village located at the foot of a 91m (278 ft.) high hill in Madhya Pradesh, central India, Sanchi is accessible via railway but the roads are deplorable and it has the worst possible public bus transportation system of all major cities in the area except Bhopal. The government-run lodge is the only decent place to stay. There is a road up to the stupa complex on the top of the hill. UNESCO declared the reliquary mound, the Great Stupa and associated structures World Heritage Monuments in 1989.

The historical Buddha was the son of a Sakyas tribal chief in Nepal in the Himalayan foothills. He was born in 563 BCE at Lumbini, now in Nepal. After ten years of meditation, at the age of thirty-five he achieved enlightenment near Bodh Gaya in the kingdom of Magadha, the present-day Bihar, south of the River Ganges. He died in 483 BCE at the age of 80 years in Kusinara, a small hill town in Uttar Pradesh.

The most powerful supporter of Buddha during his lifetime was King Bimbisara of Magadha. In its early phase Buddhism faced stiff competition with Jainism and patron kings of Buddhism were replaced by Jain dynasties. About two centuries after the death of Buddha, by gradual expansion Magadha became the kingdom of Maurya, under the first great Indian Imperial dynasty, governing all India except the southern tip. The third emperor of the Maurya dynasty, Ashoka, became a Buddhist. With the imperial patronage of Ashoka, Buddhism became a force to reckon with (from the third century BCE). Early

in the first millennium Buddhism spread to Central Asia, and China and influenced religious thought in the Middle East. Many authorities believe that Buddhism directly or indirectly influenced Christianity.

In the fourth century CE the Gupta, the second great empire of North India, came to power. The Guptas were Hindus and Buddhism slowly started to lose political and social influence in Indian society and by eighth century Buddhism lost most influence and was isolated in western India. By the eleventh century it started merging with body of Hinduism. In the twelfth century the destruction of Buddhist monasteries and libraries in Bengal and Bihar and the expulsion of Buddhist by Muslims drove Buddhism to foreign lands.

Buddhism is based on psychological, not metaphysical or theological, foundations. It is a philosophical doctrine difficult for the common mind to understand.

During 100-200 CE, the Mahayana sect branched off from the main body. Very early Buddhism absorbed the gods of the Hindu pantheon but their functions were different. Indra (Sakra) is still the king of gods. Yama, called Dharmaraja, presides over the hells. Kubera, called Jambhala, is Buddha's bodyguard. Surya assumed the role of providing light and warmth. The goddesses of the Buddhist pantheon are reminiscent of Siva Shakti. The most revered goddess is Tara.

A Buddhist Universe (Chakravala) took shape. With time, some age-old Hindu beliefs crept into the doctrine and popular Buddhism became a mixture of Mahayana beliefs, Hindu pantheon and cosmology.

The region around Sanchi in the Ganges River Valley was part of the Republic of Western Malwa (Madhya Pradesh) during the times of Buddha in the sixth and fifth century BCE, followed by the Mayura Empire from 399 BCE. The Sunga ruled the region from 187 to 75 BCE, when the Satavahana, intruding from the south, replaced them.

Buddha wandered in the Ganges River Basin for 50 years after his enlightenment, preaching Buddhism through out the year except the four rainy months — but he did not visit Sanchi. The probable reason for Emperor Ashoka to build Stupa at Sanchi was that when he was traveling to Ujjain as Viceroy governing central India he stayed at Vidisha 9 km (5.4 miles) from Sanchi, fell in love, and married Devi of Vidisha. He had two sons and a daughter from this marriage. His daughter Sanghamitta went to Sri Lanka, carrying a branch of Bodhi tree, and ordained women as nuns in the Buddhist order. One son, Mahendra, also went as a missionary to Sri Lanka. Vidisha was an influential Buddhist center and there was a Buddhist monastery at Sanchi.

Buddhist architecture and sculpture dates from the third century BCE to the eleventh–twelfth century. The Stupa at Sanchi is a relic of the era when the place of worship had not yet emerged from the cave to face the destructive forces of nature. Emperor Ashoka of the Maurya dynasty constructed the Great Stupa in 250 BCE as a funeral mound, with burnt brick interior core and mud mortar, to enshrine part of Buddha's relics amidst the community of monks on the hilltop at Sanchi. He erected a 12.6m (39 ft.) high round pillar near the south gate of the stupa. A local landlord later broke the pillar surmounted with four addorsed lions to use as a sugarcane press. A 2.4m (7.5 ft.) high stump of the pillar is still embedded in the ground and two round pieces are on the ground beside the stupa. The broken top of the pillar is deposited in the local museum. The original stone umbrella erected on the top was intentionally destroyed in the second century BCE.

Ashoka built innumerable stupas through out his kingdom to distribute and enshrine the relics of Buddha that were collected by opening eight stupas that had been erected after the death of Buddha. In 185 BCE the Sunga of Magadha in central India replaced the Maurya dynasty.

The survival of the Great Stupa as a freestanding structure is due to the piety of the rich mercantile community of Vidisha and the Buddhist community living on the top of the hill taking care of the stupa. The mound was enlarged and covered with stone slabs cut in the shape of bricks and was given a thick coating of concrete by the Sunga during the first century BCE. During the same period an almost undecorated railing of cream-colored sandstone modeled as an early bamboo fence was constructed to enclose the ambulatory passage around the stupa, with four entrances at the cardinal points. A second ambulatory passage was constructed at a height of 4.5m (17 ft.) on the stupa and the passage was enclosed by a railing. Behind the south gateway entrance, stairways

joining from opposite directions were constructed inside the first ambulatory passages; they provide entrance to the second passage. During the Sunga reign in the second century BCE, Stupa 2, located on the western slope of the hill some distance way from the Great Stupa, and Stupa 3, located near the Great Stupa, were constructed. A three-tier stone umbrella representing Buddha, his teachings, and the community of monks was erected on the top of the Great Stupa and enclosed in a small square stone railing, possibly during the fifth century CE (Fig. 1.80).

The monuments are in relatively good shape, although some intentional damage was done in the second century BCE.

Fig. 1.80. Sanchi. Great Stupa. South Gate. Ca. 250 BC-50 CE. Sandstone.

Four images of Buddha, donated by a lay female devotee, were placed behind the entrances of lower ambulatory passage facing the cardinal points before 450 CE. These carved statues, examples of the mature Gupta art of Mathura, are the only presentation of Buddha in human form at the stupa (Fig. 1.81). Buddha, seated on cushion in meditation, has smooth body contours, downcast eyes and a gentle smile on his face. A lacelike halo is centered behind the head. Celestial flying beings bearing flowers are carved in the upper corners. The attendants flanking Buddha are not the same in all the four statues. Three of these statues are damaged.

Sculpture on stone in India appeared during the second and first century BCE. In that period the carved railing of the stupa situated at the edge of the hill was created in typical Sunga style. These carvings are described as the earliest examples of indigenous relief-work in stone.

In the first century BCE the Satavahana from Krishna and Godavari Valley of southern India, in their brief incursion into northern India, replaced the Kanva (the short-lived successors of the Sunga) governing central India. The Satavahana, by constructing four glorious Gateways of the

Great Stupa, gave the monument recognition, fame and, consequently, protection. The Satavahana also constructed the gateway of Stupa 3 beside the Great Stupa. The gateways were constructed in the latter part of first century BCE. All the gateways were built in a short span of twenty years starting with the southern and followed by the northern, eastern and western gateways. The gateway of Stupa 3 was built last.

Fig. 1.81. Sanchi. Great Stupa. Statue of Buddha in lower circumambulatory passage. Ca. 450 CE. Sandstone.

The present dimensions of the Great Stupa are 16.5m (51 ft.) high (excluding the railing and umbrella on the top) and 36.6m (113.5 ft.) diameter. It is the best-preserved early stone stupa.

The last construction done at Sanchi was a wall surrounding the eastern and southern area of the complex in the twelfth century CE. Like all other monuments in India, Sanchi was forgotten after the thirteenth century. The neglect was a blessing in disguise as it possibly saved the stupa from Muslim invaders. Demolishing the gateways would have erased the beauty and attraction of the Great Stupa.

General Taylor rediscovered the Great Stupa in 1811. Treasure hunters looted the scattered sculpture pieces and Captain Johnson, the British Assistant Political Agent at Bhopal, opened up one side of the stupa from top to bottom, resulting in the collapse of the western gateway, and left it without repair. Alexander Cunningham, the First Director of the Archeological Survey of India, numbered all the monuments on the hill in 1850 and these numbers are retained till today to identify them. Alexander Cunningham opened Stupa 2 and 3 for study in 1851. Major Cole repaired all the stupas and the fallen gateway between 1881 and 1884. The antiquities scattered in the area were collected and deposited in the local museum constructed in 1919.

Both the Sunga and Satavahana were Hindus and did not finance the remodeling of the stupa directly; however,

being tolerant of other religions, they provided grants for the maintenance of these establishments. Common people, lay worshippers, monks, nuns and even carvers financed the remodeling, which was supervised by monastic authorities. The ivory carvers of Vidisha carved a number of sculptured panels and the workers of the Guild of Ivory Carvers donated a carving depicting the celebration of Buddha's turban. It is installed on left pillar of south gateway.

The stupa is a solid mass without an interior chamber. The relics of Buddha are enshrined in the center of the mound. Buddhists come to the stupa to experience the proximity of Buddha by standing near his relics. Buddha attained nirvana by meditation and did not claim to be god in his lifetime. In the early stages of Buddhist art, Buddha was not presented in human body. He is depicted on gateways by symbols like a tree, footprints, an empty seat or a parasol. An empty, long path indicates his walking presence, the stupa his attainment of nirvana, the wheel of law his teachings and the lotus his nativity. A Hindu goddess, Lakshmi, adopted by Buddhists, represents the conception of Buddha.

Statues of Buddha, first carved early in the first century, took some time to spread. As Buddha attainted nirvana after 550 rebirths, it was considered improper in early Buddhist sculpture to present him in the human body he discarded.

The artisans who created the sculpture at Sanchi were not stonecutters but were experienced craftsmen in soft media like wood, ivory and silver and they created the carvings on stone similar to delicate carvings on soft materials. There are no carvings on the stupa but all the visible surfaces of the 2000-year-old gateways are carved. Placed in front of the entrances to the ambulatory passage, possibly these gateways introduced the concept of temple gateways. On sandstone quarried from nearby hills, the artisans created delicate, detailed and realistic carvings in deep relief of the life and times of Buddha amidst charming women, plants, animals, and beautiful gestures of humans and a few gods. The carvings are not sermons but a joyful expression of life awakening forgotten memories. They depict scenes of processions and dances watched by people from balconies, women pounding grain and fetching water in the village, and animals and birds frolicking in the forest. Amidst all these joyful activities the presence of Buddha is indicated by symbols like the parasol, empty seat or ceremonial tree. The carvings also recall the spiritual and moral values by depicting events of Buddha's previous lives, his birth, death, and enlightenment. The Jatakas, the collection of memories from Buddha's previous lives, narrate how Buddha gradually acquired greater moral stature and strength as his soul passed from one incarnation to another. The problem of time and space necessary for the carving of long jatakas was solved by carving from the upper to the lower part of a panel or the continuation of the narrative from panel to panel. Men are carved, stout, fleshy, of medium stature, and wearing mostly turbans and garments wrapped on the legs. The robust but beautiful women are tall, with full, firm breasts, narrow waists, bulging hips and long cylindrical legs and fleshy thighs. They are dressed in diaphanous clothes through which their bodies are visible. The jewelry is worn below the navel, on the legs and arms. Although the figures are small, and carved in deep relief, the body contours, facial features and details of jewelry are carved realistically in minute detail. The naturalistically carved animals are treated like humans. They are carved worshipping the stupa or ceremonial tree. As incarnations of Buddha they are depicted undergoing all the trials and tribulations of life.

The greatness of the carvings lies not only in the beauty, fine finish and details but also in realistic presentation of real world incidents. It is not just the narration of incidence but also the details of the world surrounding it. Sometimes details are omitted for a purpose. These carvings are the finest of Buddhist sculpture, and are masterpieces of early Indian art.

Each gateway consist of 11.2m (34 ft.) two square pillars set 3.3m (10 ft.) apart with three wide, slightly curved architraves longer than 3.3m (10 ft.) placed horizontally one above another with a space between them (Fig. 1.82). The ends of the architrave extend beyond the pillars. Elephants, lions or dwarfs carved on the top of the pillar carry the lower architrave. Square blocks of stone similar to the square pillar below are placed between two architraves, in line with the pillar, making the pillar appear long and solid. In the open spaces between the architraves, small vertical pillars are placed to provide additional support. Additional small vertical columns carved with statues of standing horses or elephants with riders are inserted between architraves. Additional stability is provided by a supporting bracket resting on a square pillar. On the top surface of the upper architrave each pillars ends in Triratna, the holy symbol consisting of wheel of law with a trident above, symbolizing Buddha, his teachings, and the monastic order. A large wheel of law is flanked by two attendants with a Chamara (flywhisk) resting on their shoulders in the center of the upper architrave.

The general design of all the gateways was similar but the loss of certain sections or later repairs has changed the appearance of all of the gateways.

Different parts of the architraves on the gateway are carved with different subjects. The supporting brackets are carved with fertility deities leaning on trees. The vertical small pillars in the space between architraves are carved

with flowering plants and the wheel of law on pointed columns. The four square blocks of pillars placed between the architraves of the gateway are carved on the front and back surface. Eight such carvings in framed panels mostly depict decorated stupas, ceremonial trees or elephants giving a bath to Lakshmi (Fig. 1.83).

Fig.

1.82. Sanchi. Great Stupa. North Gate. Ca. 30-20 BCE. Sandstone.

In Hindu mythology possibly the most benevolent goddess, without any cruel aspect in any avatar except one, is Lakshmi. As wife of the Vedic god Varuna or Sun, she was associated with both good and bad fortune. During the Brahman era she was reborn during the churning of the Milk Ocean and became the wife of Vishnu. She remained the wife of Vishnu in all his incarnations and with Vishnu had a clear hand in the preservation of universe, reinforcing her character as goddess of good fortune and giver of wealth. She is described as a beautiful golden woman, usually sitting or standing on the lotus, which is her symbol. When shown with two hands she is considered the ideal of feminine beauty.

When worshipped alone she is considered the female energy of the Supreme Being and "mother of the world." Possibly because of her exalted position and benevolent nature, she was taken over by Buddhism to represent the conception of Buddha. Zen Buddhist literature mentions that Lakshmi once appeared in the dream of a follower and told him that she was an enemy of Buddha, but now she is enlightened and is a protector of Buddha. Carvings of Lakshmi depict her seated on a lotus flower in a lotus pond with lotus leaves and flowers surrounding her, while elephants standing in upper corners are pouring water from round pots on her head.

Fig. 1.83. Sanchi. Great Stupa. North Gate pillar block. Ca. 30-20 BCE. Sandstone.

Elephants, like Lakshmi, also emerged during the churning of the Milk Ocean. Lakshmi is carved seated in "Royal ease" with one folded leg drawn near her body and the other leg resting on a lotus below. In one carving on the north gate, the leg of Lakshmi resting on a lotus flower is wide open, exposing the flower of her sex. The elephants are carved smaller than Lakshmi and in some carvings cramped at the back. By altering the scale of physical world the artists have created a world dominated by Lakshmi. Decorated stupas with groups of worshipping men and celestial beings are generally carved on the other square block on the same architrave, possibly recalling the association of birth and death.

After Lakshmi and the stupa, the wheel of law representing the doctrine of Buddha is the object most commonly carved. The wheel is mostly carved above a shrine. It is surrounded by a decorated parasol with hanging garlands, groups of worshippers and flying celestials in the upper corners (Fig. 1.84).

Others subjects include lotus blossoms growing in beautiful vases representing the nativity of Buddha, and the tree behind the shrine decorated with flower or pearl garlands, worshipped by kneeling or standing men. A group of beautiful damsels holding offerings in raised hands in front

of a tree and flying deities above are carved on a block of the south gateway.

Fig. 1.84. Sanchi. Great Stupa. East gate pillar block. Wheel of law. Ca. 30-20 BCE. Sandstone.

The architraves are carved with different subject on different sections. The end of the arm is carved with a spiral and in few cases part of the jataka carved on the side arm is supposed to be wrapped in the spiral. The observer takes delight in identifying the jataka and remembering the part wrapped in the spiral. The body of the arm is mostly carved with part of the Jataka narrated in the mid section of architrave. Statues of standing or resting lions or elephants decorate the upper surface of the extended arms.

Sections of the architrave between pillars are carved on both front and back surfaces with two large decorated robust animals facing opposite directions. These carvings are not part of the presentation carved on the architrave. The animals include standing or squatting horses, camels, elephants, stylized lions, cattle with long or curved horns, majestic mythological lions with or without riders and mythological lions with or without wings. There are twelve such carvings on each gateway.

Carvings on the middle section of the architraves present incidents from history or the life of Buddha, but mostly the jatakas. In some early jatakas Buddha was born in animal incarnations and is depicted as such. After he attained moral stature and strength, his incarnations in human body are depicted by symbols. The most common symbols used are stupas and trees. Each gateway has at least one carving representing Buddhas as a tree or stupa, in its full length. Some gateways are carved with two such carvings. The Sakyamuni Buddha and six Manusi Buddhas that were born before the Sakyamuni Buddha are carved as the different species of trees under which they meditated before enlightenment, or as stupas. The Sakyamuni Buddha is carved as a Pipal tree (*Ficus religiosa*), with the characteristic pointed leaves, under which he was enlightened. When Buddhas are presented as stupas, the stupas are carved with different decorative designs but are not individually identified. When stupas and trees are used to present Buddhas, on an architrave, the number of stupas and trees are not same in all carvings.

None of the architraves is carved with stupas only. On the rear surface of the east gateway top architrave, all the seven Buddhas are presented as different species of the trees worshipped by a group of men (Fig. 1.85). Two trees not seen on the photograph are on architrave arms. On the same architrave front face, five stupas and two trees are carved (Fig. 1.86). The two missing stupas are on the architrave arms. A tree of Maitreya Buddha (future Buddha) is carved on the front face of the west gateway top architrave arm. The stupa and ceremonial trees are decorated with flower garlands dropped from above and pearl garlands hanging from the branches. These symbolic presentations of Buddha are surrounded with groups of worshipping men and, rarely, women.

The second most often repeated subjects on the architraves are strikingly natural elephants, which are carved on the entire length of the architraves. No other animals are carved with the elephants. Some elephants are comparatively large; all are carved deep, with a fine finish. Similar large elephants are copied on the sculptured cliff at Mamalapuram. The elephants are generally carved in herds passing beside a tree or moving toward a decorated stupa carved in the center of the architrave. The bottom architrave on the east gateway on back is carved with large herds of elephants coming toward the stupa carved in the center from both directions. The elephants are holding lotus buds and flowers in raised trunks or hanging on their tusks (Fig. 1. 87).

On the same gateway the entire surface of the middle architrave on the rear is carved with strikingly natural buffalos, deer, lions, ox, sheep, stylized lions, two cattle with human heads, a large six-headed cobra with open hood and a large bird all moving towards a tree behind the shrine in the center of architrave. Birds are carved on both the side arms of the architrave, taking gifts to the tree. They are holding baskets loaded with gifts or fruits in their beaks. There are no elephants in this crowd (Fig. 1.88). It is said that once Buddha, tired of the quarrels of his tribesmen, went to live in a forest, when the animals came with gifts to worship him.

On south gateway the front face of the upper architrave shows two diminutive elephants giving a bath to a tall Lakshmi, standing in the center of lotus pond. The surface of the pond is covered with lotus stalks, leaves, flowers, buds, and a few water fowl larger than Lakshmi. The physical scale of the objects is oddly distorted and the carving of Lakshmi is not impressive.

On the east gateway, middle architrave, front face, amidst luxurious vegetation, a finely polished wheel of law decorated with a parasol is carved. Men wearing double crowns are standing, holding hands in salutation. The men standing near the wheel are holding garlands. Deer and cattle are standing or resting on the ground, facing the wheel. The scene depicts the Deer Park where Buddha delivered his first sermon (Fig. 1.89).

The contribution of Emperor Ashoka to Buddhism has been acknowledged on two architraves by depicting his visit to religious places. The lower architrave of the east gateway on its front face is carved with Ashoka visiting Bodh Gaya shrine (Fig. 1.90). In the center of the architrave, a shrine is decorated with chaitya windows. A seat is carved in the entrance of the shrine, reminding us of the presence of Buddha. The shrine bears no resemblance to the existing shrine at Bodh-Gaya. The Bodhi tree is carved behind the shrine. On left of the Bodhi tree is the Ashoka procession with elephants and horses. After descending from a kneeling elephant, Ashoka stands with his entourage, queens, and son. Again he is carved near the Bodhi tree with his wives holding hands in salutation. On the right, a large group of nobles are offering gifts to the tree, accompanied by musicians playing various instruments. It is said that Ashoka was much attached to the Bodhi tree. Once, when one of his queens in jealousy tried to kill the tree by poisoning it, Ashoka fell ill and did not recover till the queen desisted in her effort and the tree recovered.

In one of the carving on the Great Stupa two of his queens are shown supporting an ill Ashoka by his arms on his visit to the shrine.

In the south gateway the middle architrave front face is carved with the pilgrimage of Ashoka to the stupa at Ramagrama with his entourage (Fig. 1.91). The stupa is located with luxurious vegetative growth in the background. Ashoka is approaching the stupa in a horse-drawn chariot, without any female companions, followed by elephants and an army. On the right of the stupa Nagas in human form with five-headed hoods of cobra above their heads are standing with folded arms. Nagins in beautiful female bodies with single hoods above their heads are standing with trays full of gifts in their hands. Some Nagins are touching the stupa while bowing. At the right end two naga couples are sitting in water (identified by lotus flowers and leaves). Nagas zealously guarded this stupa. Another visit of Ashoka to a stupa is carved on Stupa 3, middle architrave, front face.

Fig. 1.85. Sanchi. Great Stupa. East gate. Upper architrave rear view. Buddhas presented as trees.

Ca. 30-20 BCE. Sandstone.

Fig. 1.86. Sanchi. Great Stupa. North gate. Upper architrave front view. Buddhas presented as Stupas and trees. Ca. 30-20 BCE. Sandstone.

Fig. 1.87. Sanchi. Great Stupa. East gate. Bottom architrave front view. Elephants worshiping Stupa. Ca. 30-20 BCE. Sandstone.

Fig. 1.88. Sanchi. Great Stupa. East gate. Middle architrave rear view. Animals worshiping Buddha.

Ca. 30-20 BCE. Sandstone.

Fig. 1.89. Sanchi. Great Stupa. East gate. Middle architrave front view. Worshiping Wheel of law in Deer Garden. Ca. 30-20 BCE. Sandstone.

Fig. 1.90. Sanchi. Great Stupa. East gate. Lower architrave. Front view. Ashoka visiting Bodh Gaya.

Ca. 30-20 BCE. Sandstone.

Fig. 1.91. Sanchi. Great Stupa. South gate. Middle architrave front view. Ashoka visiting Ramagrama Stupa. Ca. 30-20 CE. Sandstone.

Fig. 1.92. Sanchi. Great Stupa. Westgate. Upper architrave rear view. Siege of Kusinara. Ca. 30-20 BCE. Sandstone.

Fig. 1.93. Sanchi. Great Stupa. Westgate. Upper architrave rear view. Malla bringing Buddha's relics to Kusinara. Ca. 30-2 BCE. Sandstone.

Fig. 1.94. Sanchi. Great Stupa. Westgate. Bottom architrave front view. Chadanta jataka.

Ca. 30 BCE. Sandstone.

Fig. 1.95. Sanchi. Great Stupa. Northgate. Top architrave front view. Chadanta jataka.

Ca. 30-20 BCE. Sandstone.

Fig. 1.96. Sanchi. Great Stupa. East gate. Middle architrave. Front view. Great Departure. Ca. 30-20 BCE. Sandstone

Fig. 1.97. Sanchi. Great Stupa. West Gate. Front view. Enlightenment of Buddha. Ca. 30-20 BCE. Sandstone

Fig. 1.98. Sanchi. Great Stupa. Westgate. Lower architrave. Front view. Vessantara leaving palace. Ca. 30-20 BCE. Sandstone

Fig. 1.99. Sanchi. Great Stupa. North gate. Lower architrave rear view. Vessantara undergoing trials in forest. Ca. 30-20 BCE. Sandstone

Fig. 1.100. Sanchi. Great Stupa. North gate. Middle architrave rear view. Temptation of Buddha.

Ca. 30-20 BCE. Sandstone

Fig. 1. 101. Sanchi. Great Stupa. North gate. Middle architrave rare view. Sujata bringing food to Buddha. Ca. 30-20 BCE. Sandstone

The siege of Kusinara where Buddha died is carved on two architraves. Malla, the ruler of Kusinara, refused to share the remains of Buddha with others seven regional kings who were devotees of Buddha. On the west gateway, middle architrave, rear surfaces, armies of seven kings with foot soldiers, cavalry, chariots and elephants are carved over the entire length of the architrave. The armies are converging on the fort and the town carved on the right arm (Fig. 1.92). The armies are extended on the left arm of the architrave. Women watch the siege from the balconies of their homes. The siege of Kusinara by the armies surrounding the fort carved in the center is a scene repeated on the rear surface of the lower architrave of the south gateway. The army of Malla is shown defending the city fort (carved in the center of the architrave) with bows and arrows from ramparts, with a few casualties in front of the fort. When Malla consents to share the relics, the attacking armies are shown retreating on the top of the

panel to the right and left of the fort. The siege of the city is depicted realistically.

On west gateway upper architrave, rear face, King Malla is pictured carrying his share of Buddha's relics to Kusinara for interment, on a magnificent elephant, with a parasol over the relics and an attendant with chamara in procession of men, musicians, elephants and horses with riders (Fig. 1.93). A tree and shrine are carved near the town to remind the pilgrims of Buddha. The town and palace shown on the right of the architrave, with men and women watching from balconies, extended to the side arm. The left extended arms of the architrave show spectators standing with hands held in salutation.

The Chadanta jataka is carved on two architraves. Buddha was born as the semi-divine white elephant Chadanta with six tusks. He had two wives. One wife was jealous and prayed to those Buddhas who had attained nirvana to be reborn as a beautiful maiden in the next generation and marry the king of Varanasi to revenge Chadanta for favoring her rival. Her wish was granted and when she grew up as a beautiful maiden she married the king of Varanasi. Pretending to be sick, she persuaded the king to fulfill her desire to bring the fused tusks of an elephant. Chadanta had three tusks, fused into one, on each side. The king hired Sonuttara, the best huntsman in the kingdom, to kill Chadanta and bring his tusks as proof. The huntsman captured Chadanta in a pit and started shooting arrows at him. When asked, the huntsman told Chadanta that the queen wanted him killed and to bring her the tusks. Chadanta understood and accepted his fate; before death he helped the huntsman to climb up to the root of the tusks. When the huntsman found the tusks too hard to cut, Chadanta took the saw, cut the tusks and fell down dead in his own blood. The queen, after hearing how the tusks were obtained, died of remorse. On the West gateway the Chadanta jataka is depicted on the bottom architrave, front face. In the carving the elephant is shown sitting, taking a bath in a lotus pool near a tree in the company of attendants at the left end (Fig. 1.94). The lotus leaves and flowers in the water are carved in normal size. Ripples indicate water in the pond and the carving is deep. Chadanta is carved again in the center near a pipal tree with all the elephants raising their trunks. The tree is adorned with flower gardens hanging from its branches and pointed pipal leaves. Chadanta can be identified by the three fused tasks. After worshiping the tree, he takes a walk and returns to the pipal tree again for worship. On the north gateway, upper architrave front face, the jataka is repeated (Fig. 1.95). The carving is similar to the previous one but the lotus leaves and flowers are relatively large and the leaves of the pipal tree are less natural. The carvings differ in the technique of execution but both are excellent. Six dwarfs sprouting lotus stalks with leaves, flowers and buds from their mouths are carved on front face of the lower architrave of the south gateway.

All the remaining architraves are carved with incidences relating to the life of Buddha. The episode of the Great Departure is carved on the east gateway, middle architrave front face (Fig. 1.96). On left of the architrave, middle section, Sidharta is emerging from the palace on a horse with a parasol hovering above. Sidharta is not shown actually on the horse. People from balconies are watching the procession. The same riderless horse followed by mourners is carved three times with a parasol above to indicate the progress of the procession. At the left upper corner, footprints on the ground with the parasol above indicate that Sidharta has dismounted. Chandaka, the loyal groom of Sidharta, kneeling before the footprints, indicates his farewell. The return journey by horse, moving in the opposite direction, towards the palace, in the lower part of the panel, indicates the departure of Sidharta on his quest for enlightenment. The story continues from the upper to lower section of panel.

The lower architrave of the west gateway in the rear view is carved with the "enlightenment" episode over its entire length (Fig. 1.97). A large multi-storied shrine is carved with chaitya windows and other decorations in the center of the architrave with Buddha presented as a tree decorated with a parasol with hanging garlands. Mara, the personification of human desires and the god of death, seeking to prevent Buddha from attaining nirvana and becoming free of desires and death, sent his army of ugly dwarf demons with thick lips and bulging stomachs, some riding horses and elephants, carrying various weapons to frighten and disrupt the meditation of Buddha. When they realize that they cannot distract Sidharta from his meditation they retreat in despair and disarray, with panic on their faces. In the commotion some demons have fallen down. Retreating, the carving shows Mara's army continuing on the right arm of the architrave. To the left of Buddha, serene and rejoicing gods, standing upright, are shown applauding Sidharta and offering salutations, accompanied by music. The assembly of gods is continued on the right arm of the architrave. The contrasts in facial expressions and stature between the gods and dwarfs flanking Buddha are overwhelming.

The Vessantara jataka is carved on both surfaces of the north gateway on the lower architrave. Buddha in his last incarnation was born as Prince Vessantara, who wanted to attain perfection in giving. His father, King Sanjaya, had a white elephant whose presence brought rain to his people. On learning that the neighbor kingdom was suffering from drought, Vessantara gives the white elephant to the neighboring king. The people, thinking that Vessantara was not concerned with their welfare, demanded that his father banish him from his own kingdom. To satisfy the people Vessantara leaves the kingdom, with his family. Vessantara's journey starts on the lower margin of bottom architrave on the front face (Fig. 1.98). He is carved emerging from the palace, riding a chariot with his family. On the way, a group of Brahmins ask for the chariot. He gives them the chariot with the horse, and walks with his family. Further up, a prince comes and begs Vessantara to give up these hardships and return to the palace; he refuses. The jataka continues on the back surface of the bottom architrave (Fig. 1.99). Vessantara, his wife and children enter the forest on the left arm of the architrave and decide to stay in a hut. He is carved sitting with his wife in front of the hut in the thick forest beside a lotus pond with a fire burning in a pot in front. An elephant is taking a bath in the pond amidst lotus flowers. The jungle is full of wild animals and fowl, including geese and peacocks. Beside the hut Vessantara is shown sitting with his children and listening, possibly to Indra. Further along, Vessantara is shown sitting in front of another hut. One day his wife was delayed from returning to the hut after collecting food in the forest; a pair of lions obstructed her way. The lions are carved near the thatched hut roof. A Brahmin approaches Vessantara and asks for his children. In the absence of the mother, the children are handed over to the Brahmin. On his way, the Brahmin meets a procession with riders on horses and elephants and sells the children into slavery. An archer sent by the prince who begged Vessantara to give up his hardships is shown with drawn bow, aiming an arrow at the Brahmin. But the Brahmin escapes after selling the children into slavery. Vessantara ends up giving away everything that belonged to him. The jataka ends on happy note. The gods, satisfied by Vessantara's lack of ego and perfection in giving, restore his wife and children. They are shown in the balcony of the palace with a beautiful garden on the right arm of the architrave.

The remaining part of the architrave is carved with the Alambusa jataka on the right arm. The carving depicts a sage sitting in front of a hut. His son Isisinga, with one horn, was born to the doe; he is standing with clasped hands. Below a doe is carved near the feet of the sage; she is looking at him, twisting her neck. Buddha in one of his previous lives was a young ascetic living in the forest. A doe fell in love with him and swallowed some of his seed together with grass and water. She became pregnant and gave birth to a boy with a horn in the middle of his forehead. The child grew up so virtuous that the gods became jealous of his merit. Indra, the king of the gods, sends a heavenly dancer, Alambusa, to seduce the youth. She succeeds and lives with the youth for three years, after which she disclosed her identity and returns to join the kingdom of Indra.

The temptation of Buddha is carved on the west gate, lower architrave, front face (Fig. 1.100). Mara, the god of human desires, sends his beautiful daughter to tempt Buddha and distract him from meditation. Mara is sitting on his throne in the center of the panel. Buddha is carved as a tree worshipped by men and women. The thick-lipped potbellied ugly demons of Mara's army (personifications of human passions) are waiting on his left to pounce on Buddha when he succumbs to the temptation. On the back of the tree, Sujata is carved holding a water pot and sweet rice in a tray that she prepared to offer to the god of the Banyan tree when her wish for a son was fulfilled. This was the first solid meal Buddha ate after six years of mortification (Fig. 1.101).

The east gateway was possibly erected during the last quarter of the first century BCE (Fig. 1.102). The strong plastic character of Indian sculpture, emphasizing supple, fluid bodies without rigid lines, is fully developed on this gateway. Beautifully decorated elephants carved in three dimensions with riders carrying banners and flags support the lowest architrave. The space between the pillar and first architrave on the right pillar is decorated with framed sculptural decorations and on the left with a flag-bearing skull.

The extended arms of the lower architrave in the front view displays a pair of finely carved peacocks. Facing opposite directions, the peacocks turn their long necks to look back at each other. The graceful twist of the necks looks natural and realistic. On the right arm a shrine is carved between the necks of the peacocks. On the upper surface of the arm a majestic lion is resting. On the left arm, a loving pair is carved between the twisted necks of the peacock. On the upper surface of the arm a statue of a majestic walking elephant is decorated on the back with drapes and bells. The upper surface of the middle architrave arm on the left has a statue of standing elephant. All the decorations on the top of the

upper architrave are lost except Triratna and the decorated elephant on the left.

Fig. 1.102. Sanchi. Great Stupa. East gate. Front view. Ca. 30-20 BCE. Sandstone

The small square pillars between the spaces of the upper architraves are carved with trees and the wheel of law mounted on a pillar on the front façade. The supporting bracket of the lower right arms is carved with a tree and Yakshi (the fertility deity) standing on a mango tree in front view (Fig. 1. 103). The yaksis on all the supporting brackets are lost except on the left arm of upper architrave.

The earlier restraint in the presentation of feminine beauty in Buddhist art gave away to provocative presentation of females. The Yakshi on the left bracket is strikingly beautiful, stunningly voluptuous, wearing diaphanous clothes through which her private parts are visible. She is wearing jewelry and scarf tied round her hips. The sensuous, provocative and curvaceous female with large firm breasts is carved with three body bends. She is hanging languidly on a mango tree with one hand wrapped around a branch and other holding a fruit-laden branch. A sense of swinging motion is suggested by the manner of placement of her feet on the branch. It is a highly sophisticated and provocative pose. She does not look semi-divine but like a living and moving person in flesh, swinging towards the observer. It is interesting to note that the females carved in frontal pose wearing diaphanous dress exposing their nude bodies are carved with beautifully designed dresses on their backs.

The three-body-bend pose of the female and the sensual quality depicted here become a standard in Indian sculpture.

A similar presentation with a different theme appeared in a seventh century carving of a dancer in Cave 7 at Aurangabad. The artists at Sanchi also excelled in modeling the female torso. A broken statue of a Yakshi with model torso is on display at the Boston Museum.

dows of the shrine, decorated with a parasol with hanging garlands. Two huge garlands are flank the tree. A parasol is carved above the tree and two *kinnaras* (birds with a human upper body) are carved holding garlands and a tray with gifts in their hands. The panel is said to present the enlightenment of Buddha.

Fig. 1.103. Sanchi. Great Stupa. East gate. Lower bracket. Yakshi. Ca. 30-20 BCE

Fig. 1.104. Sanchi. Great Stupa. East gate right pillar. Buddha walking between row of gods and Enlightenment of Buddha. Ca. 30-20 BCE. Sandstone

The pillars of all the gates are carved on three sides, all except the back, attached to the entrance. The base of all the gateway pillars facing the entrance were carved with males, some wearing foreign garments, and jewelry, mostly without weapons. They are considered to be guardians of the stupa but some viewers believe they are bodhisattvas. Most of these carvings are lost now. The outer surface of the east gate left pillar is covered with a delightful, decorative lotus vine with flowers and buds issued from the mouth of a crocodile with a fish's tail. There are water fowls amidst the lotus vines. The top panel on the front face is carved with two rows of gods with a blank strip in between — indicating Buddha walking between the rows (Fig. 1. 104).

The panel below depicts a shrine with two stories. The lower story of the shrine is carved with a shrine with Triratna on top. Two men standing on each side of the shrine are posed in gestures of worship. On the upper story a magnificent Bodhi tree has burst open from under the door and win-

The third panel depicts the Miracle of Buddha walking on water that converted the disbelieving but influential Kasyapa brothers, who were fire worshippers (Fig. 1.105). The carving is framed with a pillar on one side with a winged lion sitting on top and on other side with a band of vine with leaves, calyx, buds and flowers. A bamboo fence borders the upper and lower margins. On top of the carving two oval-shaped plants with different shaped leaves and flowers flank a course of slow-moving water with ripples. The water is filled with fishes, crocodiles, and geese. One goose is swallowing a fish. Broken lotus leaves, calyx, buds and open flowers are floating in the water. In the center the river is raging in flood, with big waves. The stems of the two different kinds of fruit trees beside the river are almost engulfed by waves. Monkeys are picking fruit on one tree. On other side broken lotus leaves, calyx buds and flowers are floating in flooded water.

Fig. 1.105. Sanchi. Great Stupa. East gate. Right pillar. Buddha walking on water. Ca. 30-20 BCE. Sandstone.

Fig. 1.106. Sanchi. Great Stupa. East gate. Right pillar. Procession of Bimbisara. Ca. 30-20 BCE. Sandstone.

On learning that Buddha was crossing the flooded river, the Kasyapa brothers, concerned for his safety and searching for him on the river, riding in a boat, saw him walking on the turbulent water in front of them. A blank space in front of the boat in the center of the turbulent stream represents Buddha walking on the water. The Kasyapa brothers, after witnessing the miracle, become believers in Buddha. At the bottom of the panel the Kasyapa brothers are seen standing amidst a row of plants on the ground, worshipping Buddha beside the river; he is symbolized as a tree behind the shrine, with pointed leaves and hanging garlands. On the other side of the river, beside a submerged tree, broken parts of lotus plants are floating in the water; ripples indicate that the flood is past.

The panel below is carved with the procession of King Bimbisara of Magadha passing through the streets of Rajagraha, his capital, on way to pay homage to Buddha (Fig. 1.106).

On the top corner Bimbisara is shown taking leave of a dignitary and emerging from a palace on an elephant, with a dignitary on horseback leading the way. The procession is watched by men and women from the palace balcony and street windows. Below, he is shown riding through the street in a chariot drawn by two horses, holding his hand in a protection gesture, accompanied by the queen. In front of the procession three men are walking, carrying gifts, followed by marching soldiers and the king's chariot. The large procession is accommodated in the panel by winding it through the street from top to bottom.

The inner face of the left pillar at the top depicts Buddha as a decorated Bodhi tree with hanging garlands surrounded by worshippers (Fig. 1.107).

Fig. 1.107. Sanchi. Great Stupa. East gate. Left pillar. Indra requesting Buddha to teach religion. Ca. 30-20 BCE.

Buddha, after enlightenment, had not yet decided to preach. The gods, wearing crowns and led by Brahma and Indra, appeared before Buddha requesting him to teach his doctrine. The upper corners of the panel are carved with flying mythological lions with riders.

A small panel below depicts Maya, mother of Buddha, sleeping in the palace when she dreamed of a white elephant entering her womb at the time she conceived Buddha (Fig.

1.108). A male head is carved near the head of sleeping Maya. The elephant symbolizing Buddha is shown standing on the moon. In Hindu mythology, one of the mighty gods of the second triad of gods was Vivasvat, eighth son of Aditi, the mother of gods. He was born as a shapeless lump and was thrown away by his mother. The divine artificer picked him up and molded him into Vivasvat. The unused parts fell to earth and became elephants. Thus elephants are made up of the stuff of gods and partake divine nature.

Fig. 1.108. Sanchi. Great Stupa. East gate. Left pillar. Maya, dreaming of a white elephant standing on the moon. Buddha visiting Kapilavastu. Ca. 30-20 BCE. Sandstone.

The panel below depicts Buddha visiting Kapilavastu. Seven years after enlightenment Buddha visited Kapilavastu at the invitation of his father. His father came out of town to greet Buddha, riding a chariot, with his kinsmen on horses and elephants, followed by soldiers and musicians on foot going before. Men and women from balconies are shown watching the procession. When they reached the outskirts of the town they saw Buddha carved as a tree. His father faced a dilemma. He was father of Buddha, as well as king, but Buddha was sovereign of the universe. Who should honor whom first? Buddha saved the situation by walking on the air, shown as a blank strip watched by his kinsmen. All were impressed by the miracle shown by Buddha. Buddha is repeatedly carved as a tree moving with the procession. The panel ends with the tree enclosed in a low railing with a group of men standing in adoration before the tree. The bottom panel shows a stout door guardian wearing an eye-popping load of jewelry and holding a flower in his hand.

The front face of the right pillar shows a part of the Buddhist heavens occupied by gods of various ranks. The Buddhist universe Chakravala has three planes: above, around and below Mount Meru. The lower plane has 136 hells, the lowest called Avici, where abusers of Buddha and of the law are sent for a time before reborn into the world. The plane around Mount Meru contains the world of animals, ghosts, demons and men. Above the peak of Mount Meru are heavens, arranged one above other. In the lower heaven guardians of the east, south, west and north reside. Further up is the "Heaven of Thirty-three Divinities," the heaven where Indra resides. It is followed by the heaven without day or night, where Yama, god of death, resides. Next is the Tusita heaven where the Bodhisattvas reside before they appear on earth as Buddha. The Maitreya Buddha is awaiting here to be born as the next Buddha on earth. The top two heavens are the heavens of higher gods.

Above these heavens on Mount Meru are the Chyana Lokas (regions of abstract meditation) and Arupa Lokas (formless worlds), reserved for spirits of high order such as Buddha. Six of the heavens, called Devalokas, shown in the carving, are inhabited with those that enjoy the pleasures of the senses (Fig. 1.109). (Two of the lower heavens have been destroyed in the carving.) The façade of each heaven is carved with four pillars. The pillars of the top heaven are decorated with lions, below the cornice, and some heavens are carved with chaitya windows on the cornice. In the topmost panel a beautiful couple, probably Indra and his wife, sit looking at each other while eating fruit. The female is holding possibly a baby near her breast. Beautiful females are standing behind. Females in all the heavens are carved with soft, well-proportioned bodies dressed similar to the Yakshi on the gateway brackets. In all the heavens the gods are sitting in a regal, easy pose in the company of beautiful females and female attendants holding parasols. All the gods are enjoying the ladies' dancing and drum music. Some gods appear to be holding a musical instrument in hand. Some appear to be holding a pot in one hand and possibly eating fruit with the other hand.

Fig. 1.109. Sanchi. Great Stupa. East gate. Left pillar. Heavens of lesser gods. Ca. 30-20 BCE. Sandstone.

The top panel on the inner surface of the right pillar depicts village life in the morning (Fig. 1.110). At one end a lotus pond is full of large flowers, leaves and buds, and a buffalo is submerged up to the neck. Some buffalo are standing in the water and some are sitting beside the pond. Some cow, sheep and goats are standing near the pond, possibly waiting for their turn to drink. A woman is bending down, filling a water pot. Another woman is standing behind, with a pot on her hip, awaiting her turn. A shrine in the center of the panel is decorated with a parasol with hanging garlands. Two men stand beside the shrine, worshipping. A beautiful woman on her way to the pond with a water pot is standing cross-legged, gossiping with a man carrying a plow on his shoulder. One woman, above, is churning milk; another is grinding grain on a stone slab with a stoneroller on a table and another is winnowing grain. In corner of a house a couple sits in intimate discussion. The woman is possibly serving breakfast on a stone slab and the man is watching her, lovingly. From beautifully decorated balconies and windows of their residences other people are enjoying watching the village. Behind the residences is another shrine. Behind the shrine a man is carrying a pole on his shoulder with a bundle tied to it; he is accompanied by a woman driving cattle. On the left a beautiful damsel is emerging from her residence carrying a bag on her shoulder to follow a man on some errand.

Fig. 1.110. Sanchi. Great Stupa. East gate. Right pillar. Village life in the morning. Ca. 30-20 BCE. Sandstone

The panel below is carved with a shrine in the center of Kasyapa village (Fig. 1.111). Kasyapa and his kinsmen were fire worshippers whom Buddha wanted to convert. Once when Buddha wanted to stay in Kasyapa hermitage, the cobra occupying the hermitage attacked him, spitting fire and smoke. But Buddha subdued him and the cobra took refuge in Buddha's bowl. In the carving behind the village is a luxurious growth of trees. Monkeys are picking fruits all over. There is a two-storied shrine in the center with fire leaping out of chaitya windows on the story above. The ascetics flanking the hermitage are wearing clothes decorated with vertical stripes. Behind the altar in the shrine is the cobra with his expanded five-headed hood. In front of the altar, a fire is burning in a pot. Below is a mixed herd of buffalo, goats and an elephant. In one corner Kasyapa is sitting in a hut with a leaf-thatched roof, with a ceremonial fire burning in a pot and a ladle for pouring oil on the fire. A man is standing in front of the hut; his folded hand indicate the status of Kasyapa. At the other corner is a river with choppy waves. There are water-fowl, lotus leaves, buds, flowers and calyx in the pond. Two boys are standing in front with raised hands to jump in the water to swim. An acetic is bathing in the pond and a woman is bent over to fill a pot with water, at the same time drinking from the river surface.

At the bottom of the pillar a guardian is standing, wearing Indian dress, decked in jewelry and holding a lotus flower in hand (Fig. 1.113). The entire outer surface of the pillar is covered with decorative motifs similar to the motifs of the left pillar.

Fig. 1.112. Sanchi. Great Stupa. East gate. Right pillar. Kasyapa performing prayer. Ca. 30-20 BCE. Sandstone.

Fig. 1.113. Sanchi. Great Stupa. East gate. Left pillar bottom. Guard at the entrance.

Ca .30-20 BCE. Sandstone.

Fig. 1.111. Great Stupa. East gate. Right pillar. Kasyapa Hermitage. Ca. 30-20 BCE. Sandstone.

In the panel below, the shrine is shown enclosed in bamboo railing (Fig. 1.112). Kasyapa and his kinsmen want to worship the fire. Kasyapa, sitting below the shrine, is pouring oil from a container and blowing on it while another person is fanning the fire; but the fire does not catch. Two devotees are trying to split wood, but the wood will not split. A third person is trying to offer his obligation to the fire by pouring oil with a ladle, but the fire does not respond. Two men are standing beside the hermitage, one carrying a load tied to the ends of a pole on his shoulder and another carrying a tree trunk on his shoulder — possibly to split more wood; but they cannot accomplish their worship.

Fig. 1.114. Sanchi. Great Stupa. Westgate. Rear view. Ca. 30-20 BCE Sandstone.

The West Gate was constructed in last quarter of first century BCE (Fig. 1.114). The lower architrave of the stupa is carried by the pot-bellied Dwarf's associated with earth — precious stones and metals subordinated to Buddha. The fat and fleshy dwarfs with bulging belly folds appear to be holding the base of the mountain in their hands, raised above their heads. Each dwarf wears a different costume and facial expression. All the supporting brackets of the arms and the decorations on top of all the arms and upper architraves are lost except the base of the wheel of law on the center of the upper architrave. Three small plain and rectangular pillars of later origin are installed between the architraves spaces.

The front face of the left pillar on the top depicts the Mahakapi Jataka, the story of Buddha when he was monkey king (Fig. 1.115). At the lower right corner the king of Benares is carved arriving in the forest on horseback, with a parasol above, accompanied by soldiers and musicians, in search of the mango tree from which a fisherman had fetched him a particularly tasty fruit. Noticing that monkeys are devouring the mangoes, the king orders the soldiers to shoot them. A soldier carved above the head of the king's horse is aiming an arrow in the direction of the monkey-king near the top of the panel. The monkey king, holding the branches of the trees on the opposite bank, has stretched across the river, forming a bridge to allow the monkeys to escape to the calm on the other side of the river, where some monkeys are frolicking and deer are sleeping peacefully. An enemy of the monkey-king, while crossing the river, jumps hard on the back of the king, mortally wounding him. Seeing that the monkey-king is injured, the king orders his soldiers to hold a stretcher below to break the king's fall. The stretcher is shown in the carving below the monkey king. At the top left corner, the king is seen sitting with a monkey under a tree, discussing the moral greatness of the king who sacrificed his life for his subjects. The comparative scale of elements, such as the trees, the men bathing on the right shore, and the river (shown as a narrow strip with fishes and the monkey king stretched over the river) is freely adjusted to narrate the story, distorting the physical world. Neither the sequence of the narrative nor the full story is evident in the panel. But for a pilgrim who knows the story, searching the scenes that are presented and filling in missing details from memory is a joyful experience.

The panel below depicts Buddha preaching religion to his mother and the gods in the "Heaven of Thirty-three Divinities." Buddha is depicted as tree surrounded by gods.

Other panels below depict the adoration of Buddha (shown as a tree with hanging garlands) by groups of two men standing on each side and *kinnaras* (half-bird half-human) hovering above. Below a row of men with hands folded

in gesture of worship and men flanking the shrine are carved in two panels. The major difference between the panels is different type of trees. One panel shows the Bodhi tree with its distinctive leaves. The tree in the other panel bears flowers, possibly depicting one of the Manusi Buddha. The bottom panel features three lions springing up in a delightful design. The entire outside panel of the left pillar is decorated with delightful, similar units consisting of two stylized beasts, with or without horns, carrying riders, surrounded by vines, large flowers, buds and leaves. Large hanging flowers are carved at the top of the unit with tendrils bearing buds and half-open flowers at the side.

Fig. 1.115. Sanchi. Great Stupa. West Gate pillar. Front face. Mahakapi jataka. Ca. 30-20 BCE. Sandstone.

The inner surface of the pillar on the top is carved with a tree under a parasol behind a shrine. Flying gods are dropping garlands on the tree. On both sides of the shrine, at a slightly lower level, two men are worshipping two small trees. Under the tree, seven men stand, carved in frontal profile with hands folded. The bottom panel is carved with a guard standing under a mango tree, wearing foreign garb, holding a spear in his left hand and his right hand on his hip. A large necklace hangs around his neck and his hands are covered with jewelry. A sword sheath hangs behind his right arm.

The right pillar on its front face may depict the paradise of heavenly love, in the top panel which is divided into two levels with a passage to the lower level (Fig. 1.117). In the upper level two *mithuna* couples are seated on a couch in each corner. A mithuna couple is standing near the stepped passage, talking. The female has hidden her face in hands, possibly feeling bashful about something whispered by the man. Two mithuna couples are seated on couches on the lower level in front of a lotus pond. The panel below, which may

Fig. 1.117. Sanchi. Great Stupa. Westgate. Right pillar. Front face. Paradise of Heavenly love. Ca. 30-20 BCE. Sandstone.

have been carved with similar scenes, is damaged. The space below was possibly not sculpted. On top of the inner surface facing the entrance is the story of young Sama, whose parents were blinded by a poisonous snake who shot venom into their eyes (Fig. 1.118). Various species of cobras that can shoot neurotoxic venom causing blindness are still found in Africa and parts of Southeast Asia. Sama was a model of parental devotion. He attended to all their needs, living with them in a hut on the banks of a river in the forest. A king who was out on a hunt saw the youth coming to the river to fetch water and shot an arrow at him, not knowing the identity of Sama. The arrow struck Sama and he dropped, mortally wounded. Learning about the helpless parents and the dutiful devotion of the youth the king was overcome with remorse and attended to the blind parents. The story ends on a happy note when the youth is miraculously cured and the parents recover their sight. In the carving on the right upper corner the residential huts of Sama and his parents are carved with the parents seated beside the entrance. A hearth with a sacrificial fire burning, a ladle and pot of oil are located between the huts. There are a few deer grazing in the center amidst a lush growth of plants. In the river lotus flowers, buds and leaves are floating and a few buffalo are wallowing. In the bottom corner the king is standing beside the lotus pond with his

bow drawn. Next, Sama is carved, fallen in the pond, pierced by the arrow. Beside him stands the remorseful king, his bow slack. Next the smiling king — without his royal robe — is standing with Sama, who has recovered sufficiently to carry a pot of water on his shoulder. In the upper left corner the parents of Sama and the king are shown standing with Indra, who came to unfold the happy ending.

Fig. 1.118. Sanchi. Great Stupa. Westgate. Right pillar. Front face. Sama jataka. Ca. 30-20 BCE. Sandstone.

The panel below depicts the episode of Naga-king Muchalinda (Fig. 1.119).

Fig. 1.119. Sanchi. Great Stupa. Westgate. Right pillar. Front face. Naga king Muchalinda and Buddha. Ca. 30-20 BCE. Sandstone.

Buddha, while experiencing the bliss of enlightenment, sat in meditation under the tree for seven days. Beneath the tree in a vast hollow lived the naga-king. During this meditation a thunderstorm arose, with pouring rain followed by a freezing gale and terrible darkness, sent by Mara. At the onset of the thunderstorm the naga-king came out of his dwelling and to protect Buddha wrapped himself around the body of Buddha seven times and spread his hood above the head of Buddha like an umbrella. The naga-king disappeared after the storm was over. When such services were not required, the Nagas appeared before Buddha as humans.

The panel depicts Buddha as a decorated tree under a parasol decorated with garlands. In the upper corners two females riding mythological lions are approaching the tree. Two men adorned with jewelry and holding garlands stand flanking the tree. To the right of the tree stand two women with a single cobra head behind their heads; one is holding a round pot and another is holding a chamara. On the left a woman accompanied by a group of female musicians playing various musical instruments is dancing. Nagas are carved with five-headed cobra hoods behind their heads and nagins with a single hood behind their heads. The hood of the cobra originates from the hips above the legs and reaches above the head from behind. Below the tree the five-hooded naga-king is seated in royal ease. On his right three females with single cobra hoods, their hair elaborately coifed and their legs ornamented with jewelry, are seated on cushions. Perhaps they are the naga-king's wives. The damaged panel below depicts a royal couple riding a boat carved with a lion head at the bow and a fish tail on the stern. The surface below may not have been decorated.

Fig. 1.120. Sanchi. Great Stupa. North gate rear view. Ca. 30-20 BCE. Sandstone.

The north gateway, constructed in 20-30 BCE, excels in the plasticity of sculpture — like the east gateway (Fig. 1.120).

Four jatakas are carved on this gateway. Most of the decorative statues are intact. The lower architrave is supported on decorated elephants. In the spaces above the elephant heads, decorative sculpture is carved. A damsel is driving one of the elephants. The supporting brackets of all the outer arms, carved with fertility deities, are intact. The Yaksis, wearing diaphanous dress, wear jewelry about the hips. The yaksi on the lower bracket is leaning back on a tree branch. The legs and one hand of the statue are broken. She does not exhibit the characteristic sophistication and beauty. The top surface of the middle and upper architrave arms bears statues of winged lions of Iranian origin sitting on their hind legs with open mouths. The upper architrave in addition to lions displays Triratna, the holy symbol, on both ends. There is a chamara bearer in attendance on the left. The chamara bearer on the right is lost. The broken wheel of law in the center is indicated only by part of the outer rim that remains. The space between the architraves bears small pillars with a tree or wheel of law carved above the pointed pillar. The space between the small pillars is decorated with elephants and horses with riders to give stability to the architraves. The arms of the middle architrave in rear view are carved with a pair of peacocks facing opposite directions but looking at each other with curved necks. A tree is carved between their necks. The shrine represents Buddha and the peacock was the emblem of the Maurya dynasty.

The front face of the left pillar in the top panel depicts Buddha visiting the "Heaven of Thirty-three Divinities" to instruct the gods and his mother (who was reborn in heaven). He is descending from the heaven after a stay of three months in the company of Brahma and Indra. Buddha is symbolized as a tree in the company of the gods at the top of a ladder and in the company of men at the bottom of the ladder.

The second panel depicts prince Sidharta visiting Kapilavastu city in a chariot drawn by horses and watched by women from the balconies. He is not seated in the chariot. During these visits he witnessed the death and sufferings of men that made him seek enlightenment. The third panel depicts Buddha carved as tree behind a shrine preaching his kinsmen in Kapilavastu. The carvings below this panel are badly damaged. The outer surface of the pillar is covered entirely with repeating units of decorative carvings with Triratna on top.

The top panel on the surface facing the entrance in the upper half space depicts kinnaras coming from four directions bearing garlands to a richly decorated stupa with a circumambulatory passage enclosed in a bamboo railing with a front entrance. Men carrying garlands occupy the ambulatory passage. Below, a group of men is coming towards the entrance bearing flags, garlands and gifts. Another group is standing with hands held in a praying gesture. One person carved in rear profile is holding his hands joined above his head in salutation. Next a group of musicians is playing music with drums, horns with serpent-like ends, double pipes and string instruments. The curly hair and different style of dress and headgear suggests that the worshipers are visitors from south Asia. The panel below depicts the story of a monkey who took the begging bowl from Buddha, filled it with honey, and offered it to Buddha. When Buddha (symbolized as a tree) accepts the offering, the same monkey is carved a second time expressing joy with raised hands. Next a group of two men and two women are shown worshipping the tree. The women are carved from the side, seated on their heels, with bent knees on the ground before the tree, their hips spread on their heels presenting beautiful side profile.

The panel below depicts the visit of Buddha to Kapilavastu. Buddha is symbolized as a tree with hanging garlands. Two kinnaras and a *karita* (half-man and half-beast) are dropping flowers from above. Beside the tree a royal couple, attended by two females (one holding an umbrella above them and another holding a *Chamara*) are greeting Buddha. Perhaps they are the parents of Buddha. The queen and another female wearing jewelry are presenting offerings to the tree. The last panel depicts a guardian wearing jewelry and holding flowers in his hand.

On the front face of the right pillar the mango tree is carved that Buddha caused to grow overnight and under which he preached. In the center of the panel an empty throne under the mango tree bearing fruits symbolizes Buddha. Four men are seated in front of the tree. Above the tree a group, possibly gods, is carved. At the top two men are beating big drums and Vidyadharas are hovering in the corners. The panel below depicts the Jetavana garden, the favorite resting spot of Buddha. It was purchased by a rich merchant, Anathapindaka of Sravasti, and was gifted to Buddha. The prominent carving in the panel is that of the merchant. Below a building with wagon-vaulted roof is carved with four openings under chaitya arches. Few people are standing in the doorways. Possibly it is the Jetavana monastery. Below is a blank strip indicating Buddha walking on air while a row of people stand below, looking at Buddha. The panel below shows King Prasenjit of Kosala going out of his capital, Sravasti, through the city gate, in a procession to visit Buddha. The last panel depicts mithuna couples, royals riding elephants, and a lotus lake below. The outer surface of the pillar is carved with

beautifully-sculptured narrow elongated leaves arranged in various designs and flowers in repeated units. Near the top of the pillar a decorated medallion and near the bottom a pair of Buddha footprints embossed with the wheel of law indicate the universal sovereignty of Buddha.

The surface of the right pillar facing the entrance is carved on the top with a rock-cut structure, possibly an early Buddhist cave, with a decorated entrance in front. There is an altar beside the entrance of the cave (Fig. 1.121). In the center of the cave a large decorated pipal tree is carved behind a shrine. A rock-cut structure with two stories is carved to the right of the tree. On the other side of the tree, the heads of a buffalo, lion, elephant and other animals are carved. Rows of well-dressed devotees wearing large turbans and earrings are standing on side and in front of the tree with hands held in praying gestures. Some devotees are holding gifts in their hands. Two beautiful females are standing in front, wearing beautifully designed dresses on their backs. Possibly the carving depicts the Indra-Sheila cave near Rajagraha. The panel below depicts a royal procession passing through the city gate while residents of the town look on. Below is a tree behind a shrine surrounded by beautiful female worshippers and men. The last panel is carved with a guardian.

Fig. 1. 121. Sanchi. Great Stupa. North gate. Right pillar. An early Buddhist cave. Ca. 30-20 BCE. Sandstone.

The south gateway was the first gateway constructed. It may have been the main entrance to the stupa. A stump of an Ashoka pillar is embedded in the ground near the entrance. Two long circular sections of the pillar lie nearby. The broken top of the pillar is kept in the local museum. Four addorsed lion standing on the decorated circular dais on top of the pillars support the lower architrave (Fig. 1.80). This motif is copied on the official seal of the Republic of India.

Fig. 1.122. Sanchi. Great Stupa. Southgate. Right pillar. Front face from top - Mounted Wheel of law in Deer park. Ashoka and below Indra visiting Deer Park. Other face from top - Buddhist shrine. Sick Ashoka visiting shrine. Ca. 30 BCE. Sandstone.

All the supporting arm brackets and ornamental statues on the upper surfaces of the architraves are lost. Rectangular plain small pillars of later origin have been installed between the architraves for stability. The mostly damaged sculpture on the architraves has lost its charm and shows more weather damage than others. On the front and side of the right pillar, few panels show carving (Fig. 1.122). The top panel on the front face is carved with wheel of the law mounted on column in Deer Park where Buddha delivered his first ser-

mon after enlightenment. Men and women are flanking the column to worshipping the wheel of law while deer are rubbing their heads on the base of column and some are licking the column. The dignitary standing beside the column could be Ashoka and his queens. The panel below depicts a king, possibly Ashoka, in a chariot with his queen and below that Indra with his wife on elephants visiting Deer Park to pay homage to the wheel of law. All the other panels below are obliterated.

The surface facing entrance in the top panel is carved with a large bodhi tree decorated with garlands. Below the tree is a realistically carved shrine with two stories. The upper story is decorated with chaitya windows. The lower story is carved with four pillars with round bases and two pilasters supporting the front porch. There is an altar in the porch. The entrance to the shrine is crowded with people. The panel below depicts the ailing Ashoka visiting the pipal tree supported by his queens. Attendants carrying an offering and holding a parasol above the king flank the queens. It is said that Ashoka was so attached to the pipal tree that he fell ill when one of his wives tried to harm the tree out of jealousy. Another panel below shows a shrine with an arch on the upper storey occupied by a few people. It represents the Heaven of thirty-three gods where Indra and other gods are worshiping the hair cut off by Buddha when he embarked on his journey for enlightenment. The gods picked up the hair and took it to heaven to worship.

The fourth panel depicts the celebration of Buddha's turban, donated by the Guild of Ivory Carvers. In the panel a turban is placed on a dais in the center with a devotee holding a parasol above it. Men wearing jewelry and decorated headwear are standing in a half circle in the back with hands folded. A few men and two women with braided hair are sitting in front of the turban. The entire gathering in the front row is carved from behind while one beautiful female is carved in side profile. In the upper left corner is a group of four females. One woman with a braid down her back is playing a drum while another is dancing. The beautiful, supple body of the dancer is wrapped below the naval with a garment. This may be the second most lovely carving of a female in Sanchi after the carving of the Yakshi languidly hanging from the mango tree. Two females wearing large earrings and beautiful hair ornaments are standing in front of the dancer. All the females in the carving have a garment draped over their lower bodies. It is said that during his Great departure to search for enlightenment, when Sidharta reached the outskirts of Kapilavastu, he sent his personal attendant back to the palace with his jewelry and all other personal belongings, removed his turban and tossed it into sky, telling himself that "if I am to become Buddha, it will remain in the air." The gods caught the turban and took it to heaven to worship. The scene possibly depicts the adoration of the relics of Buddha.

The left pillar is a replacement and has no sculpture. The original pillar, kept in the museum, is carved on one side with Muchalinda protecting Buddha from the freezing gale, Buddha turning the four bowls offered by the guardians of the cardinal points into one to receive the offering of food from two merchants, and a bullock cart traveling through a village carrying the two merchants who offered food to Buddha. The other side is carved with a bodhi tree, the jewel house built by the gods on the spot where Buddha meditated for one week after enlightenment, the grass cutter offering Buddha grass to sit on, under the bodhi tree, Sujata offering food to Buddha, and a blank strip to symbolize Buddha walking to and fro after enlightenment.

The stupa presents a sublime world full of loving and caring gods, a kind world full of grace and beauty with enchanting females and animals filling the heart with joy.

A magnificent stupa at Amaravati, the capital of Satavahana in the northwest Deccan, was built using local marblelike limestone in the second century CE (Fig. 1.123). A fragment of a polished pillar bearing Ashoka's edict, discovered at Amaravati, suggests that the foundation of the stupas were laid during the Mayura period. Shortly after the erection of the stupa a stone railing was erected but most of the elements were left plain, except a donatives inscription from the second century CE.

Fig. 1.123. Amaravati. Ruins of Stupa. Ca. 200 CE.

In the succeeding years the stupa was enlarged and decorations were added, reminiscent of the Sunga style. Buddhism ceased to be the dominant religion in Andhra after the fourth century but the stupa was kept in good repair till 1344. From the fourteenth to eighteenth century, it was totally neglected and the jungle partially reclaimed the stupa. Locally known as the Hill of Lamps, it became a quarry for limestone. In 1779, a local land owner started removing stones from the hill. The Surveyor General of India, Colonel Colin Mackenzie, visited Amaravati that same year upon learning that sculptured marble slabs were discovered in the hill. In 1818 he revisited the site with his draftsman to make drawings of the monument. By then the hill had been much excavated and the land

owner was constructing a tank on the top. Representatives from various museums started removing the sculptures.

In 1846, Sir Walter Elliot reported it as a simple round mound with a shallow depression on the top, without any indication that a magnificent stupa had once stood there. Bits and pieces of the monument are scattered in various museums. The last remaining fragments were collected and burnt to obtain lime. The stupa exists now as grass-covered flat mound surrounded with a 1m (3 ft.) high wall of recent origin. The local museum near the site has cement casts of some of the beautiful carvings that once decorated the stupa, arrayed in a sunny yard surrounded with a high wall. Photographing these casts is not permitted.

Stupa 3 was built in the second century BCE during the reign of the Sunga near the Great Stupa to transfer the relics of two of Buddha's disciples who died a few years before Buddha (Fig. 1.124). It is 8.1m (25 ft.) high with 15m (46.5 ft.) diameter with a stone block core. It is similar to but smaller than the Great Stupa. The hemispherical dome has a polished stone umbrella on the top enclosed in a stone railing designed as a bamboo fence. An ambulatory path surrounded by a stone railing is about 3m (12 ft.) above the ground. Entrance is given to the ambulatory path by stairways from opposite directions joining at the entrance to the railing. Satavahana constructed the gateway during last quarter of first century BCE. There are no supporting brackets for the arms of the architraves and no decorative statues on the top surface of any architrave. The lower architrave of the gateway, supported by pot-bellied dwarfs, is carved with the palace of Indra in paradise. In the palace, Indra is sitting with Indrani under a naga hood at the right corner, and in the left corner he is sitting with his spouse on coils of naga. Nagas, the serpents in Buddhism, were assigned the role of protectors of the teachings of Buddha. Like yaksis they are associated with fertility, wealth and abundance of nature.

Fig. 1.124. Sanchi. Stupa 3. Ca. 150-50 BCE. Sandstone.

The middle architrave is carved with an image of Ashoka's visit to the stupa with his entourage. The top architrave is carved with decorative motifs intermingled with dwarfs, demons, floral forms and a woman. Other carvings on the architraves are decorations and symbols similar to those on the Great Stupa. Cunningham in 1851 opened the stupa and found relics of two close attendant of Buddha under a large stone slab in the center of the stupa. These relics are in London now.

Stupa 2 lies on the western slope of the hill some distance away from the Great Stupa. It was constructed in the last quarter of the second century BCE during the reign of the Sunga to enshrine the remains of Buddha's priests. The top is almost flat without any crowning element. An elliptical stone railing designed as a bamboo fence encloses ambulatory passage surrounding the stupa. There are four entrances at each of the cardinal points, formed by the overlapping of the outside railing ends. There are no gateways. The posts at the entrances are elaborately carved. The railing posts are carved both inside and out in shallow relief with full medallions in the center and half medallions on top and bottom. The medallions are carved with images of men, animals, birds, plants and flowers. The human figures are depicted as awkward, with long legs, oversized feet, bulging shoulders and rough facial features. These carvings are described as the earliest examples of indigenous relief-work in stone. Captain Johnson, the British Assistant Political Agent in Bhopal mentioned earlier, almost destroyed it during his looting spree.

There are ruins of many monasteries, viharas, stupas and temples around the Great Stupa that were constructed at various time. But none are as outstanding as the Stupa. A big stone bowl is located near the ruins of one monastery. Halfway up the Sanchi hill is a small stupa with the railing dominated by carvings of a lotus medallion. By the end of the twelfth century all this construction activity ceased at Sanchi.

Fig. 1. 125. Sanchi. Temple 17. Gupta temple. 5th Century CE. Sandstone.

A few of the Buddhist temples in the complex were constructed from the Mayura era to the eleventh century. Temple 17 (referred to as the Gupta temple), near the Great Stupa, was constructed during the Gupta reign in the mid-fifth century (Fig. 1.125).

Major Cole refurbished the temple in 1850. It is considered one of the most logically designed structures, providing the basic plan for the development of future temples. This small and unimpressive temple sits on a low plinth. It consists of a front porch and square sanctum. These units are not joined properly like the sanctum in the mandapa of the early Hindu temple at Aihole. Massive stone slabs placed end to end across the sanctum and mandapa forms the flat roof, recalling a cave. The open porch is supported on four pillars placed at a uniform distance on the front of the mandapa and two pilasters in the back. The pillars are square at the bottom and octagonal above, ending in a sixteen-sided column with a bell-shaped lotus above. The abacus is mounted with a square capital crowned with addorsed lions at each corner of the abacus. Each addorsed lion has two bodies and a single head.

The entrances to the temple, unlike the front entrance of Hindu temples, go through the side of the porch. The doorjambs of the temple entrance are decorated with a band of foliate and rosette designs. The temple bears little similarity to the stupa. There is an absence of elaborate ornamentation on the temple façade, except some sculpture on the columns and doorways, no foundation, and the walls are constructed of rubble faced with stones.

In 1850 an image of Buddha seated on a lion throne was reportedly found in the sanctum. The sanctum is empty now. It is interesting to speculate what would have been the result if the front porch had been enclosed and partitioned. The builders of this temple would have created the early design of the modern temple ahead of the Chalukya, who were struggling with the open mandapa to develop the design of the Hindu temple at Aihole in southern India. Perhaps the needs and ideas of the builders of this temple were different.

Temple 18 was originally constructed of wood during the Mayura period (contemporary to the Great Stupa) (Fig. 1.126). Additions were made during the Sunga and Gupta eras. When the timber superstructure was lost in fire, a temple with Hellenistic pillars and pilaster was built on the same spot during the reign of Harsha.

The temple, built on raised platform is apsidal in shape. A flight of a few steps with a moon (semi-circular) stone in front leads to the platform. The apsidal hall had twelve imposing pillars in front; nine pillars and one pilaster are still intact. In 1912 Sir John Marshal reset the leaning 5.18m (16 ft.) tall pillars. The pillars are decorated near the top and have round edged brackets carrying architraves. A solid masonry wall surrounded the hall. The hall and the pillars were enclosed in an outer stone wall providing a circumambulatory passage around the hall. The roof may have been covered with baked tiles, as some of these were found in the rubble along with many other Buddhist relics discovered in the seventh and eighth century and in 1912. It was in use possibly till the medieval period.

Fig. 1. 126. Sanchi. Temple 18. Temple ruins. Ca. 2nd–7th Century BCE. Sandstone.

Temple 13 built in the sixth–seventh century was reconstructed in the eleventh century (Fig. 1.127). The image of Buddha in the sanctum has an elaborately carved halo. The Nagini statue standing at the right end of the platform dates from the fourth century CE. It may have been transferred here from an unknown place.

Fig. 1.127. Sanchi. Temple 13.

Ca. 6th-7th Century. Sandstone.

A little distance away from the Great Stupa amidst the ruins of the monasteries are the remains of temple 45, constructed during the seventh or eighth century (Fig. 1.128). It was furbished in the tenth century, after fire damage, incorporating some original cells. The courtyard was raised 0.76m

(2.6 ft.) above ground level and a 1m (3 ft.) high platform was added, with a molded base decorated with female figures and a few amorous couples. The temple is flanked with verandahs on three sides. The missing flat roof of the verandahs may have been supported by pillars obtained from other structures.

Fig. 128. Sanchi. Temple 45. Ca. 7th–8th Century CE. Sandstone.

At the end of the verandah on one side is an enclosed cell. A statue of Buddha seated in meditation with an oval halo behind his head is attached to the sidewall of the first cell verandah (Fig. 129). The legs and hand of the statue are partially broken.

Fig. 1.129. Sanchi. Temple 45. Statue of Buddha in Verandah. Ca. 7th- 8th Century. Sandstone.

The highly decorated door jamb of a side cell is carved with standing mithuna couples engaged in explicit sexual acts, while a third female holds the active female from behind (Fig. 130).

The main temple stands in the center of the platform (Fig. 1.131). The highly decorated façade of the antechamber has a moonstone carved with lotus, conch shells, deities, decorative designs and mythological animals carved on the base. The females in three-body-bend poses and the decorative designs carved beside the entrance are very attractive, although some of the carvings of women show a decline in the quality of sculpture.

Fig. 1.130. Sanchi. Temple 45. Carvings on door jam of a side cell. Ca. 7ᵗʰ–8ᵗʰ Century. Sandstone.

Fig. 1.131. Sanchi. Temple 45. Temple entrance.

Ca. 7ᵗʰ 8ᵗʰ Century. Sandstone.

In the square sanctum an image of a meditating Buddha is enshrined, seated on a lotus, with an oval halo behind his head (Fig. 1.132). The northern-style hollow *sikara* tower was possibly decorated with chaitya windows, *amalaka* (symbolic fruit of a tree) and *kalasa* (shaped like a water jug, it symbolized a state of plenty). The remains of a huge fragmentary amalaka and a kalasa in the shape of a stupa were found in the rubble.

Temple 40, a wooden structure with apsidal shape, was built contemporaneous with reminiscent of the shape of a water jug, symbolizing a state of plenty or bounty Great Stupa. The temple burnt down in the second century. A mandapa, or pillared outdoor hall, was constructed on the site and a small shrine was constructed in the seventh century.

Fig. 1.132. Sanchi. Temple 45. Sanctum. Buddha in meditation. Ca. 7ᵗʰ-8ᵗʰ Century CE. Sandstone.

7. Buddhist Caves at Ajanta
(200 BCE–600 CE)

Four of the Ajanta caves date back to as early as the first century BCE; there are some 29 in all. They are located 101 km (61 miles) from Aurangabad, a city which is connected to major cities of India by airways, railways and roads. It is 415 km (250 miles) from Mumbai, Central India, and has boarding and lodging, and frequent bus services to the caves.

The caves themselves are in an isolated, barren, brown, hilly region without any local facilities, except a government-run Guest House facility 5 km (3 miles) from the Ajanta caves at Faridpur, a sleepy little village. UNESCO declared the Ajanta caves Human Heritage Monuments in 1983.

The Deccan plateau is extensively covered by basaltic lava flows associated with the volcanic activity caused by continental divergence during the Mesozoic era 248 million years ago. The traps sloping from west to east have a thickness of about 2000m (6200 ft.), without inter-trap sedimentary beds; they have not undergone major deformity since the Mesozoic eon. The rock beds in the region, with its sharp vertical drop, are eminently suitable for the excavation of caves.

Buddhist caves in India were excavated for more than a millennium from the third century BCE to the eighth century. Most of the caves are located in the Sahyadri hills separating the west coast from the inland. The sub-ranges of the Sahyadri hills also run on an east–west axis. In the third century BCE, Ashoka and his grandson Dasaratha excavated the first seven caves in the Barbara and Nagarjuni hills, sub-ranges of the Sahyadri hills, near Gaya, in Bihar, to provide shelter in the rainy season for wandering non-Vedic religious sects, "as long as the sun and moon shall endure."

The first type of cave excavated by Buddhists was probably a chaitya cave. The chaitya is essentially a large hall with an apse-shape at one end, with a stupa, for the monks to mediate by. A stupa is a burial mound for the deposit of the mortal remains of Buddha or his followers. Mostly stupas represent the demise of Buddha.

In the second century BCE, the excavation activity shifted to what is now Maharashtra, in the coastal region, and caves were excavated at Bhaja. Buddhists excavated 29 caves at Ajanta from the first century BCE to the fifth century CE on a 76m (236 ft.) high hill in the western coastal hilly region of central India. The caves were excavated in the wall of a narrow horseshoe-shaped gorge hewn out of the bedrock by the Waghora River (Fig. 1.135). The river is now mostly a dry sandy bed except in the rainy season.

Buddhism underwent profound changes after the death of Buddha. Most of these changes can be seen in the Ajanta caves. Buddha ordained monks to roam in countryside, preaching; they were to use shelters for meditation in the rainy season. In addition to protecting shrines from natural destruction, caves were suitable residences for monks, who are the essential pillar of Buddhist faith — after Buddha and his teaching (The Law). Soon residential cells were dug out of the sidewalls of the cave by elimination of a stupa, and the caves started serving as a sanctuary for the monks. A small shrine on the rear wall was provided for worship. Such caves are known as *vihara* caves. These caves also had an assembly hall in the center where monks could mediate or receive instructions.

In its early stages Buddhist sculpture considered it improper to present Buddha in a human body, since he had discarded his after 550 births, described in the Jatakas (the stories of the previous lives of Buddha). He was presented as a stupa, footprint, or parasol, or other symbols.

In the second century BCE, a people of Central Asia, collectively called the Kusanas, invaded and settled in India. Their migration continued over a period of 200 years. Iranian and Western influences grew stronger. Possibly under this influence the desire to revere Buddha in human form surfaced. The first image of Buddha in India with a few characteristic features was carved during the last quarter of the first century CE. The image spread slowly all over the country.

The image of Buddha reached the Ajanta region during the first phase of excavation and was carved in chaitya caves 9 and 10, but images of the Bodhisattvas were not carved. In later developments, a sitting or standing Buddha was carved in deep relief on the stupa facing the entrance. In the vihara caves an image of Buddha was carved in the shrine for worship.

The split that occurred in Buddhism one century after his death, during the first council of the Buddhist order, resulted in Buddhism branching into two traditions which brought the most profound change in Buddhist philosophy.

The essential difference between Theravada (Hinayana) and Mahayana Buddhist tradition is in the doctrine of Bodhisattva. In Theravada tradition, the emphasis is on attainment of nirvana and escape from the cycle of births and deaths. In Mahayana, the aim is to attain Buddha-hood but to take birth again, forgoing nirvana to help others to achieve salvation. A new group of divine beings called Bodhisattva, the Buddhas-to-be, appeared. Bodhisattvas first appeared as attendants of Buddha. The most popular Bodhisattva is Avalokiteshvara, protector of travelers from the eight great perils of mankind: lions, elephants, snakes, fire, thieves, water, shipwreck and demons. Another Bodhisattva, Vijarapani, associated with the thunderbolt, gained importance. He carries a totem in his hand which is considered by some to be a phallus.

There may be no limit to Bodhisattvas. They can appear any time and their functions may vary. Buddha did not ordain women in the Buddhist religious order but female Bodhisattvas slowly appeared as spouses of male Bodhisattvas, and later attained independent status equal to that of their male counterparts. Some attained the status of goddess, like Mahamayuri, the goddess of learning, and Tara, the spouse of Avalokiteshvara.

The next to-be-born Buddha, Maitreya, and Manusi Buddhas who attained nirvana before Sakyamuni Buddha appeared, were carved in both the chaitya and vihara caves at Ajanta.

Caves were excavated here in two phases. The early phase of cave excavation occurred from first century BCE to first century CE when the Satavahana ruled the region. They had invaded central India for a short period from the south and replaced the Sunga. During this early phase two chaitya caves, 9 and 10, and two vihara caves, 12 and 13, were excavated near the center of the existing row of caves.

Buddhist imagery had reached central India by this time and his picture was carved in these chaityas. But there are no carvings of any Bodhisattvas, possibly because Bodhisattvas were not very popular yet or their presentation was still resisted by Theravada traditions. Building activity ended abruptly after excavation of these four caves and silence fell over Ajanta.

The second phase of excavation started with a burst of activity in the fifth century during the reign of the Vakataka dynasty. The Vakataka were feudatories of the Gupta dynasty that ruled northern India and were also related to the Gupta by marriage. After the fragmentation of the Gupta empire, they emerged as the rulers of central India. Harishena ascended to the Vakataka throne in 460 CE, inheriting a huge empire in central India with a stable economy. The second phase, which lasted for short period, started with the regime of Harishena, during which almost all the remaining caves were constructed in a span of about fifteen to twenty years from 460 CE to 475 or 480 CE. Some minor work continued for one more century.

Out of a total of 25 caves excavated during the second phase, only two caves, 19 and 26, are chaitya; the remaining caves are viharas. Nine of the caves were partially excavated. The spurt of activity during the second phase was due to the patronage of ministers, princes, and high officials of the court of the Vakataka kings, particularly Harishena. The emperor himself was the sponsor of vihara Cave 1. The prime minister of Harishena sponsored the excavation of vihara Cave 16. The King of Rishika, a feudatory of Harishena who was actually governing the Ajanta region at the time, sponsored chaitya Cave 19. An official of the court of Asmaka, another feudatory of Harishena, sponsored chaitya Cave 26. The caves began to be painted in 462 CE and by around 500 CE the painting of all the caves was completed.

Soon after the death of Harishena, in 480 CE, his son was killed in internal strife. His grandson fled to an adjacent regime and the Vakataka era ended. After 483 CE, not a single image was carved at Ajanta. The Vakataka sculpture and paintings in these caves show the influence of the Satavahana tradition.

Fig. 1.135. Ajanta. Caves. Ca. 100 BCE-500 CE. Basalt.

The general layout of the vihara was standardized in the second phase under the Mahayana influence. All the vihara caves excavated during the second phase have a similar basic plan providing a small verandah, single or multiple entrances and an assembly hall with pillars arranged in square. The shrine on the rear wall featured a pillared portico, vestibule and sanctum with a statue of a sitting or standing Buddha flanked by Bodhisattvas. Residential cells for monks were cut into the sidewalls with a raised rock bed and head rest. A niche was provided in the cell wall for an oil lamp. Most vihara caves accommodated six to twelve monks. Cells cut on the rear or side walls were converted into additional shrines as the complexity of the religion increased.

Chaitya caves were excavated with a window above the entrance facade imitating the wooden windows of the time. The windows were covered with wooden screens to filter sunlight into the caves. Some caves were excavated with a verandah in front. Allowing additional exterior space for carving.

The craftsmen employed in the second phase were inexperienced; large-scale cave excavation was not undertaken in the region from the second to the fifth century CE. A few simple Hindu one-chambered caves were excavated a few

hundred miles away at Udayagiri some fifty years before the excavations were started at Ajanta. The caves excavated at the initiation of the second phase are ambitious but do not stand out. The emphasis was on decoration rather than grand execution, at least in the early caves. For the decoration of the caves, painting was preferred rather than sculpture by inexperienced craftsmen.

The plans of many caves were altered after start of excavation. The work may have abruptly stopped in all the caves for some time with the end of Harishena lineage. A fragmentary record on cave 26, left by the Rashtrakuta dynasty ruling from Ellora, indicates some activity at Ajanta in the eighth and ninth century. When the works stopped after the death of Harishena, the craftsmen and their descendants moved to Elephanta Island in the sea of Oman near Mumbai, where they excavated Siva Cave. After Siva Cave they went to Ellora, where they excavated and painted the Ellora caves. Finally, the craftsmen may have moved to northern Karnataka to construct structural temples. By this time the creative impulse of the sculptor had died.

A few centuries after the work stopped at Ajanta, the caves were forgotten and neglected except by a few monks; they were soon engulfed by the forest. Fortunately the damage done by the overgrown forest was not as severe as that wrought by the huge roots embracing the freestanding monuments at Angkor, Cambodia. In 1817 a group of soldiers on a tiger hunt rediscovered the caves at Ajanta, and the caves were given identity numbers before the date of excavation of each cave was determined.

The Satavahana and Vakataka kings were Hindus but they provided grants of lands and endowments for the maintenance of monasteries out of political expediency and religious tolerance. Harishena and his Hindu feudatories sponsored a few caves, but the excavation and painting of most caves was made possible by donations from lay worshippers and Buddhist merchants.

These caves are the product of sculpture on a grand scale, but are not rock-cut architecture. Few or no architectural principles were involved in cave excavation. The technique for hewing caves in basaltic lava, sandstones and granite is described in the chapter on Religious Monuments. The absence of faults and deposits of sedimentary rocks in basalt lava was a divine bonus. These caves are carved in imitation of thatched roofed huts of central India with non-functional accessories.

Ajanta is renowned for wall paintings. Ample talent for painting was available in the persons of those local craftsmen who were decorating local monuments constructed of more perishable materials like wood and bricks. The walls and ceilings of 25 caves at Ajanta were covered with lavish paintings narrating the jatakas, the legends from previous lives of Buddha.

The earliest paintings created in the first century BCE during the time of Satavahana rule, in cave 10 exist in patches. Unfortunately the paintings created the during second phase have survived only in caves 1, 2, 16 and 17. All the remaining paintings have faded to a large degree and most have chipped and peeled. One can imagine what a paradise Ajanta was when all the paintings were visible. In 1984 the caves were not fully electrified and the guides use to show the paintings by kerosene light. In a cave they use to turn off the light and the pearls necklaces worn by females would come to life possibly due to a radioactive element in the pigment. These paintings are full of life and rich in composition.

The late fifth century paintings in caves 1, 2, 16 and 17 are the glory of Gupta era. The artists have used females as their best decorative asset, like the sculptors of later Hindu temples. It is said that modern art has not succeeded in paying tribute to women as successfully as it is paid at Ajanta. Paintings in cave 1 and 2 are sensual and restless. The paintings on the ceilings are generally flat, like designs on textiles.

The surface to be painted was prepared by applying two layers of mud plaster mixed with sand, paddy husk, grass and rock-powder over unpolished stonewalls to smooth the surface and this was overlaid with lime wash. After the wash dried, the outlines to be painted were sketched using red paint. Pigments were applied in a binding medium of glue or gum. Color was applied using brushes made of animal hair.

Except for lapis lazuli imported from Afghanistan for the color blue, local minerals were used. White was used to reflect light. Blue was sparingly used. Light pigments were used to give body to the figures. In cave 1 and 2, white pigment was used to highlight and to pick out the subject. The paintings are dominated by scenes from the jatakas.

Cave 1, excavated under the patronage of Vakataka King Harishena (460-478 CE), has a pillared verandah. The top of the columns and cornice of the cave roof are decorated with sculpture (Fig. 1.137). The entrance door jambs are carved with females standing with body bends, loving couples, and decorative sculpture. The interior of the cave is rectangular. The large hall excavated in 468 CE has twenty decorated pillars arranged in a square. There are twelve residential cells on the sidewalls and five cells on the rear wall. The central cell on the rear wall is the shrine, with an antechamber. The paintings were completed in 477-478 CE.

Fig. 1.137. Ajanta. Cave 1. Facade. 460-478 CE. Basalt.

The sixteen-century-old paintings in the cave have mostly faded. The dim light of the cave and a ban on flash photography makes it difficult to capture the remaining splendor. The most attractive painting on the walls depicts Bodhisattva Padmapani standing in three-bend body poses. He has a well-proportioned torso, broad chest, thick arms and beautifully arched eyebrows, and wears rich pieces of jewelry; he holds a blue lotus (Fig. 1.138).

His expression is one of remoteness and calm in the midst of a crowd. On the right of Padmapani a curvaceous, sensual, naked black female with a flowing plastic body and bulging breasts is drawn sitting leaning on a man (Fig. 1.139).

Fig. 1.138. Ajanta. Cave 1. Bodhisattva Padmapani. 460-478 CE.

On left wall is the Nanda jataka. Prince Nanda is surrounded by a queen and the beautiful ladies of the palace (Fig. 1.143).

Fig. 140. Ajanta. Cave 1. Bodhisattva Vijarapani. 460-478 CE

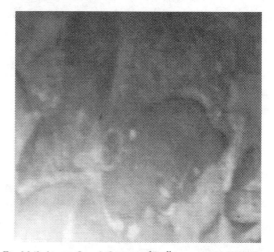

Fig. 1.141. Ajanta. Cave 1. Consort of Bodhisattva. 460-478 CE

Fig. 1.139. Ajanta. Cave 1. Lovers. 460-478 CE

At the right of the antechamber entrance an elegant Bodhisattva Vijarapani with a narrow waist, strings of pearls looped around the chest, a beautiful decorated crown, sleepy eyes, bow-like eyebrows and lotus-petal lips is created by modulation of colors rather than use of lines (Fig. 1.140).

The beautiful consort of Bodhisattva is drawn with large half-closed eyes, a narrow, pointed nose and lotus-petal lips (Fig. 1.141). The jatakas painted in the cave depict the splendors of royal courts, pious rulers and naga kings. In the painting of the Mahajanaka Jataka, a shipwrecked prince is sitting with a beautiful queen on a throne on the star studded floor of a palace with female attendants staring at the couple. The queen is trying to seduce the prince, but he is unmoved (Fig. 1.142).

Fig. 1.142. Ajanta. Cave 1. Mahajanaka Jataka. 460-478 CE

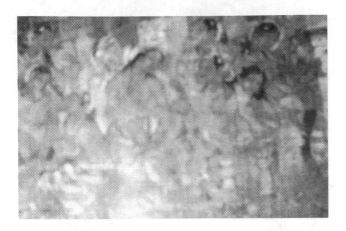

Fig. 1.143. Ajanta. Cave 1. Conversion of Nanda. 470-478 CE.

Fig. 1.144. Ajanta. Cave 1. Palace scene. 460-478 CE.

Fig. 1.145. Ajanta. Cave 1. Palace scene. 460-478 CE.

The handsome prince wearing a crown and a band of pearls on his arms is drawn with large half-closed eyes sitting beside his beautiful wife Sundari. The prince has decided to leave the luxuries of the princely life, palace and beautiful wife behind, to join the monastic order of Buddha. He is disclosing his intention to his wife, who sits beside him, her right hand raised as though to caress him. Her lovely almond-shaped eyes under arched eyebrows gaze at the prince, full of love, sympathy and sadness. She is wearing a beautiful crown and pearl jewelry on her arms. Her flowing, supple body, narrow waist, delicate hands, full hips and thighs are bursting with radiant beauty. Her bosom is accentuated by the strands of jewelry that have disappeared between the breasts and reappeared below. Expressions of shock can be seen in the eyes of other queens standing behind them. The surrounding court ladies, with sorrow in their eyes, drawn according to the Indian ideals of feminine beauty, show the mastery of the Ajanta artists.

Many other scenes depict the luxuries of court life, fully exploiting the beauty of the female form. A dancing scene depicts an exquisitely charming dancer with a long, slender neck and attractive headdress wearing jewelry on her delicate body and dancing amidst the musicians playing drums and flutes. She is wearing an apron-like robe cut to expose the sides of her narrow waist. The long sleeves made of a textile printed with flowers add drama to her form. Another scene depicts the interior of a palace filled with beautiful women in different costumes, hairstyles and poses.

In another painting a beautifully decorated princess is sitting cross-legged in the company of other attractive women. A sensual black female standing beside is holding Chamara (Fig. 1.144). A tall, finely built female is standing with a prince under a royal umbrella amidst royal ladies (Fig. 1.145).

A sensual black female standing beside them is holding a chamara. Above, in the balconies, women are standing watching the royal pair (Fig. 1.146). Among them a beautiful black female with full hips, narrow waist and a striped cloth hanging from her hips to her knees stands, leaning on a wooden pillar (Fig. 1.146). She is wearing pearl jewelry on her hips, thighs and neck. The woman mixing a sandalwood paste for the princely bath is remarkable for the rhythmic bend of her seductive body.

Fig. 146. Ajanta. Cave 1. Palace scene. 460-478 CE.

On the left of the main entrance the Sivi jataka is depicted. In a previous life Buddha was born as a prince in the neighboring kingdom of Sivi; he offers his own flesh in weight to save a pigeon from hawk. On the right the pigeon is shown nestling in the lap of the prince. Beyond a pavilion, the prince is shown standing beside a pair of scales. Three jatakas, the Sankhapala, Champaka and one with unknown name, depict stories of the naga kings. Harishena traced his genealogy to the Naga kings. In the Champaka jataka a Naga king caught by a snake charmer is released on the intervention of the Benares king. The king is shown seated in the palace, watching a dance, then talking to the cobra king who has assumed human shape, and finally with the gifts given to him by his new friend. The center of the ceiling is painted in a grid-like pattern with seated males and females, abstract motifs, playful elephants in a lotus pond, birds touching beaks and lotus flowers (Fig. 1.147). White is abundantly used on the ceiling, possibly to reflect light, in contrast to the earth tones of wall paintings.

Fig. 1.147. Ajanta. Cave 1. Painting on ceiling. 460-478 CE.

Cave 2, a vihara excavated in the second half of the fifth century, is smaller than Cave 1; it has a pillared verandah. The verandah, interior walls and hall ceiling were painted. The cave entrance door is carved with females in three body bends and loving couples (Fig. 1.148).

Fig, 1.148. Ajanta. Cave 2. Entrance. Ca. 5th Century CE.

In the verandah only fragments of the painting on the ceiling have remained. The hall has twelve lavishly carved pillars arranged in a square. There are ten cells in the sidewalls and three cells on the rear wall. The central cell in the rear wall is the main shrine with a seated Buddha with hands in preaching gesture (Fig. 1.149).

Fig. 1.149. Ajanta. Cave 2. Buddha in main shrine. 5th Century CE. Basalt.

Profusely ornamented Bodhisattva flanks him and two flying apsaras are hovering above, carrying garlands in their hands. The pedestal is carved with the wheel of law in profile, flanked by two deer and some early disciples of Buddha. The two cells to the sides are additional shrines. The right cell has large seated sculptured images of Pancika and Hariti, flanked by a chamara-bearer and a female caressing a bird on her hand. They are heavy but are remarkably beautiful. A child is sitting on Hariti's thigh. Hariti, the patron of children, was an ogress who devoured the children of Rajagraha until Buddha concealed one of her favorite children to make her feel the pain of such a loss. While attacking Buddha to find the lost child, she repented. Buddha assured her food in every monastery. To honor the promise, an image of Hariti is installed in the dining room of monasteries. The cell on left has two large yaksa images.

The painting on the left wall of the antechamber depicts the attempt of the beautiful daughters of Mara to distract Buddha from his meditation. On the right wall multiple images of Buddha with various hand gestures refer to the miracle when Buddha multiplied into countless Buddhas. The ceiling of the antechamber has been painted in bright colors in a grid-like pattern containing floral and abstract motifs. White is abundantly used. On the left wall of the hall Maya, mother of Buddha, is shown standing in a palace garden in Lumbini where Buddha was born. On the extreme left of this wall is the Hamsa jataka. A golden swan king is captured and released by the King of Varanasi and Queen Khema after hearing the discourse on law by the swan king. In the painting a bird catcher and a companion are shown approaching a lotus lake filled with geese and further along he is shown leaving the pond, holding the swan in hand. The next scene shows a sage preaching in the king's court, then a lake full of lotus flowers, lilies and geese. Individual artists have painted the ceiling of the cave in a variety of styles.

The Jatakas painted in the hall includes the Vidhurapandita jataka. It depicts the Naga princess Irandati with full firm breast; narrow waist and large hips swinging while two attendants are watching her (Fig. 1.150).

Fig. 1.150. Ajanta. Cave 2. Vidhurapandita Jataka. 5ᵗʰ Century CE.

Perhaps the most attractive female body drawn at Ajanta is the one kneeling before the feet of Buddha on the ceiling (Fig. 1.151). Her body is as supple as a new shoot emerging from a seed.

One scene depicts a loving couple standing together (Fig. 1.152). Loving couples sitting in balconies, with erotic overtones still glow with tints of blue pigment.

Fig. 1.151. Ajanta. Cave 2. Devotee kneeling before Buddha. Ca. 5ᵗʰ century CE.

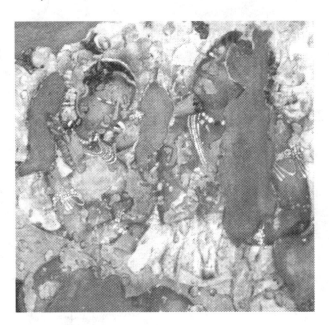

Fig. 1.152. Ajanta. Cave 2. Lovers. 5ᵗʰ Century CE.

Cave 3, excavated during the fifth century, is a small, incomplete vihara. On the façade of the cave is one of the most beautiful pieces of sculpture carved at Ajanta. A delicately built damsel with all the attributes of feminine beauty is standing under a tree (Fig. 1.153). As she leans her bent elbow on a tree branch and rests her weight on one leg, her hips are thrust to one side, creating a sensual and sophisticated pose. There are no paintings remaining in the cave, but this one sculpture makes up for their loss.

Cave 4 is a large vihara with large square hall in the center and a few residential cells on the sidewalls. Cave 5 is a small vihara squeezed between Cave 4 and Cave 6, which is a vihara with two stories. The first floor has a square hall with sixteen pillars arranged in four squares. There are a few residential cells in the sidewalls. The second story is similar to the design of Cave 2 except that the cell at the right end of the rear wall has an additional shrine with antechamber. The main shrine in the center of the rear wall is carved with a seated Buddha with hands in a teaching gesture and flanked by two decorated Bodhisattva and various deities. Three Manusi Buddhas are carved on each sidewall of the sanctum. The cells on the right and left of the verandah are converted into additional shrines. Cave 7 has two adjoining square halls with four pillars. Each hall has a shrine at the end of the sidewall. The main shrine is located in the center of the rear wall.

Fig. 1.153. Ajanta. Cave 3. Apsara on Façade. 5ʰ Century CE. Basalt.

On the sidewall a sculptured frieze depicts the miracle when Buddha multiplied himself a thousand times. A heretic sect in Rajagraha, the capital of Magadha, ruled by Bimbisara, refused to acknowledge the superiority of Buddha. They resolved to make a great display of their supernatural powers to convince the multitude of their mastership and superiority. As Bimbisara was a staunch supporter of Buddha, they decided to challenge Buddha in Sravasti, in the neighboring kingdom of Kosala. On the day fixed for the showdown, a large crowd gathered. The king of Kosala, Prasenjit, came to the gathering with great pomp and took his royal seat. On the invitation of the king, Buddha, in preliminary miracles, rose into the air and caused flames of fire and streams of water to gush forth alternately from his upper and lower body. Then with the assistance of Brahma and Sakra (Indra), he multiplied a thousand times, seated in a meditation posture

on a cartwheel-sized corolla of a golden lotus flower of a thousand petals, created by two serpent kings, Nanda and Upananda. Above this lotus he caused another lotus to appear which likewise showed Buddha seated in meditation. Thus he filled the sky with a multitude of Buddha figures. He seemed to walk, to stand, to sit or lie down. The Buddhas issued forth flames, flashes of lighting and streams of water. Some of them asked questions and others answered them. The heretical teachers were so confounded that they remained silent when the king invited to display their magical powers.

Cave 8 appears to be an incomplete vihara. Caves 9 and 10, excavated in the first century BCE to the first century CE, are chaitya caves with a row of pillars following the apsidal shape of the caves and a stupa at the rear, with a circumambulatory passage. By the time these caves were excavated, the idea of portraying the image of Buddha had reached Ajanta. The façade of Cave 9 is dominated by a window carved with an imitation of wooden rafters and a standing Buddha on the sides. It is believed to be one of the oldest chaitya.

Cave 10 is the largest chaitya at Ajanta. There are patches of the oldest known wall paintings in India, from the first century BCE, painted during the Satavahana reign in the cave. Fragments of one painting show a king with his retinue (including musicians and group of lovely ladies with expressive eyes) visiting a tree. On the right wall, the Sama and Chadanta jataka can be recognized.

In the painting of Sama jataka the king is shown aiming arrow at Sama holding a pitcher on his shoulder. The next scene depicts repenting king and the devastated parents beside the body of Sama. The painting ends with Sama sitting under a tree with a pair of deer grazing and the king near a hut. The painting of Chadanta jataka is much damaged but in broken patches depicts the favorite resort of the elephant, a lotus pond under pipal tree, and his presenting of lotus to other wife that enraged the jealous wife, hunter spying elephant from behind the rocks and sawing of the tusks. The chaitya pillars are painted with standing Buddha (Fig. 1.154).

The stupa is dome shaped with barrel shaped base and a square pedestal supported on a long square neck (Fig. 155).

Cave 11 excavated during the first phase inserted between cave 10 and 12 is uncomfortably close to cave 12. It has a small rectangular hall in the center with four pillars. The main shrine is on the rear wall. The cell to the right of shrine is converted into additional shrine with antechamber.

Caves 12 and 13 excavated during the first phase are closely packed viharas without pillars in the central hall.

Residential cells are cut on sidewalls. Excavation of cave 14 was attempted but was left incomplete. Cave 15 a vihara has square interior without pillars, shrine on the rear wall and few residential cells on the sidewalls.

Fig. 1.154. Ajanta. Cave 10. Paintings on pillars.

Ca. 1ˢᵗ Century CE. Basalt.

Fig. 1.155. Ajanta. Cave 10. Stupa. Ca. 1ˢᵗ Century CE. Basalt.

Varaha Deva, the prime minister of Harishena financed the excavation of vihara Cave 16 in later half of fifth century. It has a large reservoir of water which is still in use. The interior of the cave has a large hall with pillars arranged in square, a large shrine on the rear wall and residential cells on the sidewalls. The interior of the cave is decorated with sculptures and paintings. The statue of seated Buddha with apsaras hovering above is detached from the rear wall in the shrine. Varaha Deva compares the cave to the palace of Indra.

A flying couple carved on the bracket of a pillar is remarkable for the impression of weightlessness. The female leaning on the man with bent legs and flowing hairs suggests flying motion but does not appear to exert any weight on man. The walls are painted with Nanda, Mahaummagga, and few other Jatakas. An enchanting figure of black princess on the wall is memorable for her elongated beautiful thin face, half closed almond eyes, lotus petal like lips, long neck, beautiful jewelry and headdress (Fig. 1.156).

Fig. 1.156. Ajanta. Cave 16. Black Princess. 5ᵗʰ Century CE.

Beside cave 16 is carving of Naga king in a niche. The queen seated beside has broken off.

Upendragupta a feudatory ruling adjacent Rishika kingdom was the patron of cave 17. It is considered a standard Mahayana vihara. The pillared verandah is accessed by flight of steps. The entrance to the cave is carved similar to Cave 1, but above the door lintel loving couples sitting with erotic overtones wearing different costumes and jewelry are painted in separate panels (Fig. 1.157). Above the lovers a row of vines bearing white flowers separates a row of Buddha painted in panels. Buddha is seated in meditation with halo behind head indicating attainment of nirvana and with hands in gesture of reassurance and protection. The ceiling of the verandah is painted with attractive floral designs with a circle in the center drawn with busts of beautiful apsaras with their heads pointing towards the periphery.

On the sidewall is a much damaged painting of Vessantara jataka. A fragment of painting depicts Vessantara sitting with his consort on throne (Fig. 1.158).

Fig. 1.157. Ajanta. Cave 17. Entrance door lintel. Ca. 5th Century CE.

Fig. 1.158. Ajanta. Cave 17. Painting on veranda sidewall. Ca. 5th Century CE.

The black prince with queen in his lap informs her that he is banished from his father's kingdom. She sags in the prince's lap, throwing her head to the side with almost expressionless eyes. Her fingers are shown nervously manipulating the chain of the dangling pendent around her neck, while anxious attendants are hovering around with carafes in hand on the star studded floor of the palace. Another patch of painting depicts a tall, delicately built, beautiful queen with happy face standing with a cup in her raised hand on the star studded floor (Fig. 1.159).

An elegantly dressed female standing beside the queen appears to be obstructing an approaching Brahmin carrying a basket in his hand. A man seated beside an attendant on

the other side of the queen, holding a parasol, appears to be oblivious to the surroundings. Behind the queen two ladies are peeking through a palace window.

Fig. 1.159. Ajanta. Cave 17. Painting on Veranda Sidewall. Ca. 5th Century CE.

Vessantara is again shown standing in somber mood beneath a palm tree under a beautiful parasol held by an equally beautiful attendant in a palace garden. There is a pavilion at the far end of the painting. The large hall inside the cave has pillars similar to the hall of Cave 16. The rear wall has five cells. The shrine in the center of the rear wall has a statue of Buddha, with his hands in a teaching gesture, detached from the back wall. Ornamented Bodhisattvas with chamara and flying figures on the upper corners flank Buddha. The pedestal of the statue is carved with the wheel of law in profile, in the center flanked by foreign devotees and deer. Residential cells are on the sidewalls.

The cave contains the highest number of murals, most considered masterpieces. The Simha Avadana jataka covers a complete wall. Simha was a virtuous merchant. On one of his voyages he was shipwrecked, but with his companions reached an island inhabited by witches. The witches disguised as beautiful damsels entertained the visitors during the day, then, reverting to ogresses, devoured them during night. In a scene with erotic overtones, shipwrecked Simha is sitting in the tent with a beautiful damsel (Fig. 1.160). Simha, apprehending danger, accepts the offer of a flying horse; and escapes with a few companions from the island and reaches his native land. The witches follow Simha, disguised as beautiful women, and the witch who entertained Simha claims him as her husband. When refuted in court, she approaches the king who, enchanted by her beauty, takes her as his wife — and is devoured. Other ogresses devour the inmates of the palace. Simha notice vultures hovering over the palace, with its closed doors. He climbs over the walls and chases out the ogresses. Later, with the army of the king, he invades the witch island to punish them and ultimately is crowned king of the island. The main incidents of the story have to be searched out in the painting.

Fig. 1.160. Ajanta. Cave 17. Simhala entertained by a witch. Ca. 5th Century CE.

Near the Simha jataka is the renowned dressing room scene (Fig. 1.161).

Fig. 1.161. Ajanta. Cave 17. Toilet scene. Ca. 5th Century CE.

The painting depicts a tall, sensual, seductive black damsel with arched eyebrows, half-closed eyes, pointed nose and flared lips standing with three-body bends accentuating the full, firm hips and thighs by crossing her legs. Holding a

mirror in one hand she is giving the final touches to her make-up after a shower. Most of her body, including the thighs, is decorated. By a touch of white paint, various parts of her body including her thighs, legs, nose, breasts and nipples are highlighted. Her buxom body appears to be radiating the warmth of flesh. In a nearby painting the beautiful damsels listening to Buddha's teaching are equally radiant. A painting in the antechamber shows Maitreya Buddha. Maitreya, the future Buddha, in the top register, is residing in Tusita, the heavenly paradise, awaiting his next birth. In the center register he is shown after descending from Tusita to preside over the earthly paradise of great tranquility, Ketumati, to the welcome of his devotees. The bottom register shows him preaching.

Another scene depicts a seated king giving alms. Men and women in varied costumes, some in rags, holding bowls in extended hands, are standing in front and beside the king. Another man standing in the street, holding a tray in his hand, is also distributing alms. A woman in the gathering wearing a tight-fitting garment to cover her upper body and holding a child on her hips, is remarkably beautiful. Besides her is another woman in a long striped robe.

The Vessantara jataka has been repeated on the left wall of the hall. The main incidents drawn in the paintings are the farewell to Vessantara by his parents, followed by Vessantara driven in a chariot drawn by four horses through the town streets. The next scene shows them living in a hut, followed by the gift of the children to a Brahmin in the absence of the mother. The redeeming of the children by the grandfather is followed by the return of prince and the queen to the palace.

Below the Vessantara jataka is another version of the Mahakapi jataka. Buddha, born as the monkey king, is shown leading a man away from a deep abyss where he had fallen from a tree, while looking for a stray cow. The ungrateful man tries to kill the seated monkey king by dropping a stone on him from behind. The king escapes by jumping aside. When approached, the king forgives the man.

In the Machchha jataka, Buddha born as fish induces the god Indra by his good deeds to send rain to save his kindred fishes who were being devoured by birds as the pond bed dried up. Most of the painting is damaged. Only one large fish is seen, surrounded by small fishes and other aquatic animals in the pond.

Another Mahakapi jataka is depicted on the front wall. The depiction of nature is realistic, compared to the carving of the jataka on the Great Stupa at Sanchi. The river is full of fishes and other aquatic animals and some people bathing in the river. A panel below presents the Hasti jataka. Travelers are shown feasting on the carcass of an elephant. Buddha, born as an elephant, throws himself from the top of a precipice to die and serve as food to the hungry travelers.

In the Nigrodhamiga jataka, Buddha born as deer is trapped and kept with other deer in the Royal Park to be killed for meat when required by the king. The deer decide between themselves to select a member for slaughter by casting lots when the king requires meat. One day the lot falls to a pregnant doe. Buddha offers himself as a substitute for the doe. The astonished cook reports the incident to the king who, moved by Buddha's sense of compassion, lets all the deer go free. The painting depicts the deer in Royal Park, a deer in the kitchen for slaughter, and the astonished cook reporting to the king. The king is shown speaking to the deer near the kitchen hut. The next scene depicts the deer delivering a sermon. In the last scene a stupa with a congregation of birds and animals is shown expressing gratitude to Buddha.

Cave 18 is the smallest vihara. Cave 19 a splendid chaitya excavated in the second half of the fifth century by Upendragupta, a regional feudatory king of Asmaka. It is considered the perfect specimen of Buddhist rock cut temples. It has an elaborate façade with projecting pillared portico (Fig. 1.162).

Fig. 1.162. Ajanta. Cave 19. Façade. 5ᵗʰ.Century CE. Basalt.

Flanking the entrance to the portico are number of carvings of standing and seated Buddha; none of the carvings are alike. The panel to the right of entrance is carved with a standing Buddha offering his hand to his son Rahul. The next panel depicts Buddha standing under a stupa. A large number of panels on side walls of the cave, separated by pilasters, depict seated or standing Buddhas wearing diaphanous garments, holding hands in various gestures. A large circular window

with stone beams carved in imitation of wooden windows of the time is located on the portico. Bulky attendants with dressed hair and attractive poses flank the window. The images of Buddha are somewhat heavy and some are lifeless, although some are awe-inspiring. The interior of the chaitya hall has closely-set thick pillars crowding the space. Panels on the rim above the pillars are carved with Buddha images flanked with foliate and architectural motifs (Fig. 1.163).

Fig. 1.163. Ajanta. Cave 19. Buddhas carved above pillars. 5ᵗʰ Century CE. Basalt.

A few of these Buddha are supposedly from other worlds (Budhalokas) presumed to exist by Mahayanists. The ceiling is carved with an imitation of rafters. The stupa at the far end is almost a vertical structure. Above the dome of the stupa three discs like umbrellas are carved one above other. Under each disc a miniature stupa is carved (Fig. 1.164). The front of the stupa is carved with figure of standing Buddha under a pilaster arch.

Fig. 1.164. Ajanta. Cave 19. Stupa. 5ᵗʰ Century CE. Basalt.

Fig. 1.164. Ajanta. Cave 19. Naga King & Queen. *5th Century CE. Basalt.*

In addition to the lavish sculpture on the façade of the cave, a magnificently conceived sculpture of a royal couple in regal pose with a female chamara-bearer standing beside them is carved outside the cave on the left of the entrance (Fig. 1.165).

The couple are the king and queen of the serpents. Both are seated on a raised platform with one leg pulled close to the body and other leg resting on the floor in "royal ease." The full-breasted nagini wearing jewelry and her hair tightly bound in braids is sitting slightly behind the king, holding a flower in her hand. The king's head is under the multi-headed cobra hood.

Cave 20 and 22 are small viharas with shrines on the rear wall. Cave 21, 23 and 24 have large pillared halls. Cave 21 and 23 have three shrines on the rear wall with varying numbers of residential cells on the side walls, some servings as shrines. Cave 24 has no shrine on the rear wall. Caves 25 and 27 are excavated above Cave 26, as the right and left wings. Cave 25 was roughed out and not completed.

Buddhabhadra, a Buddhist monk, excavated chaitya Cave 26 with right and left wings. He obtained funds for construction of the chaitya from the court of the King of Asmaka, a regional feudatory. The verandah providing passage to the cave from courtyard has partially collapsed, disfiguring the façade (Fig. 1.165).

Fig. 1.165. Ajanta. Cave 26. Façade. *5th Century CE. Basalt.*

The façade of the cave is dominated by a ribbed chaitya window flanked by guardians and a multitude of sitting and standing Buddhas. In addition a seated Buddha is carved in small panels above the window. The cave is similar but wider and more elaborate than chaitya Cave 19. The hall is 25m (75 ft.) deep and 13m (40 ft.) wide with twenty-six pillars. The interior is elaborately decorated with sculpture. The stupa is carved with the image of Buddha seated on an elevated platform with legs resting on a pedestal, possibly depicting Maitreya Buddha, the future Buddha (Fig. 1.166).

Fig. 1.166. Ajanta. Cave 26. Buddhas on façade of stupa. *5th Century CE. Basalt.*

Maitreya Buddha was in existence when Buddha gave his first sermon. Five thousand years after the death of Buddha and more than five hundred rebirths, he will be born as

Buddha. The wall of the ambulatory passage along the perimeter on the left is carved with 7m (22 ft.) long statue of Parinirvana Buddha, representing the demise of Buddha, after which he has no more births (Fig. 1.167). The wailing of the mourners carved below on a plinth enhances the calm and detached expression on Buddha's face — similar to the sleeping Buddha in Bangkok. The cave is unique in depicting the demise of Buddha as well the to-be-Buddha.

Fig. 1.167. Ajanta. Cave 26. Parinirvana Buddha. 5th Century CE. Basalt.

Another beautiful sculpture depicting the victory of Buddha over Mara is carved in the passage (Fig. 168).

Fig. 1.170. Ajanta. Cave 26. Temptation of Buddha. 5th Century CE. Basalt.

Buddha is carved seated under a Bodhi tree surround by the threatening army of Mara. Mara is seated on an elephant on the right. His voluptuous daughter, carved in front profile, is dancing, accompanied by a musician, to distract Buddha. Buddha, unmoved, has his hand in the gesture of calling the earth to witness.

All of the remaining caves are incomplete viharas. Cave 27, without pillars in the hall, has three shrines on the rear wall and three residential cells on one side and one cell on other. The middle parts of the verandah pillars are broken. The top of the pillar is hanging, attached to the roof, and the bottom stub is sitting on the verandah edge.

8. THE SIVA CAVE AT ELEPHANTA
(540–555)

An outstanding early Hindu cave temple, displaying the best of Hindu temple sculpture created in the sixth century, is located on the island of Elephanta in the Sea of Oman, at a distance of 10 km from the Gateway of Mumbai. It can be reached by public motorboat in one hour. The Portuguese changed the name of this commercial, military and religious center in the sixteenth century from Gharapuri to Elephanta, after a large stone elephant statue that was on the shores of the island. The statue is now in a British museum. During the temporary occupation by the Portuguese, zealots of another religious persuasion used the interior of this most impressive cave for gunnery practice. UNESCO declared the Siva cave at Elephanta a World Heritage Monument in 1987.

After the demise of the Vakataka dynasty in the sixth century, one of their feudatories, now called the Early Kalacuri, rose to power in the Maharashtra region. They remained in power till the end of the sixth century when the western Chalukya of Karnataka eclipsed them.

It is possible that the craftsmen who excavated the caves at Ajanta and Aurangabad also excavated the Siva cave, under the patronage of the Kalacuri, and then returned to Ellora to excavate the caves there.

King Krishnaraja (550-575) of the Kalacuri dynasty, an ardent Pasupata Saivite, commissioned the construction of this rectangular mandapa temple to celebrate his conquest of the region. The history of the cave temple is not well known. A stone that some believe may have been inscribed with that history was found — and lost — by the Portuguese. The artistic style of the sculpture in the cave is said to suggest the period of excavation in 540-555. It was earlier believed that the Chalukya of Badami excavated the monument between 600 and 645.

The Siva cave at Elephanta appears so open, light and airy that one rarely gets the feeling of confinement in a cave. Providing residence to the monks was not an important function of Hindu caves. The development of freestanding stone structural temples was in progress in South India at Aihole. The desire to break the temple out of the confinement of the dark cave and restricted hilly regions appeared first at Elephanta.

The cave was excavated with three large openings, one serving as entrance and two leading to flanking subsidiary shrines. The subsidiary shrines were constructed in sunken, open courts without any roof, allowing more light to enter the main cave as well as to provide sufficient height in the matrix for the tall façade of the subsidiary shrines. The courts with subsidiary shrines have no independent exit to the exterior.

The craftsmen who moved to Ellora after completing the Elephanta cave made radical changes in cave design. In Ellora they excavated a cave similar to the Siva cave in layout, with an exit to the exterior from the side subsidiary shrines. Cave 14 at Ellora is excavated with an open veranda similar to the open verandah of the side shrines of Siva cave. Cave 15 has an open veranda with a monolithic hall. Finally, unable to completely shake off the concept of a cave temple, the construction of Cave 16 was started as a grand monolithic structure. It has no roof and so is exposed to the sun; but it is still confined in a pit.

After Ellora, interest in cave construction waned and soon the temple confined in hilly regions was liberated and freestanding stone structural temples were constructed in the vast plain regions. Siva cave in addition broke the shrine free from attachment to the cave walls and added four entrances to the shrine.

Of all the monuments constructed by the Kalacuri, the Siva temple is the finest. The most distinguished feature of this cave are the monumental sculptured panels. There are no decorative designs carved on the walls of the cave or decorated borders around the panel to distract attention from the beauty of the monumental panels. The three-dimensional carving of large panels with large figures was introduced here. It started with the relatively flat Siva of Ardhanari and evolved to the almost detached Siva in the Andhaka panel. The same artists took three-dimensional carving to a climax in carving the episode of "Ravana shaking Kailas" at Ellora. Some of the panels in this cave are elevated to the status of secondary shrines.

The entrance to the cave is located on the east, facing the harbor in the Sea of Oman (Fig. 2.1).

Fig. 2.1. Sea of Oman seen from the cave. 2002.

The cave is essentially a mandapa with a narrow porch in front. From a slightly sunken court, possibly excavated to obtain sufficient height for the façade with a minimum of rock removal, a few steps lead to a pillared porch entrance with two pillars and two pilasters (Fig. 2.2).

2.2. Elephanta. Siva cave. Cave entrance. Ca. 540-555. Basalt.

The pillars are similar to the pillars in the mandapa and similar to the pillars in the Ellora caves. They are thick,

relatively plain, square up to mid-height and then end with fluted cushion capitals (Fig. 2.3).

Fig. 2.3. Elephanta. Siva cave. Pillars in cave. Mahadeva on back wall. Ca. 540-555. Basalt.

The pillars bear longitudinal ridges on the upper half. The central hall of the cave is 40m (124 ft.) long on the north-south and east-west axes. With the addition of extensions on three sides for entrances and for second shrine on the back, the total area of the cave is 5246 sq. m. (17,200 sq. ft.). The three huge heads on the bust of Siva carved on the back of the cave are visible from the main entrance. Some consider this panel as a secondary shrine within the cave. The 5m (16 ft.) high square shrine still attached to the roof of the cave is moved slightly to the side instead of being placed in the center of the hall or on the rear wall. This provides an unobstructed view of the three monumental Siva heads on the back wall of the cave from the main entrance (Fig. 2.4).

Fig. 2.4. Elephanta. Siva cave. Sanctum. Ca. 540-555. Basalt.

The square sanctum has undecorated entrances on all faces. Giant doorkeepers wearing highly decorated hair and crowns flank all the entrances. Like all the figures in the cave they have heavy lower lips and downcast eyes. A few steps lead into the sanctum enshrined with a lingam appearing as though it were standing on a pedestal, carved without a spout.

From the main cave two large openings on north and south open to sunken courts with subsidiary shrines. A short flight of steps connects the main cave to sunken courts with subsidiary shrines. The sanctum in the main shrine of the cave is placed in line with the exits to the north and south sunken courts without mandapa pillars obstructing the line of view. Standing on the steps of the north opening outside the main cave one has a clear view of the lingam in the main sanctum (Fig. 2.5).

Fig. 2.5. Elephanta. Siva cave. Lingam in Sanctum seen from north court entrance. Ca. 540-555. Basalt.

The courts, without roof, are enclosed within high walls with drains for rainwater to the exterior on the east. There are no independent exits from the courts to the exterior.

It is a Siva temple. The walls of the hall are carved with nine large reliefs alluding to various attributes of Siva. Other gods, when present, are diminutive spectators to the glory of Siva. The subject matter of the panels has been dreadfully damaged by artillery practice and would be very difficult to understand without prior knowledge of the episode depicted. Centuries of dirt and dust deposits and encrustation with leaching minerals have also taken their toll. On the back wall of the cave three monumental sculpted panels are framed in pilasters carved with 4m (12 ft.) high guardians and dwarfs. The damaged central panel is carved with a bust of Mahadeva with three giant heads depicting different attributes of the god in a single form (Fig. 2.6).

On a 1m (3 ft) high base, the 5.5m (19.5 ft.) high heads carved 3.5m (11 ft) deep on the rear wall appear to emerge from the wall itself. The broad shoulders belong to the central head but can be attributed to other heads. The central, impassive head of Mahadeva, serene, supreme, beneficent and all knowing, is wrapped in self-absorbed inwardness indicating concentration and a store of energy. The right

hand of the statue is broken and the left hand is holding a citron. The left face, with its bulging eyes, twisted moustache, angry eyebrow, matted locks of hair on the head entwined with snakes and skull represents the destructive aspect of Siva, Aghora-Bhairava, the disruption of energy. He is holding a snake in one hand. The right head, female, decorated with pearls and with flowers in her hair, has a blissful, soft face, soft curls, full lips and a lotus bud in hand, represent the creative activity and continuity of space and time. The pilaster on the right of Mahadeva is carved with a 4m (12 ft.) high standing male with a female squatting beside him. The dwarf standing with a female on the pilaster on the left of the central panel is similar to the dwarf in Aurangabad Cave 7; perhaps it was carved during the same period.

Fig. 2.6. Elephanta. Siva cave. Mahadeva. West wall. Ca. 540-555. Basalt.

The panel to the right of Mahadeva is carved with Ardhanari: Siva, fused with his beautiful spouse Parvati, representing the fusion of male and female energies (Fig. 2.7).

The living beings created by Brahma failed to reproduce because he failed to create women. When he approached Siva for help, Siva transformed the right side of his body into a female and took the form of Ardhanari. The two parts separate and merge in sexual union to produce living creatures. According to most Hindu thought, the male component, purusa, is inactive. The female, personified in Prakriti, is the active urge for creation. Siva as Ardhanari manifests as the unifier of the inactive male with the active female. Together they represent all of creation

Ardhanari has four arms. The left half (male) has the strong and firm contours of a man's body, and matted locks of hair piled high on the head. One of his arms is resting on the back of Nandi, his vehicle. The right half, female (Parvati), is holding mirror in one hand and the other hand is lazily resting on her hip. The mirror is supposed to reflect the glory of the male (Siva) as the moon reflects the light of the sun. She has a soft jaw line, hair arranged in curls bulging to the side, a full, firm bosom, narrow waist and curvaceous, sensual hips — dramatically different from the hips of Siva. A four-headed Brahma sits on his throne of swans to the right; Vishnu on his mount, or vehicle, Garuda, and Varuna on his mount Makara, to the left, are sculpted at one quarter the size of Siva; they are applauding Siva for this manifestation. Flying figures occupy the upper corners. The flying couple on the left corner is exquisitely beautiful. Flying is generally indicated by pieces of garment or hair floating in the air. The female has nothing on her beautiful body to indicate forward motion; still, she appears to be floating in the air like a dream. Her right hand with a feather-light touch is resting on the shoulder of the male, without exerting the slightest pressure on him, and her left hand is resting on her hip. The female figure is more natural and attractive than the flying pairs on the sculptured cliff at Mamalapuram. The lower portion of the relief is badly damaged.

Fig. 2.7. Elephanta. Siva cave. Ardhanari. Ca. 540-555. Basalt.

The sculpted panel to the left of Mahadeva represents the legend of the river Ganges descending from her abode in heaven to earth to sustain life and for the disposal of human ancestors' ashes in water (Fig. 2.8). Ganges is carved as a three-headed female, above Siva, as union of three rivers forms the Ganges. Weightless flying couples are hovering above. The descent of Ganges on Siva's hair implies the union of male and female components. To spare the earth from the

shattering impact of her fall, and to unify earth and heaven, Siva permitted her to descend on his hair where, after meandering for ages, she lost her impact and descended gently to the earth.

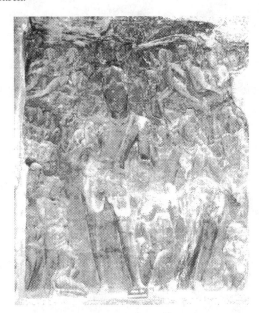

Fig. 2.8. Elephanta. Siva cave. Descent of Ganga. Ca. 540-555. Basalt.

Ganga was the second love of Siva. To express her displeasure, Parvati is standing at some distance from Siva, surrounded by dwarfs, with Vishnu, on Garuda, beside her. The thrust of her torso away from Siva, legs bent at the knees and her left hand away from Siva, implies her displeasure. The gods witnessing the event are carved in one quarter the size of Siva and Parvati. The scalloped margin of clouds above is characteristic of Chalukya sculpture.

The panel on the sidewall of the north entrance is carved with the legend of Ravana. In the panel the entire group of figures including the dwarf and Bhringin, the skeleton son of Siva, are completely detached from the concave back wall. This much-crowded panel in overall appearance would have been immensely impressive but for the heavy gunnery damage; the carvings may have suffered particular damage because most of the figures in the panel were detached from the background and were more exposed to the force of impact.

Ravana, the abductor of Sita, was the demon king of Lanka. In one version Ravana, while traveling in the mountains, could not cross the boundary of a place where Siva and Parvati were making love. Unable to bear the insult, Ravana tried to uproot Kailas, the abode of Siva, and throw it away. For this impudence Siva imprisoned him in a cave under Kailas, where he raged and raved like a wild animal. With light pressure from his leg Siva kept Ravana imprisoned for ages in the cave. After Ravana repented for a thousand years in captivity, Siva released him and allowed him to go to Lanka. Ravana is the bearer of chaos in the universe but Siva effortlessly subdues him and restores calm. Unlike the Ravana sculpture in Kailas temple at Ellora, the six-armed Siva is sitting with crossed legs on his throne, with one leg drawn near the body and his left leg folded at the knee. The folded raised leg, by exerting pressure on the roof of the dungeon, kept Ravana imprisoned. Siva is calm, leaning towards Parvati (who is sitting beside him), to reassure her. The head and hands of the Parvati figure are broken but the remaining exquisitely carved torso with its outstanding bust is comparable to the marvelous torsos carved at Sanchi. The necklace dangling beside her naval indicates she is leaning towards Siva. Her sitting on a flat surface with one folded leg drawn near the body and the other leg with knee lifted to rest the foot flat on the ground is a common sitting posture of Indian women. Ravana is whirling beneath like a ferocious animal in the cage.

The panel on the right side wall of the north entrance, carved with legend of the gambling scene, is also sadly mutilated. In the panel Siva is seated cross-legged with a female attendant, Bhringin, his skeleton son, on the back and flying couples hovering above. The beautiful Parvati is sitting with two female attendants and a guardian is standing beside. Siva's married life was not harmonious. The grievances caused by the yogi aloofness and the persistent adulteries of Siva habitually erupted into quarrels when Siva and Parvati played the game of dice, because Siva regularly cheated to win. During these quarrels Siva use to leave Parvati in anger and roam around, bolting out all the stars or extinguishing the sun or moon or committing other acts of cosmic hooliganism until Parvati transformed into a beautiful mountain maiden to win him over. The cycle of cataclysmic events and serenity in the universe reflect the innate nature of the gods.

The panels on the side walls of the south entrance depict the marriage of Siva, and Siva impaling the demon Andhaka. The legend of Siva's marriage with Parvati is romantic. Parvati, the beautiful daughter of the Himalaya Mountains, saw Siva, fell in love and decided to marry him. She fought with her parents, who did not approve her selection. Siva was a yogi, leading a chaste life; but determined to marry Siva, Parvati preformed penance for years to attract him. This persuaded Kama (the love god) to shoot an arrow at the heart of Siva and shake the yoga of Siva. Siva went to Parvati disguised as an old Brahmin and uttered disrespectful remarks about Siva. When Parvati defended Siva in a spirited way, Siva fell in love, and asked Parvati to marry him. She agreed, and asked him to obtain the consent of her parents, which they ultimately granted. In the much-damaged panel

Parvati is standing beside Siva surrounded by gods and flying couples (Fig. 2.9).

Fig. 2.9. Elephanta. Siva cave. Marriage of Siva and Parvati. Ca. 540-555. Basalt.

With the thrust of her voluptuous hip towards Siva and the forward motion of her right shoulder toward him, she is turning away from her protective father, who stands behind them. Vishnu, on the right of Siva, gives away the bride. Four-headed Brahma acting as priest is sitting in front of the couple to offer oblations to the fire. All the gods are witness to the ceremony.

On the right side wall Siva is depicted slaying the demon Andhaka by impaling him on his trident (Fig. 2.10).

In a playful mood, once Parvati covered Siva's eyes. Darkness fell over the universe. A drop of sweat that came from his eyebrow fell in one eye, got heated, and turned into an angry child called Andhaka. Andhaka grew up in the underworld, adopted by a demon, Harianyanetta. Years later he saw Parvati, fell in love with her and wanted to carry her off (under the oedipal impulse?). Siva caught and impaled him on his trident and began to dance. The flesh and sins of Andhaka were burnt away by the fierce gaze of Siva. When Andhaka praised Siva he took him home and both Siva and Parvati accepted him as their son and gave him the name of Bhringin. The blood of Bhringin drained away when he was impaled and left him a skeleton. The panel is much damaged by the gunners. In the panel the huge, almost three-dimensional figure of Siva wearing a crown decorated with a skull plunges out and soars upwards. Flying apsaras are hovering in the corners. The damaged figure of Siva with fangs protruding from his mouth, bulging eyes and a multitude of broken arms looks terrifying. He is carrying a sword in the only hand which remains intact. The figure of Andhaka impaled on the trident is also broken. In the palm of a broken left hand Siva, is holding a cup in which the blood of Andhaka was collected — bringing an end to Andhaka's cycle of death and resurrection.

Fig. 2.10. Elephanta. Siva cave. Adhaka impaled by Siva. Ca. 540-555. Basalt.

On the side walls of the main entrance panels depict Siva as the Lord of yogi and Siva dancing his eternal dance. Both the panels are badly damaged. In the panels a weightless Siva is sitting crossed legged on a lotus with long lotus stalk coming out of turbulent, muddy waters (Fig. 2.11).

Fig. 2.11. Elephanta. Siva cave. Siva. Lord of Yogi. Ca. 540-555. Basalt.

A similar panel in Cave 1 at Aurangabad, carved in the late fifth century, depicts Buddha sitting on a lotus in similar style. The image of Siva represents the ideal human yogi form. From the beginning, Siva is associated with meditative as well as sacrificial religion. He is a solitary god who withdraws into the mountains and meditates for countless years and accumulates energy to maintain the cosmic order. Other gods seek help or advice, and he obliges them. This panel may represent Lakulisa, the founder and teacher of the Pasupata cult (also considered the seventeenth incarnation of Siva, favored by early Kalacuri). According to the Pasupata belief the seemingly disparate aspects of creation are ultimately unified in Siva. This belief permeates through all the panels in the cave. The panel on the right side wall depicts Siva as Nataraja (Fig. 2.12).

Fig. 2.12. Elephanta. Siva cave. Nataraja. Ca. 540-555. Basalt.

His erotic dance with erect phallus is associated with the creation of the world and Tandava, the violent aspect, is associated with destruction of the world. The dance represents the single aspects of Siva where he creates to destroy and destroys to create, thus unifying destruction and creation. According to a legend told in relatively late Sanskrit texts, a group of sages were living in a forest with their wives. To prove that the yogis had not subdued their anger and lust, he went to their wives as a handsome beggar, with his hair nicely styled, and started dancing amidst them with erect phallus, exciting their wives. The yogis on seeing him dancing thus amidst their wives cursed him, in a blind rage, to be castrated. The phallus of Siva fell to the ground and the universe was plunged into darkness. The yogis realized that the beggar was Siva and begged his forgiveness. He agreed

— on the condition that they would worship his phallus forever. Another version of the legend does not mention castration. The yogis in anger hurled everything they could lay their hands on at Siva but he trampled everything and kept on dancing, compelled by thwarted erotic impulses to destroy everything thrown at him. The image of Siva in the panel is sadly mutilated. His legs and most of the six arms are broken. By the thrust of his right shoulder carved out of the background Siva is turning towards the main entrance. With his only unbroken hand he is lifting a veil. With little space left above his head and the ceiling, he appears compressed from above. Amongst the spectators are his elephant-headed child Ganesha, and Kattrikeya. A three-headed Brahma on a throne of swans with a male and female devotee behind and apsaras beside are spectators.

In the sunken court on the south, a subsidiary shrine is located. A huge cistern on one side of the court collects water. A lingam with a square base is enshrined in the sanctum. The pedestal, like the pedestals in the other shrines, is lost. A huge doorkeeper guards the sanctum. The doorkeeper on other side is lost. A small hall in the shrine is carved with panels. Siva depicted as Lord of the yogi is badly damaged. The hall contains sculptured panels of Ganesha, Kattrikeya and seven mothers.

The image on the south wall is badly mutilated; Ganesha can barely be recognized. Flying apsaras, female attendants and possibly rats flank him. On Siva's refusal to beget a son, Parvati creates Ganesha from piece of her sari. Siva gazed at the beautiful child in anger and the head of the child fell off. On Parvati's pleas, Siva sent his mount Nandi to bring a new head. After a long battle with the royal elephant of the god Indra, Nandi brought an elephant head and Ganesha came to life when the head was placed on him. In another version of the legend, Parvati posts Ganesha at the entrance of her quarters to prevent visitors entering at will. Once, while Parvati was bathing, Siva arrived. Ganesha obstructed his entry. In anger Siva cut off his head.

Ganesha is worshiped before any undertaking to remove obstacles. According to one legend, the gods complained to Siva for granting boons to the demons that became his devotees, making it impossible for them to control the demons. To help the gods, he created Ganesha to overcome evil spirits. His mount, the rat, is well suited to gnaw through any obstacle.

The history of the eight mothers carved on the side wall is obscure. They may be the mothers of Kattrikeya or bloodthirsty killer servants of the murderous goddess Kali. The eight standing women are much damaged. One legend ascribes their origin to Siva's attempt to kill the demon And-

haka. The drops of blood falling to the ground from Andhaka while Siva was fighting him created new demons. To help Siva, other gods sent their Shakti in the form of mothers to suck the blood drops and prevent the sprouting of new demons.

Fig. 2.13. Elephanta. Siva cave. Kattrikeya. South side subsidiary shrine. Ca. 540-555. Basalt.

The image of Kattrikeya on the west wall has not sustained much damage. The large figure of Kattrikeya has a beautiful headdress. His hands and legs are partly broken. A dwarf accompanies him, while flying apsaras hover above (Fig. 2.13). Once, when Siva was making love to Parvati, Agni, the god of fire, interrupted his love play in the disguise of a chattering parrot. Furious at the interruption, Siva caused Agni to take his seeds in his mouth. Agni is mostly carved with a big belly. Unable to bear the seeds, Agni gave the seeds to Ganga, who could not bear them and cast them ashore on a clump of reeds where six matrikas were taking bath. The matrikas got pregnant all at the same time and give birth to Kattrikeya. To suckle milk from six mothers, he sprouted six heads. At the birth of Kattrikeya, a stream of milk started flowing from Parvati's breast, making her aware of birth of a son. The multiple parentage of Kattrikeya by Siva and Parvati, Agni, Ganges and six mothers possibly represent the mixing of several cult myths. As the son of Siva he became the head of the army of gods.

In the north, sunken, roofless court a subsidiary shrine facing east has been excavated in the rear wall of the open courtyard (Fig. 2.14).

Fig. 2.14. Elephanta. Siva cave. North court. Subsidiary shrine. Ca. 540-555. Basalt.

The entrance to the subsidiary shrine, which is larger than the entrance of the main cave, bears four pillars and two pilasters similar to the pillars of the cave.

Fig. 2.15. Elephanta. Siva cave. North subsidiary shrine. Sanctum. Ca. 540-555. Basalt.

The entrance is followed by the sanctum, which is guarded by seated lions flanking the entrance. Possibly the doorkeepers on the façade of sanctum have been lost. A lingam is enshrined in the sanctum. Part of the square base of the lingam is visible on a nontraditional pedestal. A mutilated panel of Yogi Siva, similar to the panel in the main cave, is seen in the subsidiary shrine.

9. The Buddhist Caves at Aurangabad
(1st Century BCE–6th Century)

Aurangabad, an ancient city in Maharashtra, central India, is the commercial center of the region. The caves here present all the developmental stages of Buddhist cave layout, architecture and philosophy.

During Mughal rule the name was changed from Khidki to Fatah Nagar, and finally it was renamed after the last Mughal emperor, Aurangzeb (1659-1707), who is buried here. It was the capital of two southern dynasties, the Satavahana, in the second century CE, and the Yadva, in the twelfth century. For short periods it was the capital of Rashtrakuta, and Muhammad Taughlak, a sultan who temporarily shifted his capital here from Delhi.

The caves at Aurangabad were excavated in three phases. Chaityas, the earliest Buddhist caves, with stupas, provided monks a place to worship and meditate. Converting the chaitya into the vihara cave eliminated the stupa and provided space in the center of the cave where the monks could meditate and assemble to receive instructions to preach. A shrine in the rear wall met the need of worship. Small residential cells excavated on the periphery of the cave combined the need of worship with residence. With the increasing complexity of worship, more shrines were added by converting the residential cells of the vihara into shrines.

Cave layout took a step forward at Aurangabad. Hindu custom gave rise to a strong desire for circumambulation of the sanctum. The image of Buddha was detached from the rear wall at Ajanta, but to meet the desire to circumambulate the sanctum, the sanctum was moved to the center of the cave in the space of the vihara hall originally meant for the congregation of monks to meditate or

receive instruction. The community of monks played an important role in guiding the average people on the path of enlightenment by personal example. By eliminating the vihara hall, the monks may have been sidestepped as devotees were encouraged to develop a direct relationship with Buddha, with the help of Bodhisattvas and female deities like Tara, similar to the Hindus' development of an intense personal loyalty to a chosen god and his female counterpart. Tantrism, which had crept in Buddhism took firm root at Aurangabad.

About 9 km (5.8 miles) from Aurangabad are two groups of caves excavated in basaltic lava outcrops. The first group, comprising five caves, is located on a small hill (Fig. 2.20). The period of excavation of Caves 2, 4 and 5 is not certain. Caves 2 and 5 are viharas and Cave 4 is chaitya. It is possible that these caves were excavated during the Satavahana dynasty, coinciding with the excavation of early phase of Ajanta caves from first century BCE to the first century CE. Aurangabad was under the rule of the Satavahana during the early part of the first millennium.

Cave 1 and 3 were excavated during the Vakataka regime, coinciding with the second phase of cave excavation at Ajanta. The carvings of these caves show the influence of Satavahana and Vakataka art. The caves are numbered in standing sequence, as in Ajanta and Ellora, not on the basis of the date of excavation.

Fig. 2.20. Aurangabad. First group of caves. Ca. 1st BCE-5th Century. Basalt.

Cave 2 has a verandah with a row of sitting Buddhas on left wall and two decorated pillars in front of the sanctum. Buddha is seated on a lotus, similar to the carving of Siva as Lord of yogi in the Elephanta cave. Two nagas with human bodies and their heads under a naga hood are holding the lotus stalk and supporting the flower with their heads (Fig. 2.21).

Fig. 2.21. Aurangabad. Cave 2. Buddha seated on lotus. Ca. 1ˢᵗ-3ʳᵈ Century CE. Basalt.

Cave 4 is the only chaitya at Aurangabad. The similarities with the chaitya cave at Karli suggest the first century BCE as the time of excavation. The complete façade of the chaitya has collapsed, leaving only the outline of the chaitya window on one side and an open nave (Fig. 1.22).

Fig. 2.22. Aurangabad. Cave 4. Chaitya. Ca. 1ˢᵗ Century CE. Basalt.

The chaitya has thick, plain, octagonal, perpendicular pillars along the aisles. Decorative sculpture is carved above the pillars and the vaulted nave is carved with beams. The stupa at the rear end of the nave has a drum-shaped base and bulbous dome with a square, long neck sitting on the drum base like a pot. The neck is carved with four floating square

horizontal plates above. The superstructure above the neck is missing.

Between Cave 4 and 5 is a shallow cave with a large statue of Buddha seated on a lion throne with legs resting on lotus flower. His hands are broken. He is flanked by two attendants. One attendant is lost and the extant attendant is possibly a female, suggesting Tara, the spouse of Avalokiteshvara (Fig. 2.23).

Fig. 2.23. Aurangabad. Shallow cave. Statue of Buddha. Ca. 1ˢᵗ-3ʳᵈ Century CE. Basalt.

Fig. 2.24. Aurangabad. Cave 5. Vihara. Ca. 1ˢᵗ-3ʳᵈ Century CE. Basalt.

The façade of Cave 5, which is a vihara, has collapsed, exposing the skeleton of a residential cell on the left side of the verandah (Fig. 2.24). There are three openings on the façade bearing sculptured lintels. The sanctum, located in the center, bears three door jambs carved one behind another and flanked with beautiful females and decorative sculpture. The layout of the vihara was still evolving at this point; inside the sanctum a large image of a meditating Buddha with a halo behind the head is flanked by chamara bearers carved on the rear wall.

Cave 1 and 3, excavated during the regime of the Vakataka in the late fifth century CE, shows advanced features of Buddhist vihara caves. They are contemporary to the late Mahayana cave excavation at Ajanta. The unfinished Cave 1 is 23m (71 ft.) deep with a verandah. An antechamber has two decorated round pillars on eight-sided bases, ending in round tops bearing two side brackets (Fig. 2.25). A side bracket of the left pillar is broken.

Fig. 2.25. Aurangabad. Cave 1. Vihara. Pillars in front of sanctum. Ca. 3ʳᵈ-5ᵗʰ Century CE. Basalt.

On the outer side of the other bracket a female, resembling the females of Ajanta, is carved near the base of the bracket. A large statue of Buddha in a shrine is seated with his legs on a lotus flower and hands in preaching gesture.

Cave 3 is 25m (78 ft) deep and 19m (60 ft.) wide, with twelve pillars in the hall. The intricately carved pillars are square at the base, round at the center and square at the top, bearing short side brackets. The carvings in the hall resemble the carvings in Cave 1 and 26 of Ajanta. The shrine with portico is moved to the center of the hall. The entrance to the shrine is flanked with huge figures of Avalokiteshvara holding a lotus in hand and Vijarapani holding a vijara in hand (Fig. 2.26).

Fig. 2.26. Aurangabad. Cave 3. Vihara. Sanctum. Ca. 3ʳᵈ-5ᵗʰ Century CE. Basalt.

In a large statue Buddha, seated on a lion throne in the sanctum, holds his hands in a preaching gesture, his legs resting on a lotus. The side walls of the ambulatory passage are carved with small statues of Buddha sitting in various postures. The cells on the sides and back of the passage are residential, whereas the cells on the rear corners of the passage are subsidiary shrines.

Across the same hill, the second group of four caves (Fig. 2.27) is located 1½ km (1 mile) from the first group.

Fig. 2.27. Aurangabad. Second group of caves. Ca. 6ᵗʰ Century. Basalt.

After the collapse of the Vakataka dynasty at the end of the fifth century, the Kalacuri rose to power and ruled central India till 600, when the Western Chalukya of Karnataka eclipsed them. During the later half of the sixth century the second group of four caves was excavated by the Kalacuri dynasty (Fig. 2.28). A road connects the two groups of caves. Excavation of Cave 8 was attempted. Possibly due to the hardness of the stone, the rough surface of Cave 9 was plastered. There is no noteworthy sculpture in Cave 9 but there is a shallow, incomplete carving of Tara holding a lotus in her hand. Cave 6 and 7 show Vakataka and Kalacuri traditions. Cave 7 shows some influence of Eastern Chalukya sculpture.

At this time the Pallava, a Hindu dynasty from Tamilnadu, were experimenting with the excavation of small caves and monuments in exposed granite outcrops and were developing decoration for temple exterior. The Chalukya of Karnataka were excavating caves in sandstone and developing freestanding stone temples in Aihole.

The style of sculpture in caves of the second group is similar to the sculpture in Elephanta. The craftsmen and artists and their descendents, after excavating the caves of the second phase at Ajanta and the excavation of Elephanta cave, moved to Aurangabad during the Kalacuri regime in the later half of the sixth century to excavate the caves of the second group. These caves are advanced in style and iconography over the caves of the first group, with large panels and monumental figures to convey the messages effectively. The females carved under Kalacuri influence are robust, with well-proportioned bodies, and are strikingly beautiful. A visitor who rushes on to Ajanta and Ellora will miss two masterpieces of Indian sculpture located in Cave 7, surpassed nowhere.

From the middle of the fifth century, coincident with the decline of the Gupta empire, interest increased in the cult of feminine divinities and religious rites connected with magic, known as Tantrism. It surfaced in organized form in the seventh century, in Buddhism, with two main forms, known as Right handed and Left-handed. The Right-hand sect, devoted to masculine divinities, became very influential in China and Japan. The Left-hand sect, led by Vijarapani (Vehicle of Thunderbolt), is devoted chiefly to the feminine counterparts or wives of Bodhisattvas and other divinities of later Buddhist mythology.

The chief feminine deity Tara is the spouse of Bodhisattva Avalokiteshvara. The magical practices were believed to lead to salvation or to superhuman power.

The verandah of Cave 6 has two subsidiary shrines at the ends. There are fragments of painting on the roof of the verandah. In the right shrine Ganesha with the Saivite pantheon is carved on the walls. On the left shrine wall, six females and Siva are carved. The main shrine has a huge statue of Buddha flanked by attendants. An ambulatory passage surrounds the antechamber and shrine. Some of the cells on the side walls of the passage have stone beds. The shrine at the left corner of the ambulatory passage at the rear has a statue of Buddha with hands in meditation gesture and in the right corner shrine a statue of Buddha has his hand in a teaching gesture. Bodhisattva

Vijarapani, carrying a *vijara* in his hand, and Padmapani flank the doors of both the shrines. A vijara is an implement with an even number of hooks at both ends, which, according to some, represent the phallus.

Avalokiteshvara, holding a blue lotus in hand, is also known as Padmapani. Professor John Huntington states that the guarding of the shrines by Vijarapani and Padmapani and presence of Hindu Saivite pantheon in Buddhist cave strongly suggest the possibility that Buddhism (either identical to or very closely related to Shingon Buddhism) was being practiced in the second quarter of the sixth century at Aurangabad.

Cave 7, excavated around 560, is adorned by two superb pieces of sculpture depicting Bodhisattva Avalokiteshvara and a dancer; they are outstanding in the entire wealth of Indian sculpture. The pillared verandah of the cave has subsidiary shrines at the ends. The subsidiary shrine on the left has carvings of Hariti and her consort Pancika, flanked by attendants (Fig. 2.28).

They are bulkier than those carved at Ajanta. The attendant standing at left is caressing a bird held in hand. The shrine on the right has a group of consorts of Bodhisattvas carved in three-body bend poses with all the attributes of feminine beauty. All the females carved by the Kalacuri have full-figured but well-proportioned bodies and radiate beauty.

Fig. 2.28. Aurangabad. Cave 7. Sub-shrine in hall. Hariti and Pancika. Ca. 6th Century. Basalt.

Fig. 2.29. Aurangabad. Cave 7. Avalokiteshvara and Vijarapani flanking entrance. Ca. 6th. Century. Basalt

The rear wall of the verandah has a central and two corner entrances leading to a small hall. The side entrances continue in the circumambulatory passage around the sanctum. Doorkeepers guard central entrance and small carvings of seated Buddha are carved on the façade (Fig. 2.29). The decorated central entrance on the right is carved with a larger-than-human Bodhisattva Vijarapani accompanied by his consort and flying couples.

On the left, the large panel is carved with a larger-than-human sized Avalokiteshvara, the protector of travelers. Nowhere in Buddhist sculpture is Avalokiteshvara presented more majestically (Fig. 2.30).

He has a benevolent smile radiating from his face. His graceful body shows broad shoulders and round hips. Curly hair is piled up high on the head and some tendrils falling to the shoulder spread like meandering streams in the valley. He is standing on a lotus with his right hand in a protection gesture. A lotus bud on a long stalk adorns his side.

Four small panels on each side depict two travelers in each panel praying to the Bodhisattva to save them from the perils confronting them. He is carved flying in front of each small panel with his right hand raised in protection gesture. The carving on the right depicts travelers confronted with fire, a sword in the hand of their enemy, chains, and shipwreck. On the left side travelers are confronted with a lion, snakes, a mad elephant, and death — depicted as a demon snatching a child form its mother's lap.

Fig. 2.30. Aurangabad. Cave 7. Avalokiteshvara flanking Hall entrance. Ca. 6th Century. Basalt.

The hall behind has a large shrine in the center of the cave with an antechamber surrounded by a narrow circumambulatory passage connected with the passages from the corners of the verandah wall. The principal shrine, by occupying the center, has eliminated the vihara hall. The side walls of the main shrine entrance have a large panel carved with Tara, principal consort of Avalokiteshvara, and her reflections on her sides.

Fig. 2.31. Aurangabad. Cave 7. Tara flanking entrance to sanctum. Ca. 6th Century. Basalt.

Prominent female images as attendants of Bodhisattvas or of Buddha represent sexual symbolism and are associated with the Tantrism that flourished at Aurangabad in the sixth century. These voluptuous figures with elaborate hairdos have proportionate soft bodies, round, full breasts, large, round hips thrown slightly to one side, and bulging thighs. The Goddess Tara is full-figured but radiantly beautiful (Fig. 2.31).

Fig. 2.32. Aurangabad. Cave 7. Main shrine. Buddha. Ca. 6th Century. Basalt.

Fig. 2.33. Aurangabad. Cave 7. Bodhisattva and his consort. Ca. 6th Century. Basalt.

The dwarfs on the left of Tara, with five knots of hair on their head, represent the active male principal. They resemble the dwarf attending the Mahadeva statue at Elephanta, personifying compassion. The female dwarf to the right personifies wisdom. The flying celestials with garlands in their hands, in the upper corners, are bearers of supreme wisdom. They are set on clouds with scalloped margins, a characteristic of Chalukya sculpture. Inside the main shrine a huge figure of Buddha is carved, seated on a lion throne, his legs resting on a lotus and hands in a teaching gesture (Fig. 2.32). Three Manusi Buddha on each side flanks the figure of Buddha.

oval face with chiseled nose, flared lips and downcast eyes bears a faint smile. She wears a diaphanous garment covering her lower body. She is depicted in a Bharatanatyam dance pose, which enhances her radiant beauty and sexuality.

Dance developed a huge vocabulary of visual language by the seventh century. Her slender delicate left arm with palm turned upward denotes some sort of duality, or a long slender object that could be understood in context of presentation. As the fingers are directed towards her genital area, not far away, she may be inviting cohabitation. Her prominent breasts and slightly large lower abdomen representing her creative ability may be indicate her right to motherhood.

The sanctum is surrounded by a narrow circumambulatory passage. In the passage three residential cells on each side and subsidiary shrines at each back corner are excavated. Buddha, in each shrine, is carved seated on a throne with his legs on a lotus and hands in a teaching gesture.

Fig. 2.34. Aurangabad. Cave 7. Dancer. Ca. 6th Century. Basalt.

A large panel on the right of Buddha is carved with a slightly bulky, voluptuous female with an elaborate hairdo, firm, large breast, round hips and thighs, flanked with Bodhisattva and a dwarf (Fig. 2.33). On the left wall a group of six female musicians playing different instruments accompany an extraordinary beautiful dancer (Fig. 2.34). Her hair is piled up high on her head in an attractive arrangement. Her

10. EARLY WESTERN CHALUKYA MONUMENTS AT AIHOLE, BADAMI, MAHAKUTA, ALAMPUR AND PATADKAL

(535-756)

The free-standing, structurally modern temple was pioneered in Andhra Pradesh, where Chalukya monuments are located at Aihole, Badami, Mahakuta, and Patadkal in North Karnataka and Alampur. These are the earliest group of extant temples in South India.

The temple building activity of the Western Chalukya ended at Patadkal. UNESCO declared the group of monuments at Patadkal to be World Heritage Monuments in 1987.

The small town of Badami lies 96 km (60 miles) from the twin cities of Hubli and Dharwar, the commercial and academic centers of South India. From there to Badami is a 3-hour trip by road or railway. Badami has developed boarding and lodging facilities. Small villages in the Malaprabha River Valley — Aihole 43 km (27 miles), Patadkal 16 km (10 miles), Mahakuta 5 km (3 miles) from Badami, can be visited by daily road trips from Badami. Alampur is located 256 km (159 miles) from Patadkal near Karnul in Andhra Pradesh and can be reached by train from Hubli.

Tribes living in the rugged Deccan plateau were in constant conflict over the fertile lands of Tamilnadu and Andhra. The Satavahana ruled the region from the second century BCE to 300 CE. The Pallava feudatories of Satavahana appeared in Tamil lands in 325 CE and dominated much of peninsular India by 600. They ruled parts of south and central India up to 800. The Chalukya, possibly one of the feudatories of Satavahana, gained prominence in the mid-sixth century and ruled Karnataka in south India for about two centuries.

The founder of the Chalukya line, Jayasimha, and his son Ranaraga, governed Aihole in the early sixth century. During the rule of Ranaraga, Aihole and Mahakuta started developing as religious centers. In the mid-sixth century, Pulakesin I (535-566) founded the Chalukya dynasty in the eastern Deccan with Badami, a settlement of the Kadamba, as capital. He gathered the talent to excavate the cave temples and the Buddhist chaitya at Aihole. His son Kirtivarman I (566-597) conquered parts of Maharashtra, Tamilnadu and Karnataka. Possibly he constructed the Mahakuta temple. Mangalesha, his brother, constructed the first Brahman cave at Badami during the regime of Kirtivarman I. On the death of Kirtivarman I, Mangalesha (597-610) became regent to Pulakesin II, the minor son of Kirtivarman I. During the rule of Mangalesha, Mahakuta emerged as great Siva center. It may have been him who constructed the Jain cave at Badami. Mangalesha tried to install his son as successor to the throne. A civil war broke out that temporarily disrupted the temple building activity. Pulakesin II (610-642), after his uncle was killed in the civil war, gained power and conquered the south Indian kingdoms of Kadamba, Ganga and Alupa. After conquering parts of the Godavari River Valley in Andhra, he installed his younger brother as ruler in the Godavari district, establishing the Eastern Chalukya dynasty, which survived the demise of the Western Chalukya regime and ruled till 1070.

Pulakesin II repulsed the attack of Emperor Harsha from north India. He attacked and defeated the Pallava king Mahendravaram I, but failed to take the capital; this started the feud with Pallava that lasted till the end of Chalukya rule. When he attacked the Pallava the second time, he was killed, and Badami was under Pallava occupation for nearly 13 years. During Pulakesin II's reign the Meguti temple and a Jain temple at Aihole and the Upper

Sivalaya temple at Badami was constructed, before the temporary fall of Badami in 642.

The Chalukya of Badami returned to power after 13 years under Vikramaditya I (655-681), son of Pulakesin II, after taking refuge in parts of Andhra Pradesh during the occupation of Badami by the Pallava. Vikramaditya I regained control of territories including Alampur in Andhra Pradesh in 658. The Chalukya were worshipper of Vishnu, but they also worshipped the seven mothers and Kattrikeya, son of Siva, and revered Siva. Vikramaditya became a Saivite. The Malegitti Sivalaya temple at Badami was constructed during his rule. His successor Vinayaditya (681-696) constructed Svarga Brahma temple at Alampur, and his queen Vinayavati may have constructed Jambulinga temple at Patadkal. His son Vijayaditya (696-733) continued the temple-building activity at Alampur and built Sangameshvara temple at Patadkal.

The longest, most peaceful and prosperous Chalukya reign was that of Vijayaditya. Vikramaditya II (733-744), the next king, defeated the Pallava king Nandipotavarman. He built a couple of temples at Aihole and Mahakuta and continued the temple building activity at Alampur. He married two princesses of the south Indian Kalacuri dynasty, who built Virupaksha and Mallikarjuna temples at Patadkal. The Durga temple at Aihole was also built in the middle of the eighth century. Kirtivarman II (744-766) built several small temples at Mahakuta and completed construction of the Papanatha temple started during the reign of Vikramaditya II. Dantidurga, a feudatory of the Chalukya, defeated Kirtivarman II (744-776) and seized Badami, ending the rule of the Chalukya and terminating their temple building activity.

Kirtivarman II tried to seize the power upon the death of Dantidurga, but was prevented by Krishna I. Descendants of the early Eastern Chalukya survived as subordinates of Rashtrakuta and appear to have retained significant prestige and resources. When the Rashtrakuta regime ended in the tenth century, the late Eastern Chalukya dynasty rose under Taila II in 974 in Andhra Pradesh, but merged with the Cola royal family in 1070. Rashtrakuta and the late Eastern Chalukya of Andhra also constructed temples in the region. The temples constructed by the late Eastern Chalukya resemble the early temples.

The Chalukya engaged in cave excavation in the second half of the sixth century at Aihole and Badami. But within a century they gave up cave excavation and directed their energies towards development of freestanding stone structural temples that could be built in the vast plain regions of India. Chalukya temple building activity, after the start at Aihole, oscillated between Badami, Mahakuta, Alampur and Patadkal.

Most of the Chalukya temples were built in a small triangular area with Badami and Aihole at the base and Patadkal at the apex, in the 20 km (12 miles) long Malaprabha River Valley, which is partly lined by standstone hills; there are a few comparatively well developed temples at Alampur in Andhra Pradesh. The temples were constructed of large red sandstone blocks, laid without mortar disguising the joints. Large temples were constructed with flat roofs over multi-pillared halls and ceilings were carved with large separate panels. Most of the temples are of modest size and appear heavy. Some Jain temples were also constructed.

Aihole, standing on the banks of the Malaprabha River, was possibly the capital of the early Chalukya rulers when they were feudatories. It was a large city spread over five miles and has still retained a massive old city wall, almost circular, with many entrances. About 130 stone temples were built in a three-square-mile area of Aihole between 450 CE and 650. About fifty are in various state of preservation; the rest are in ruins. Buddhist chaitya and vihara caves enriched with local elements inspired the design of these temples. The transition taking place at the time from rock cut cave temples to free-standing structural temples necessitated experimentation to develop a plan for long lasting stone temples suitable for the plain regions. In imitation of the caves excavated in the hills, the Chalukya constructed temples with a massive appearance in the early stage. Gradually they developed all the basic units of the free-standing structurally modern temple. The development of all the basic units of the temple can be traced in the extant Chalukya temples at Aihole.

The rectangular sanctum of early temples was changed to square in temples constructed near the end of the temple-building period at Aihole. Evolution of the temple tower started with a four-sided indistinct mass on the center of the temple roof. The tower was later moved over the sanctum. The curvilinear tower of the northern temple, complete with crowning elements, was developed. A distinct decorative feature developed at the base of the tower façade is called the *gavaksa*. It consists of a circular enclosure carved with the image of a dancing Siva or other deity. In a further development, a projecting element with a wagon vaulted roof with a gavaksa on the façade was added at the tower base. It is called Sukanasa. A distinct pyramidal Kadamba-Nagara tower with multiple receding flat square tiers decorated with the *kalasa* (pitcher) on a flat top was also developed at Aihole. It led the Chalukya on the road to development of the four-sided south Indian temple tower refined at Badami.

The breakthrough in development of temple towers occurred when a hollow chamber was added on the tower of the Upper Sivalaya temple, enabling construction of tall towers by lessening the load on the tower. Further refinement of the tower took place at Mahakuta. The finalization of the south Indian temple tower and decoration on the temple exterior were completed at Patadkal. Many of the early experimental temples stand at Aihole, Badami, Alampur, Mahakuta and Patadkal. Unfortunately the date of construction of most early temples is not known.

The Chalukya oscillated between developing and constructing south- and north-Indian style temples, possibly due to their strong affiliation to Andhra Pradesh. Andhra Pradesh, which may have been their original home, was very receptive to central and western influences, possibly a legacy of the Satavahana. In addition, a line of the Chalukya dynasty was governing parts of Andhra Pradesh conquered during their expansion by Pulakesin II (610-642). After the finalization of the tower, the south Indian dynasties of the Cola, Hoysala, late Chalukya, Vijayanagara and Nayakas adopted the pyramidal south Indian tower with regional modifications. It is interesting to note that temple towers popular in south India are decorated with designs developed by the Pallava in Tamilnadu. The early designs of these towers were carved first on the pilaster ends flanking the sanctum entrances of most of the temples at Aihole. The surge of temple building activity at Aihole may have even helped write or finalize the codes for construction of future temples.

The badly weathered sculpture at Aihole is distinctly different from, and inferior to, the sculpture at Sanchi, Ajanta and Mamalapurum but glimpses of the influence of these centers is seen in some carvings. The females generally lack gentle curves and body bends. They are carved in awkward poses, occasionally with distorted bodies, particularly the breasts, hands and legs, although some carvings are good. Above the Guadar-gudi sanctum door lintel a highly-decorated chaitya window is carved with a seated Lakshmi bathed by elephants. It is similar to the carvings of Lakshmi on the Sanchi gateways. The sculpture in the Ravana Phadi cave shows Pallava influence. The females are tall and delicate, but slightly rotund. By the eighth century the carving style had matured, as seen on Durga temple. Some distinct features are the carving of large sculpture panels of gods on the ceiling slabs in the early Aihole temples. This was possibly done to make the devotee feel surrounded by the gods or to enshrine the gods on the walls as well as above the head. This practice appeared again in the temples constructed near the end of the building activity at Aihole. The most often repeated carving is Man-Garuda, a human upper body with wings, carved on the lintels of the temple doors. The coiled bodies of the snakes held by Garuda in both hands decorate the doorframe. In the Ravana Phadi cave, the drapery of the

females is indicated by deeply scored parallel lines. Some females are carved with a distinct loincloth and few carvings show the females in an extremely agitated sexual mood. Amorous couples are seen on the first temple constructed at Aihole, but the near-human size copulating pair on Huchchappaya Matha is possibly the first large erotic display in an Indian temple.

Many of these temples were neglected and used as residences or cattle barns till recent time. One temple is still in the custody of private individuals. The early Chalukya temples at Aihole are called *gudi*, meaning "temple" in the local language. These temples are classified into an early group that includes simple temples like the Konti-gudi, Guadar-gudi and Lad Khan temples, and an intermediate group that includes the Galaganatha, Huchchimalli-gudi, Durga and other temples exhibiting a few advanced temple features.

Jayasimha and his son Ranaraga, who ruled Aihole in the first half of the fifth century, may have built Konti-gudi, the earliest-built group of free-standing stone temples, in the beginning of the fifth century and Guadar-gudi in the first quarter of the fifth century. The modern temple was evolved from a mandapa with an open facade. Konti-gudi, a group of three small, similar, early temples are essentially open mandapa (Fig. 2.30).

Fig. 2.30. Aihole. Konti-gudis. Pillared portico. Ca. 5th Century. Sandstone.

The first temple facing east in this group has a rectangular verandah. The sloping roof of the verandah is supported by six pillars on the front. Two parallel rows of four squat pillars located on a wide axis in the middle of the hall behind the verandah bear the weight of the ceiling. A wall constructed on the back and sides of the temple supports the sloping roof. The space between the two rear squat pillars is clumsily blocked with a wall with an entrance in the center. Two walls join the rear pillars and back wall to form the sanctum. The façade of the sanctum entrance is richly decorated. Man-Garuda is carved on the lintel of the sanctum door. The sanctum, guarded by doorkeepers, is empty. Vishnu and Nataraja are carved on the exterior walls of the sanctum. The ceiling slab is carved with a three-headed Brahma, seated on a lotus, and Siva seated on a dwarf. A panel is carved with a four-armed Narayana sleeping cross-legged on a coiled naga. In the carving Narayana is sleeping with his head under a Naga hood and possibly Brahma wearing a crown is seated beside his legs (Fig. 2.31).

Fig. 2.31. Aihole. Konti-gudi. Mandapa ceiling. Narayana sleeping on Ananta. Ca. 5th Century. Sandstone.

In the second temple there are two sets of two pillars in the center. The two rear pillars are used to create the sanctum. One of the spaces left beside the sanctum is similarly blocked to form an additional sanctum, starting the trend to construct more than one sanctum in a temple. The pillars are carved with beaded festoons, a floral band, and circular medallions carved with amorous couples.

The third temple is similar to the first in its floor plan, with two additional features. On the roof of the third Gudi, a five-foot high square structure with miniature carvings is constructed in the center of the roof. This unimpressive structure was the beginning of the temple tower. The process of dividing the interior space, leading to the development of various interior temple components, was first introduced here.

A wall with perforated windows and entrance in the center separates the sanctum from the verandah, which in later developments became the mandapa. The space between the pillars of the verandah façade and the wall with perforated windows is still open but the sanctum is behind the wall. A pillared portico is constructed between the two shrines; it is not a passage between the shrines. Such pillared porticos were constructed as a front porch of advanced temples.

A second line of approach in developing the temple format appeared in the building of a mandapa open on all sides with a sanctum in the center; this type did not gain ground. The Guadar-gudi was constructed in the first quarter of the fifth century on an elevated molded platform in a pit with steps to climb to the temple (Fig. 2.32).

Fig. 2.32. Aihole. Guadar-gudi. Ca. 5th Century. Sandstone.

Four open undecorated squat pillars on each side on the periphery bear the sloping roof. A low parapet wall decorated with vases connects the pillars to the periphery. The two parallel rows of pillars running in the center of the mandapa on the long axis support the ceiling. The space between the two pillars of the first and second parallel of rows is blocked with an entrance in the center to form sanctum. The space left at the back of the sanctum introduced a circumambulatory passage around sanctum. Man-Garuda with spread wings is carved, holding a naga in each hand, on the lintel of the sanctum. Above the highly decorated lintel of the sanctum entrance, three chaitya windows are carved with pyramidal *sikara*-like structures ending in *amalaka* and *kalasa*. In the large central chaitya window, elephants are bathing Lakshm, who is seated on a lotus. The two small pyramidal sikara flanking Lakshmi are carved with females standing with three body bends in the chaitya windows. The sanctum is empty. On the flat roof of the gudi a three-course masonry block with chaitya motifs is constructed above the sanctum that makes up the tower.

Lad Khan temple, constructed in the second quarter of the fifth century, is named after the last resident of the temple (Fig. 2.33). The cave-like massive appearance of the temple and the carving of a fish motif (similar to the carving in Badami Cave 2) suggest the temple was constructed during the regime of Pulakesin I (535-566). It is essentially a large square mandapa, where all the units of the temple except the porch and tower are enclosed in the large mandapa. Four tall massive pillars support the flat roof of the mandapa at the center; two peripheral rows of twelve and twenty pillars of lesser height support the two-tiered sloping roof of stone slabs. Stone slabs on the back, on the temple corners and the outer peripheral pillars support the temple roof on the sides. Windows carved in geometric designs close the space between the pillars and allow air and light inside. Stones cut in the shape of a split coconut tree trunk are added to cover the spaces between stone slabs, introducing the local feature of coconut leaf-covered residential huts.

The enclosure of open space around the temple gave rise to the modern mandapa. A new unit, the open front porch (similar to the pillared portico of the early temple parapet wall with its sophisticated open front porch) is added, with a low parapet wall between the pillars.

Fig. 2.33. Aihole. Lad Khan temple.Ca. 535-566. Sandstone.

The entrance pillars of the front porch are carved on the façade with loving couples. The hand of the female on the left pillar is distorted. Beautiful Yamuna, standing on a tortoise, and Ganga on her mount *makara*, are carved on the corner pillars. A seated bull occupies the center of the mandapa between the four tall massive pillars. The rectangular sanctum is constructed between two back pillars attached to the back wall. The lingam is enshrined in a rectangular sanctum without a circumambulatory passage.

A later development was to extend the mandapa in the back of the sanctum, giving rise to the designs of the Alampur temples. The flat roof above has a small square cell carved with pilasters on the exterior walls and at the front entrance. The stone ladder kept in the second Konti-Gudi suggests that access to the cell above was given a similar stone ladder, now lost. Niches on each side of the cell are carved with reliefs of Vishnu, and incomplete carvings of Surya and Ardhanari. It was possibly an experimental tower or secondary shrine above.

The Tarabasapa, Narayana and Galaganatha temples have well-developed front porches and a well-defined doorway entrance from porch to mandapa. The well-conceived sanctum with its entrance door is a separate distinct unit attached to the rear of the mandapa. The mandapa of the Tarabasapa temple has two-tier roof. Lattice windows on the side walls of the mandapa allow light and air into the interior. The shrine door is flanked with pilasters decorated with chaitya windows at the top and the door lintel is carved with Man-Garuda. A sculpture on a stone slab depicts Durga killing the buffalo-demon. The tower is curvilinear with amalaka pieces between the moldings and a very short *sukanasa* at the base.

A similar tower is carved on the top of the shrine door lintel. The Narayana temple is similar to Tarabasapa. The sanctum of Narayana is enshrined with a statue of Surya, carved from black stone, flanked by Usha and Pratyusha, the female attendants, with bow and arrow to drive away darkness. The curvilinear tower bears the image of Surya inside a chaitya window on the façade.

Huchchappayya-gudi is similar to Tarabasapa. Siva is carved as Nataraja in the porch and as guardian of the sanctum enshrined with the lingam. The sanctum exterior walls bear a three-eyed Siva in the north side niche and Nrsimha, the lion incarnation of Vishnu, in the west side niche.

In Huchchappaya Matha the walls on the periphery and two rows of 6 pillars on vertical axis support the sloping roof. A seated Nandi is located between the last four pillars of the vertical row of pillars with a squat square tower on the roof. The front porch is missing (Fig. 2.24).

Fig. 2. 34. Aihole. Huchchappaya Matha. Ca. 5ᵗʰ Century. Sandstone.

Fig. 2.35. Aihole. Huchchappaya Matha. Exterior pillar. Erotic couple. Ca. 5ᵗʰ Century. Sandstone.

The sanctum is located at the rear of the mandapa. An exterior pilaster on the facade wall of the temple depicts a female with the loose end of her open loincloth hanging behind her. She is so impatient that she is pulling the hair of the man who is standing with her, with a short, pendulant phallus, pulling her folded leg. Her breast appears distorted (Fig. 2.35). The ceiling of the mandapa is carved with Siva and Parvati seated under parasol with a host of attendants and many other gods.

The main temple of the Mallikarjuna group lacks an antechamber and circumambulatory passage. The most interesting feature of the temple is the Kadamba-nagara style tower.

Chikka-gudi is similar to Guadar-gudi but is better organized, with the layout of the Alampur temples. It has a rectangular pillared portico, interior columned mandapa and sanctum with aisles on the sides and back. The mandapa columns and beams are decorated with the lotus. A circumambulatory passage surrounding the sanctum has three latticed windows. The exterior walls are undecorated. The ceiling slabs are carved with flying figures, Vishnu sleeping on Ananta with Brahma springing out of Vishnu's navel, and Trivikrama. Siva is carved as Nataraja, and as Andhakasura killing the demon elephant. The base of the ruined sikara stands on the roof.

Huchchimalli-gudi, located near the Travelers Bungalow, has the layout of the Alampur temples (Fig. 2.36).

Fig. 2.36. Aihole. Huchchimalli-gudi. Ca. 6th Century. Sandstone.

The temple, standing on a high plinth, consists of entrance porch, mandapa, and an antechamber that is not completed separated from the mandapa. The front porch has low parapet walls carved with delicate vase-and-foliage motifs. The ceiling of the portico is carved with Kattrikeya seated on a peacock, holding a sword in one hand and flowers in other hand, surrounded by flying figures. The exterior of the mandapa is devoid of niches and has very small windows. There are four pillars arranged in a square in the mandapa. The space between the two rear pillars of the mandapa is blocked by a stone grill with a door in the center (Fig. 2.37).

Fig. 2.37. Aihole. Huchchimalli-gudi. Wall separating sanctum from mandapa. Ca. 6th Century Sandstone.

In a later development, when the mandapa was completely separated from the sanctum, the antechamber was formed. The entrance door to the sanctum located behind the stone grill is decorated with floral designs, and Man-Garuda holding nagas in his hands. Ganga and Yamuna are carved at the base of the door lintels. The square sanctum enshrines the lingam. The ceiling of the mandapa is carved with Siva, Indra, Vishnu and Brahma with their mounts and the ceiling of the antechamber is carved with the lotus. The circumambulatory passage around the sanctum has perforated windows on the back and side walls. The curvilinear tower on the sanctum is carved with a sukanasa bearing a chaitya window carved with Nataraja. There is a tank a few yards in front of the temple.

There are thirty temples in the Galaganatha group situated on the bank of the Malaprabha River. Most of them are dilapidated. The main Galaganatha temple has a pillared portico, mandapa, antechamber, detached sanctum and curvilinear tower similar to the Tarabasapa temple. Similar temples with well-defined antechambers are located in adjoining Chikka-gudi and Ambiger-gudi. All the basic units of the temple are evolved and the basic internal design of the modern temple was complete and has remained the same, except the division of these basic units to serve various needs.

Near the top of Meguti hill, Pulakesin I (535-566) in the mid-sixth century excavated a two-storied Buddhist chaitya with open façade at Aihole. The only surviving sculpture in the chaitya is the carving of Buddha on the second storey ceiling — Buddha with a halo is sitting cross-legged in an undefined posture. There is a three-tier umbrella above his head. On the crest of the hill, Pulakesin II (610-642) constructed the Meguti temple in 634. The temple is dedicated to Mahavir (Fig. 2.38).

Fig. 2.38. Aihole. Meguti Temple. Ca. 6ᵗʰ Century. Sandstone.

It is the first temple built with the body of the south Indian temple. The south Indian temple features are basement moldings decorated with friezes in between and kudus cornice. The friezes are now empty. The twelve pillars and four pilasters of the large porch bear the flat roof with curved eaves. The small parapet wall on the top is decorated with a faded Kaputa and other decorations. The large porch in front of the temple with opposite steps to climb the basement has sixteen pillars with faint impression of carvings. The low parapet wall of the porch is decorated with friezes and kudus above. The niches on the temple's exterior walls and friezes on the porch parapet wall are empty now. An entrance from the portico leads to a chamber divided by a wall in the middle, similar to the mandapa of advanced Hindu temples which are divided into a front and rear mandapa. The second chamber, situated at a slightly higher elevation, is reached by a flight of steps. A door from the second chamber leads to a large hall with four pillars in the center. The sanctum is set in the center of the pillars, enclosed in walls. At the back of the sanctum is a crude image of Tirthankara. The circumambulatory passage around the sanctum is made up of connected chambers. The wall of a chamber at the back is blocked, making the ambulatory passage non-functional. A huge slab, possibly dislodged from one of the chambers, with a carving of Jain Yakshi Sidhiaka, attendant of Mahavir, is located in Aihole local museum (Fig. 2.39).

She is seated on a throne with one crossed leg resting on the other and is crowded by attendants and a seated lion beside. The carving of Sidhiaka, with a soft and proportional body, is outstanding in beauty and naturalism. Possibly this is the only carving of Sidhiaka carved in the nude. From the portico a stone staircase leads to the roof with a dilapidated, rectangular cell placed above the ground floor sanctum. The cell is enshrined with a Tirthankara image and has lost the roof. This structure is similar to the cell on the Lad khan temple roof. It is possibly an experimental tower or a second sanctum on the roof. It may not be the original struc-

ture. The Meguti temple added the new element of mandapa division. The external design and decorations of Dravidian south Indian temples, mostly borrowed from Pallava sculpture, started to take final shape. The fully developed temple towers at Aihole were limited to the curvilinear (nagara) and Kadamba-nagara style.

Fig. 2.39. Aihole. Meguti Temple. Sidhiaka. Ca. 6ᵗʰ Century. Sandstone.

The Ravana-Phadi cave temple was excavated possibly around 550, simultaneously with the cave excavation at Badami, in a small granite outcrop. The Saivite sculpture of the cave suggests it was excavated during the reign of Vikramaditya (655-668). A huge monolithic fluted pillar with square base stands in front of the cave, followed by Nandi seated on a platform facing the cave. The cave stands on a high platform reached by a flight of steps. On the platform's front corners there are small-pillared halls with front entrances. Fat potbellied Pancika, guardian of wealth, stands by the cave entrance. A flight of steps from the platform leads to the entrance with two decorated pillars in the center (Fig. 2.40).

Fig. 2.40. Aihole. Ravana Phadi. Ca. 7ᵗʰ Century. Sandstone.

The ceiling of the rectangular mandapa inside is decorated with a huge intricately carved lotus flower. The entrance side wall is carved with Ardhanari standing with a trident, her hip to the side (Fig. 2.41). On the other side, Siva with three eyes is guarding the entrance. The wall facing the mandapa has large opening leading to antechamber with carvings on both sidewalls. On one side of the sanctum entrance Siva is carved, standing under the three heads of Ganga , alluding to the episode of the descent of Ganga to the earth from heaven (Fig. 2.42).

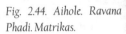

Fig. 2.43. Aihole. Ravana Phadi. Nataraja.

Ca. 7th Century. Sandstone.

Fig. 2.41. Aihole. Ravana Phadi. Ardhanari.

Ca. 7th Century. Sandstone.

Fig. 2.44. Aihole. Ravana Phadi. Matrikas.

Ca. 7th Century. Sandstone.

Fig. 2.42. Aihole. Ravana Phadi. Descent of Ganga. Ca. 7th Century. Sandstone.

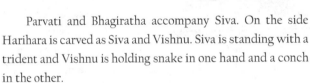

Parvati and Bhagiratha accompany Siva. On the side Harihara is carved as Siva and Vishnu. Siva is standing with a trident and Vishnu is holding snake in one hand and a conch in the other.

Two side chambers flank the rectangular mandapa. A flight of few steps on the left leads to a very narrow side chamber with a powerful image of Nataraja with ten long slender arms appearing like vines emerging from the back of Siva (Fig. 2.43). He is holding a snake in two hands raised above his head and wearing a snake on his neck.

Ganesha is carved on the right and on the left Parvati is carved, with a firm breast, narrow waist, rounded hips and thighs. Her dress reaching the ankles; this is different from the short dress of the Matrikas. Siva and Parvati are also accompanied with seven Matrikas in two groups. Three Matrikas stand between Parvati and Nataraja. They are all tall, with shapely bodies in three body bends, wearing short dresses covering only their thighs, and tall headdresses. In the group of three Matrikas, one looks bored, one is wearing a headdress carved with a skull and another is wearing a headdress carved with peacock feathers (Fig. 2.44).

Four Matrikas are carved after Parvati. All the females are tall, with slightly robust cylindrical bodies with the bends and curves of the females of Pallava sculpture.

The right chamber is not carved, possibly because of a fissure on the roof. A flight of steps from the mandapa leads to small antechamber with carvings on the side walls. Durga, carrying a long sword, bow, trident and multitude of emblems in her hands, is slaying a buffalo demon. The carving does not differ much from her carving on Durga temple. Her trident has pierced the body of the demon kneeling on the ground.

Another panel on the opposite side depicts Vishnu in his Varaha incarnation. Goddess earth is sitting on the raised arm of Vishnu (folded at the elbow) with her legs resting on the palm of another hand. The ceiling of the antechamber has three big circles carved with Vishnu on Garuda, a lotus, and Indra on his mount, the elephant; the beams are carved with flying apsaras. The rectangular sanctum is enshrined with the Lingam.

After the Meguti temple the last temple constructed at Aihole was the Durga temple, which is a synthesis of Hindu temple and Buddhist chaitya forms. The Buddhists had built a freestanding apsidal chaitya amidst the Jain caves on Udayagiri hill near Bhubanesvara, now in ruins. Temple 18 at Sanchi, constructed originally in wood during the Mayura dynasty in the third to first century BCE, was apsidal shaped. But this is possibly the first and last Hindu temple built on the apsidal chaitya design built in the eighth century. Probably it was consecrated to Surya. The temple stands on a high, ornately molded base, more attractive than the basement of the Meguti temple (Fig. 2.45). The flight of steps leading to the porch on the east are hidden behind a short wall resembling the molded base of temple. The porch surrounding the temple on the sides and apsidal back has thirty-three pillars standing on a low parapet wall (Fig. 2.46).

Fig. 2.45. Aihole. Durga Temple. Apsidal end.

Ca. 8th Century. Sandstone.

Fig. 2.46. Aihole. Durga Temple. Façade.

Ca. 8th Century. Sandstone.

All the pillars of the porch are decorated on the exterior face with well-built and good-looking females and couples with the lovely females in three body bends, resembling the Pallava females. There are graceful females in various postures including intoxicated females in their lovers' arms, single females, and amorous couples and dancing pairs. The

female member of a dancing couple is shown wearing a loin cloth (Fig. 2.47).

Fig. 2.47. Aihole. Durga Temple. Carving on verandah pillar. Ca. 8th Century. Sandstone.

Fig. 2.48. Aihole. Durga Temple. Durga on temple wall. Ca. 8th Century CE. Sandstone.

Some mithuna couples in the act of love exhibit extreme passion. A number of Dravidian and northern-style niches on the exterior walls of the temple in the porch are decorated with robust images. The eight-armed Durga killing the buffalo demon is standing beside her mount, the lion, carrying a trident and a multitude of emblems in her hands (Fig. 2.48). Her body appears stretched sideways, with two large ball-like breasts placed wide apart on her chest. A small, unimpressive buffalo demon with upturned head is placed between her legs, appearing to have distorted her hips and legs. Her trident has broken away or has not pierced the neck of the demon.

Vishnu, standing as a boar with one leg on the coiled body of Sesha, is carrying the mother goddess on his bent right hand (Fig. 2.49). The spouse of Sesha is sitting beside them.

Fig. 2.49. Aihole. Durga Temple. Vishnu as a boar. Ca. 8th Century. Sandstone.

Another niche is carved with Harihara, accompanied by attendants, looking up, and beautiful females in body bends in the upper corners. Multi-armed Siva is leaning on Nandi in the company of a dwarf in a niche.

The flat roof of the temple has four tiers. The first forms the eaves around the temple; the second tier forms the sloping roof of the porch and the remaining two tiers make up the rest of the roof. The roof of the sloping porch is carved with flying couples.

A flight of steps from the porch leads to the portico with carved ceiling and pillars. The door leading to the mandapa is decorated with Man-Garuda with spread wings on the lintel and holding nagas in both hands. The coiled tails of the nagas decorate the length of the doorframe. Bands of floral motifs and females in amorous postures are carved beside the band of naga tails. There is an indistinct temple tower carved above the door lintel.

Inside the mandapa two parallel rows of pillars on the long axis support the ceiling and divide the mandapa into central nave and side aisles. The side aisles serve as a circumambulatory passage round the sanctum. A Lingam is installed in the sanctum. The general belief is that the temple was originally dedicated to Durga. A partially-damaged, relatively plain northern-style curvilinear tower with clumsily fitted tiers carved with chaitya-arch motifs stands over the apsidal end. The crowning elements are possibly lost.

Other Hindu temple groups at Aihole are Jyotirlinga (sixteen temples), Mallikarjuna (five temples), Veniyavar (ten temples), Maddin (four temples), Tirambakesvara (five temples) and Ramalingam (five temples). Most of the temples are in ruins. There are ten Jain temples in three groups. Charanthi Matha has three temples, Yoginarayana has four temples. On Meguti hill are three temples.

Pulakesin I (535-566), the founder of the Chalukya dynasty, captured Badami from Kadamba in the middle of the sixth century. He fortified and made Badami his capital because of its advantageous defensive location. By damming the river between outcrops of red sandstone the present large lake was created and the town grew up around it (Fig. 2.50). The scenic Badami Lake seen from the porch of Cave 2 has a group of temples on the shore on the right, the Sivalaya temples on the hill on the left, and the town of Badami in front of the bank.

Badami is the southern-most region of the western hilly range in south India where rock cut-caves were excavated. The early Chalukya excavated four caves in the red sandstone hills bordering Badami town in the sixth century and built five stone structural temples in the seventh century. The caves may have been excavated using techniques similar to that used in the Buddhist caves at Ajanta and Aurangabad. The caves are similar to the open-pillared mandapa resembling the early temples at Aihole, like Konti-gudi. The open front façade, lack of any large structures in the cave, and comparatively soft sandstone possibly made the excavation of the caves easier than the Buddhist caves in basaltic rocks. The sanctum is excavated in the rear wall of the caves.

The inclined causeway leads to four caves in the cliff towering Badami. The caves are numbered serially. Cave 1 is possibly the earliest. Cave 3 was excavated during the reign of Kirtivarman I (566-597) and was consecrated to Vishnu by Mangalesha in 578. Cave 2 and Jain Cave 4, the last cave in the series on the top of hill is of uncertain date.

In basic lay out the caves are transverse aisles separated by columns standing on raised floor strips separating aisles. The square pillars of the façade have fluted cushion capitals elaborately decorated with brackets and beams. Inside the mandapa the pillars are carved in two different styles. Though small and simple the caves have fine carvings and decorative motifs particularly on ceiling. The females carved are in general more attractive and beautiful than at Aihole. They are tall, lightly built with body curvatures similar to females at Mamalapuram and body bends like Sanchi females.

Cave 1, possibly excavated a few years earlier than Cave 3, is dedicated to Siva (Fig. 2.51).

Fig. 2.50. Badami. Badami Lake. Group of temples on lakeshore. Ca. 7th Century.

Fig. 2.51. Badami. Cave 1. Ca. 6th Century. Sandstone.

Fig. 2.52. Badami. Cave 1. Nataraja. Ca. 6th Century. Sandstone.

It is similar to Cave 3 but smaller. The cave stands on a high plinth and the molded columns are decorated with medallions and jeweled garlands. The outer aisle is treated like a porch. The right exterior extension of the porch is carved in deep relief with a large panel depicting a multi-armed Siva dancing, watched by Parvati, Nandi, Ganesha and a drummer (Fig. 2.52). On the left extension of the porch Siva is standing in a large panel with a trident in one hand and the other hand resting on his hip.

Another panel is carved with Siva as Ardhanari leaning on his mount Nandi, with a pronounced tilt of the hips. His richly decorated spouse Parvati is standing beside him and his son Bhringin is standing in the background. Flying figures hover in the upper corners. The overall effect of the panel is not overpowering. The females of all the flying couples in the caves are shown sitting on the legs of the flying males, unlike other examples where the female flies behind the male, with one hand touching his shoulder. One panel is carved with a standing Vishnu holding a conch and chakra. He is accompanied by the beautiful Lakshmi, an attendant holding a flower, a dwarf, and another dwarf standing by who has a human body and a Nandi head.

Cave 2, dedicated to Vishnu, has the verandah cut into an overhanging cliff (Fig. 2.54).

Fig. 2.53. Badami. Cave 2. Ca. 535-561. Sandstone.

The molded basement is decorated with a row of dwarfs. The façade pillars are decorated similar to the pillars of Cave 1. The ceiling of the outer aisle is carved with a fish wheel and swastika motifs, similar to the motifs in the Lad Khan temple at Aihole, suggesting the cave was excavated during the reign of Pulakesin I (535-566). Vishnu is carved standing with a flower in his right hand. A beautiful, diminutive female is standing beside him, holding a flower with a long stalk in her left hand. Vishnu as multi-armed Trivikrama carrying a multitude of weapons is standing with one leg on earth and other resting on heaven (Fig. 2.54).

Fig. 2.54. Badami. Cave 2. Trivikrama.

Ca. 535-561. Sandstone.

A group of worshippers is carved below. The dead body of King Bali is falling on their heads. Four-armed Vishnu in the Boar incarnation is standing with one leg on earth and other leg on the coils of Sesha (Fig. 2.55). The spouse of Sesha is sitting to the side. Vishnu is holding the mother goddess in the palm of his right hand, supporting her back with another hand. Vishnu, carved as a boar by the Chalukya, has a proportionally long snout and is comparatively slender to those carved in other south Indian temples. The hall is orientated towards the sanctum. The sanctum set in the back wall bears decorated carvings on the door.

Cave 3, the largest cave, was excavated during the reign of Kirtivarman (567-597). Mangalesha, younger brother of the king, dedicated it to Vishnu in 578 (Fig. 2.56).

*Fig. 2.55. Badami. Cave 2.
Vishnu as Boar.*

Ca. 535-561. Sandstone.

Fig. 2.56. Badami. Cave 3. Ca. 566-597. Sandstone.

It has a large spacious verandah. Dwarfs are carved on the decorated niches of the molded plinth. There is a band of unrecognizable decorations above the dwarfs. The columns of the cave are carved in three different styles, like all the other caves. The square columns on the cave façade bear a medallion near the base decorated with loving couples and decorative sculptures near the top. Inside the hall, some of the columns are round with parallel longitudinal grooves, a narrow neck bearing a square, decorated top and abacus supporting beams on short brackets. Some similar square columns are plain. The brackets of the façade row are decorated with superb loving and mithuna couples standing beneath trees in various postures (Fig. 2.57).

Fig. 2.57. Badami. Cave 3. Bracket. Mithuna couple. Ca. 566-597. Sandstone.

Fig. 2.58. Badami. Cave 3. Bracket. Mithuna couple. Ca. 566-597. Sandstone.

One female has entangled her leg with the leg of her lover while holding him by his shoulder. She has placed her other hand on his chest (Fig. 2.58).

Fig. 2.59. Badami. Cave 3. Bracket. Loving couple. Ca. 566-597. Sandstone.

Another beauty is leaning on her lover's chest; her hip has tilted to the side and her body weight has shifted due to her crossed legs. The male holds her by the shoulder and she is balancing herself by holding a rope held by both (Fig. 2.59).

Another is exhibiting all the curves of her body by throwing her hip to one side and shifting her body weight on one leg, leaning on the folded hand of her lover (Fig. 2.60).

Her lover appears to be pulling her by the hand while she tries to pull herself away — all the while looking at him lovingly. Another couple is carved with the female displaying all the curves of her delicate, slim body. A female with long legs is standing with downcast eyes, holding a stick in her hand, with a child standing beside her. When looked at from the other side, the child looks like a monkey standing on his hind legs. All the females carved on the brackets are tall and slim with long arms and legs.

Fig. 2.60. Badami. Cave 3. Bracket. Loving couple. Ca. 566-597. Sandstone.

A superb image of Vishnu with four arms sitting on the coils of a serpent with his head under the naga hoods is carved at the end of the outer aisle (Fig. 2.61).

Fig. 2.61. Badami. Cave 3. Vishnu seated on coiled Sesha. Ca. 566-597. Sandstone.

Trivikrama, the incarnation of Vishnu pacing the cosmos in three steps, is carved in almost three dimensions at the end of extended aisle. Vishnu is surrounded by devotees; and the dead body of King Bali is falling above their heads. On the protruding corner of the cave, Vishnu is standing in all his grandeur. The lion incarnation of Vishnu, Nrsimha, is carved at the end of the second aisle (Fig. 2.62). Worshippers stand near his feet and flying couples hover at the corners. Vishnu is standing majestically with a conch in one hand and a pointed artifact and snake twisted around the other hand.

Fig. 2.62. Badami. Cave 3. Nrsimha. Ca. 566-597. Sandstone.

As the Boar incarnation, Vishnu is standing with one leg on the coils of Sesha and holding a standing Mother Earth in the palm of his hand. The carvings of standing Vishnu are self assertive with inflated legs, oversized arms and erect posture. His jewelry is carved in great detail. The ceiling features intricately carved medallion friezes. In one carving Vishnu, in the center of the medallion, is riding his vehicle, Garuda. He is surrounded by eight guardians of the space (directions) carved inside medallions. Another carving, under the eave of the passage entrance, depicts a seated deity flanked by flying couples. The overhanging eave of the cave has the only remaining patches of original cave painting. The sanctum at the back is decorated with loving couples beside the entrance.

A further climb through a gateway leads to Cave 4. It is a small cave, dedicated to Mahavir. The façade columns in the transverse aisles are decorated similar to the façade columns of Cave 2. The columns inside are decorated with carvings of various Tirthankaras (Fig. 2.63).

Fig. 2.63. Badami. Cave 4. Pillars in mandapa. Ca. 6ᵗʰ Century. Sandstone..

At the end of the aisle is a large panel of a standing Bahubali, with vines entwined on the limbs and thick strands of hairs on his head. Beautiful female worshippers, attendants, and snakes are carved near his leg (Fig. 2.64).

Fig. 2.64. Badami. Cave 4. Bahubali on sidewall.

Ca. 6ᵗʰ Century. Sandstone.

In another carving at the end of the aisle Tirthankara Parshvanath is standing under a naga hood accompanied by an attendant holding a parasol above his head and a devotee seated at his feet. A Tirthankara with a crown above his head is carved standing under an arch (Fig. 2.65).

Fig. 2.65. Badami. Cave 4. Mahavir on sidewall.

Ca. 6ᵗʰ Century. Sandstone.

The arms of the arch are carved horizontally with Jain teachers. The sanctum is enshrined with a meditating Mahavir. He is sitting on a throne with a halo behind his head. A three-tiered umbrella above the head and beautiful attendants holding chamara beside him, and flying figures above, surround the Tirthankara.

The Chalukya constructed five structural stone temples at Badami in the seventh century. The dates of construction are not known with certainty, except for the Jambulinga temple. All the temples at Badami have a high plinth with elaborately carved figures of mostly mythical animals. The temple towers have a limited number of receding tiers and various crowning elements. One of the temples has a north Indian curvilinear temple tower with *amalaka* and *kalasa* as crowning elements. Other extant towers on the temples are a four-sided Dravidian type with a square-to-dome or octagonal-to-dome superstructure, with or without *kalasa*. A brick tower superstructure foreshadowing the future Vijayanagara temples is also seen at Badami.

A group of three Sivalaya temples stands on the North Fort hill (Fig. 2.66).

Fig. 2.66. Badami. Sivalaya temples on North Fort Hill. Ca. 7ᵗʰ Century. Sandstone.

The Dravidian temple style was further developed in Upper Sivalaya, at a temple constructed in the early part of the seventh century. The temple has a molded plinth. Scenes from the Ramayana and the legends of Krishna, including Rama shooting the golden deer and Ravana abducting Sita, appeared for the first time in Indian sculpture on the plinth relief. The exterior walls bear pilasters and a *kaputa* cornice on top. The parapet wall above bears a barrel-vaulted *sala* and square-domed *kuta*. The carvings on the temple exterior walls, set in pilasters, depict Krishna holding Mount Govardhana, Rama subduing Kaliya (the king of serpents) and Nrsimha tearing open the stomach of a demon. The columned mandapa has disappeared. The square sanctum has an ambulatory passage. The imposing massive four-sided tower on the sanctum has a hollow lower chamber and repetitive units above, ending in a square-to-dome superstructure carved with figurative sculpture. The *kalasa* is missing on the tower. Inclusion of a hollow chamber made it possible to construct imposing tall towers; the repeated hollow chambers lessened the weight of the tower on the sanctum.

The Malegitti Sivalaya temple (possibly constructed after Upper Sivalaya) sits on a gigantic weathered sandstone boulder. It has a richly carved front porch, square-columned mandapa with aisles, sloping slab roof and sanctuary without circumambulatory passage. The exterior of the temple is similar to the Upper Sivalaya temple but the parapet wall elements are better articulated. The exterior walls of the mandapa bear sculpted panels and the windows in recesses are surmounted by foliated aquatic monsters. Siva and Vish-

nu are carved between the windows. The super structure of the tower is octagon to dome.

The almost-ruined Lower Sivalaya has a massive four-sided Dravidian tower with two receding units and an elongated-square-to-dome superstructure topped with a kalasa. The superstructure is highly decorated with figure carvings. It bears some resemblance to the tower of the Upper Sivalaya temple.

The Bhutanatha temple, surrounded by structures of later origin, stands in a picturesque locale on the shores of the lake. It was probably constructed in the sixth century. The temple has an entrance porch, square-columned hall, sanctum and pyramidal tower with square, flat tiers with a square-to-dome superstructure topped with a kalasa. The porch with sloping eaves was a later addition. The sculpture on the columns has been mutilated.

Jambulinga temple, built in 699, is hidden behind the dwellings of the modern town. Brahma, Vishnu and Siva were installed in three sanctums with openings to a common large hall with elaborately-carved ceiling panels. The evolution of more than one sanctum in a temple, started in Aihole, matured in this temple with shrines for three gods. Brahma is carved accompanied with a flying couple in the central bay, Siva is carved with Parvati and Nandi on the ceiling in front of the Siva shrine with Lingam. Vishnu is carved with his consort. In addition to the fish wheel, a naga with human upper body and flying couples are carved on the ceiling. The brick tower is disfigured. Brick was used to lessen the load on the tower. Most of the temple towers in Vijayanagara are constructed of bricks.

In the late seventh century, possibly contemporaneous with the Alampur temples, the Chalukya constructed twenty small- and medium-sized temples in a developing Dravidian style at Mahakuta, 5 km (3 miles) from Badami. The residence of a Saint Agastya, who destroyed the legendry demon Vatapi, made the place famous and sacred.

All the temples situated at the base of the hill are enclosed in a compound with a gateway facing east. All the temples are Saivite. Lingams are installed and stored everywhere in the compound. The two medium-sized temples, Mahakuteshvara and Mallikarjuna, and a small, well-preserved Sangameshvara temple face east. Small temples located on the periphery of the compound wall face the tank in the center of the enclosure. All the temples except two have northern-style towers, in contrast to those at Badami. Most of the temples are of later origin and some utterly neglected temples have dark interiors. The exterior walls of some temples are carved with beautiful sculptured panels.

A large tank in the center of the complex, surrounded by a low parapet wall, has a continuous supply of water from a natural spring (Fig. 2.67).

Fig. 2.67. Mahakuta. Temple tank. Mahakuteshvara & Sangameshvara Temples in background. Ca. 6-7ᵗʰ Century. Sandstone.

The continuous flow of spring water to the tank is channeled to another tank outside the temple complex so that the level of water in the tank remains the same all the time. A small, open square mandapa is constructed in the tank above the water level and installed with a Lingam. Outside the parapet wall of the tank a small circular shrine in the shape of the lingam is constructed. A small window near the top is the only opening in the temple providing light and air to the interior. The floor of the shrine is well below the water level in the tank. At the bottom of the shrine a tunnel dug deep below the standing water level in the tank floods the shrine up to the water level in the tank. Inside the shrine a Lingam is installed above water level, which remains constant, controlled by the water level in the tank. The Lingam can be reached for worship only by swimming through a tunnel connecting the shrine to the tank. Another small, open mandapa beside the tank has an enshrined lingam carved with beautiful female faces on the top.

Mahakuteshvara, a whitewashed temple constructed in the sixth century, is still in use. It has concrete porch of recent origin. The location of the temple in crowded structures around does not permit the front full view of the temple. An inscription dated 601 on column removed to Bijapur Museum, states authority of Mangalesha (579-610) to increase the grant to the temple suggesting that the temple existed before 610. A seated bull in detached pavilion faces the entrance porch. The layout of the temple is similar to the Badami temples. The moldings on a raised basement in addition to chaitya windows are carved with a frieze narrating episodes from the Ramayana (Fig. 2.68).

Fig. 2.68. Mahakuta. Mahakuta temple. Side wall.Ca. 7ᵗʰ Century. Sandstone.

A pierced stone window on the exterior walls allow light to enter the hall and sanctum. The parapet on the wall top bears a *sala* and *kuta*. The exterior walls of the sanctum on three sides are decorated with gods carved in southern-style panels framed in decorated pilasters and a decorative band. A decorated Ardhanari is carved in a niche standing with a trident and a snake wrapped around her waist (Fig. 2.69).

Fig. 2.69. Mahakuta. Mahakuta temple. Sidewall. Ardhanari. Ca. 7ᵗʰ Century. Sandstone.

The sanctum has an incomplete ambulatory passage. The four-sided whitewashed tower with pilaster and parapet elements between stories resembles the towers of the Sivalaya temples at Badami. It has a square-to-dome superstructure and a finial.

Mallikarjuna, a southern-style temple, was possibly constructed after Mahakuteshvara temple, which it resembles (Fig. 2.70). The colonnade wall constructed at the side of the entrance does not permit a full frontal view of the temple. The side walls are carved with Vishnu standing majestically and Ardhanari, short and bulky, with three body bends and four hands. Siva is carved on the left of the façade, standing with a trident. The mandapa has two rows of thick, square, decorated pillars and the sanctum is enshrined with the Lingam. The southern-style four-tiered tower is decorated with kudus, kaputa cornice and pilasters similar to the tower of Mahakuteshvara temple. The tower ends in an eight-sided dome structure, bearing large chaitya windows on four side and a round kalasa above.

Fig. 2.70. Mahakuta. Mallikarjuna temple. Tower.

Ca. 7th Century. Sandstone.

wall bearing vase and foliage decorations. The plinth of the ruined Nandi mandapa in front has a statue of a seated Nandi. The square sanctum follows the porch. The niches on the exterior walls of the shrine bear superb sculptures. The niche on the north is carved with Harihara. Ardhanari, in the west niche, with her pronounced tilt of the hips and body bends is beautifully decorated (Fig. 2.72). Her feminine features contrast well with the male.

Fig. 2.72. Mahakuta. Sangameshvara temple. Ardhanari. Ca. 7th Century. Sandstone.

Sangameshvara, a small, well-preserved temple with minimal carvings, was possibly constructed in the mid-eighth century. It was constructed with a southern-style body and northern-style tower.

Fig. 2.71. Mahakuta. Sangameshvara temple.

Ca. 7th Century. Sandstone.

The molded base is decorated with kudus and kaputa cornice on the parapet wall. The sidewalls bear

pilasters with carvings in between (Fig. 2.71). The temple has a small porch with four decorated pillars with a low parapet

The niche on the south has a carving of Lakulisa, with a graceful, well-proportioned body and erect phallus, standing on a dwarf (Fig. 2.73). Lakulisa is considered the incarnation of Siva.

Fig. 2.73. Mahakuta. Sangameshvara temple. Lakulisa. Ca. 7th Century. Sandstone.

Lakulisa was the founder of the Pasupata sect, with which this shrine may have been affiliated. The curvilinear northern-style tower is crowned with a ribbed *amalaka* and finial. The carving of Gavaska on the front façade of the tower appears to have

been erased. The tower is similar to the towers of the Jambulinga and Kadasiddhesvara temple towers at Patadkal.

The tower of the Bananti temple resembles the tower
of the Upper Sivalaya temple at Badami and may be contemporary to it. The temple is almost unadorned. The four-sided
tower with four tiers is carved with shallow, empty niches
between tiers. The almost-round, ribbed tower with flat top
lacks a finial.

11. CHALUKYA II

The Chalukya, after establishing their rule at Badami, conquered the area surrounding Alampur, Andhra Pradesh during their expansion period and constructed numerous temples around Alampur. These temples, though not well known, are considered finest monuments of the time and have some of the best Chalukya sculpture.

Andhra Pradesh may have been the original home of the Chalukya. Starting with the reign of Vijayaditya (696-733) till the end of the dynasty during Kirtivarman's rule (744-755), the Chalukya constructed nine temples in a group near the southern banks of the Tungabhadra River at Alampur in addition to several other temples in the surrounding area. Three of these may have been built by Vikramaditya (733-744). Kirtivarman (744-755), the last king of the dynasty, possibly continued construction of the last temple, Taraka Brahma, started by Vikramaditya, but could not complete it. All nine temples facing east are dedicated to Siva. Eight of them are located in the dilapidated Fort area and the Taraka Brahma temple is built outside the Fort area.

The Taraka-Brahma is the only temple built in southern style. Perhaps the northern style was preferred due to the broader influence of the north at this time, to which this area was very receptive. All the temples at Alampur, with minor differences, are similar to Sangameshvara temple at Kudaveli, to which Pulakesin II (619-642) made a grant in 637.

The date of construction of all the temples at Alampur except Svarga-Brahma is not known for certain; it is possible that most of the temples were built after the reign of Pulakesin II (619-642), which would indicate that temples of similar design were in existence before most of the Alampur temples were constructed, and the Chalukya continued the legacy of their original homeland.

The original name of the temples is not known. All the temples are collectively called as the Nava (nine) Brahma. In basic layout all the temples in Alampur have a long rectangular mandapa enclosing a sanctum near the rear, with Nandi sitting between the pillars in front of the sanctum in most cases. The layout is reminiscent of the early mandapa temples at Aihole. Most have an front open entrance porch and a few have open or blind porches on the sides. The layout of the temples differs in size, number of pillars and the orientation of pillar rows in the mandapa, presence or absence of a front porch, and side porches with or without entrance.

The exterior walls of the temples have regularly-spaced niches built in the northern style with interlocking half or full *gavaksa* (circular enclosure) decorations. Most of the niches have lost their carvings. The majority of the temple entrance doors are carved with multiple divisions of lintel and jambs, with flying couples on the upper portion of wall. Some temples bear large lattice windows on the side walls, some with entrances.

All the temples except one have northern-style *Vimana* (towers) with four tiers. The towers on two of the temples are missing and the one southern-style tower is dilapidated or was not fully constructed. All the towers have a wagon-roof-shaped extension, the *sukanasa*, at the base of the tower with a circular or horseshoe-shaped blind arch on the façade enclosing a carving of Nataraja. Some towers have lost the carving of Nataraja. Full or half interlocking *gavaksa* (circles) and pieces of ribbed flat stone on the tower add to the beauty. The top of the northern-style towers are decorated with *amalaka*, a flat, almost round stone with ribs carved on the margins and a *kalasa* (a pot-shaped structure) above.

The date of construction is known only for Svarga Brahma, built by one of the sons of Vinayaditya (682-696). The basement of the temple is decorated with geese on blocks and niches. The sculpture on the temple walls includes Siva, Saivite deities with dwarfs, Vedic gods, musicians, dancers, and monster masks. Guardians with clubs flank the entrance doorways. There is an abundance of flying figures on the walls below cornice. Some of the flying figures on Svarga Brahma temple are unique. In one carving a flying couple appear to be making love while in flight.

Visva-Brahma, a massive temple with the tallest tower in Alampur, bearing an empty *gavaksa* on a *sukanasa*, was possibly built in 696-733 during Vijayaditya's reign (Fig. 2.74). The basement is divided into blocks. The central division consists of square blocks with carvings on the front square face. Seated Nandis decorate the roof corners of the temple. There is no front entrance porch. The lintel of the entrance door of the temple is carved with flying man Garuda, and Ganga and Jamuna with body bends decorate the ends of the door jambs.

Fig. 2.74. Alampur. Visva Brahma Temple. Ca. 696-733. Sandstone.

One of the side porches bears a carving of Nataraja flanked with small lattice windows (Fig. 2.75).

Fig. 2.75. Alampur. Visva Brahma Temple. Nataraja in side porch. Ca. 696-733. Sandstone.

Most of the northern-style niches on the exterior walls are empty. The exterior sides and back walls bear blind porches.

Large lattice windows installed on sidewalls provide air and light to the interior. Most of the surviving carvings are of mithuna couples. The mandapa pillars bear some decorative sculpture. The façade of the sanctum is decorated beautifully with Nandi sitting in front. The sanctum is enshrined with the Lingam. The pilasters beside the entrance on top are carved with tall, slender beautiful females with three body bends. The ceiling in front of the sanctum is carved with lotus.

The Vira-Brahma is similar to the Visva-Brahma in layout and decorations, with fewer decorated niches on exterior walls. The majority of the niches are empty. There are no side porches on the exterior walls. Three large lattice window on the exterior wall on each side of the sanctum provide access, light and air to the sanctum area. The interior pillars and ceiling are decorated. The sanctum is enshrined with the Lingam. A sitting bull is positioned in front of the shrine. The tower is stout and comparatively short, with four tiers. The *amalaka* and *kalasa* are missing from the top of the towers.

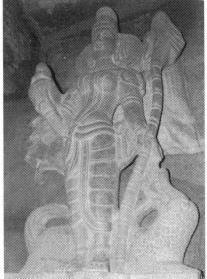

Fig. 2.76. Alampur. Akra Brahma Temple. Rita.

Ca. 7-8th Century. Sandstone.

Some loose sculpture possibly collected from various temples is lying on ground; one of these is perhaps the most beautiful sculpture at Alampur. It depicts Rita, the spouse of Kama (Fig. 2.77). The sculpture embodies a sublime beauty with the ideal feminine body standing on a decorated pedestal. Her curvatures are accentuated by the garment she is wearing. She is sparsely decorated, but wears a high headdress and her abundant hair spreads like a fan beside her head. She is standing in front of a crocodile-like mythological creature near her feet, holding a sugarcane plant in one hand and possibly a sweets-filled pot in another hand.

Fig. 2.77. Alampur. Kumara Brahma Temple. Ca. 7-8th Century. Sandstone.

Akra-Brahma, a copy of Visva-Brahma, was possibly constructed during the reign of Vikramaditya (680-696). The main entrance to the temple bears worn-out door guardians. The tower is lost. The sanctum is enshrined with the Lingam and a seated Nandi in front.

Kumara-Brahma is possibly the oldest temple constructed by the Chalukya at Alampur (Fig. 2.77). The four pillars of the front porch on the upper half are intricately carved. There are large lattice windows on the side wall. Most of the carvings on the exterior are lost. The ceiling is decorated and the sanctum is enshrined with the Lingam, with Nandi sitting in front. The tower, with gentle curves, appears light.

Fig. 2.78. Alampur. Bala Brahma Temple. Ca. 7-8th Century CE. Sandstone.

The Bala-Brahma temple was probably constructed during the reign of Vikramaditya (Fig. 2.78). The front whitewashed mandapa, of recent origin, was constructed using old Chalukya pillars. It two sub-shrines dedicated to the seven

mothers and Mahesamurti flanking the front end. Outside the mandapa on the left a pillar carries an elephant standing on the top. The vestibule and sanctum follow the mandapa. Three niches around the sanctum exterior walls are carved with Parvati, Siva and Parvati and Ganesha. There are four projecting niches and a large lattice window on the exterior walls. The *vimana* bears an elongated *sukanasa* and almost round *amalaka*. On the back of the temple a low wall has two sub-shrines bearing sculptures of Nataraja and Durga. Multi-armed Durga, in three body bends holding weapons and various attributes in his hands, is standing pressing the head of the buffalo demons with one leg and pulling up the tail of the buffalo with his other hand for leverage.

The Garuda-Brahma temple was possibly built during Vijayaditya reign. A modern temple built in front of it hides the full front view and another structure built on the left has covered the face of the left wall. It is very similar to Vira-Brahma, with four decorated pillars in single row on the front porch. The pilasters of the porch are carved with doorkeepers. The highly decorated entrance with a multi-jamb entrance has an image of Vishnu on Garuda on the lintel and Ganga and Jamuna carved with three body bends at the jamb ends. The entrance door to the vestibule bears a flying figure on the lintel. The decorated niches on the temple façade are empty. The *sukanasa* on the northern-style tower bears an empty *gavaska*.

Of all the temples at Alampur, Svarga-Brahma is the most beautiful (Fig. 2.79).

Fig. 2.79. Alampur. Svarga Brahma temple. Ca. 682-696. Sandstone.

An inscription on the temple states that it was constructed in honor of the queen of Vinayaditya (682-696) by one of her sons, presumably in the early eighth century. The temple porch has four pillars in a row on the façade with an entrance between the middle pillars, and a pillar and pilaster on side. The pilasters are carved with doorkeepers standing with clubs.

In addition to Vishnu, Siva and Brahma, Vedic gods like Indra, Varuna, Agni and Vayu are carved on the temple walls. Below the cornice on the exterior walls flying couples are carved. On one side of the temple façade Siva, Vishnu and Brahma are carved in three decorated niches (Fig. 2.80).

Fig. 2.80. Alampur. Svarga Brahma temple. Left temple façade. Ca. 682-696. Sandstone.

Vishnu is carved standing in the central niche holding a conch and chakra. On the left niche Siva is emerging from the Lingam. Three-headed Brahma and Vishnu are carved flanking the Lingam at the top, in the middle, and near the bottom. At the bottom they are carved diving below the Lingam. In the right niche Siva is carved again as Nataraja. The image is badly damaged.

Various small carvings around the niches are lost or partially broken. On the other side of the temple façade Indra is carved standing with a baby elephant in a highly decorated central niche, flanked on one side with Siva living as a beggar in repentance for cutting off the fifth head of Brahma (Fig. 2.81).

On one side of Indra, Siva is carved receiving Ganga on his head. The carving is much damaged and only the presence of the skeletal ascetic Bhagiratha in the lower corner suggests the carving as a depiction of Gangdharmurthi. The broken multiple arms on one side of Siva appear like a spreading wing. A seated Nandi is carved at one lower corner. Another carving depicts a furious six-handed Siva riding the chariot driven by the three-headed Brahma to slay the three demons. The doorway of the shrine has multiple divisions of jamb and lintel. The exterior walls are carved with gods in decorated northern-style niches, interposed with latticed windows, loving and mithuna couples, and flying figures below the cornice. There are three blind porches on the exterior walls surrounding the sanctum. In one of the porches a multi-armed Siva is carved as Nataraja, with a group of musicians playing the drum and flute, accompanying a dancer (Fig. 2.82). Beautiful Parvati with body bends is standing beside them.

Fig. 2.82. Alampur. Svarga Brahma temple. Nataraja carved in side porch. Ca. 682-696. Sandstone.

Fig. 2.81. Alampur. Svarga Brahma temple. Temple façade. Right. Ca. 682-696 CE. Sandstone.

Fig. 2.83. Alampur. Svarga Brahma temple. Carvings on wall. Ca. 682-696. Sandstone.

The next carving depicts a female standing under a tree, holding the trunk of the tree to resist the man who is pulling her toward him. All the while, the expression of love on her face, slight bend of her head in modesty, and her other hand resting on the thigh of the man indicate her deep love for him.

Fig. 2.84. Alampur. Svarga Brahma temple. Carvings on wall. Ca. 682-696. Sandstone.

Another niche is carved with a deity holding a rosary in one hand and an unrecognizable object in other hand (Fig. 2.84). Beside the deity a loving pair is standing side by side. The male is offering food to the female, holding it in his hand near her chin, and pulling her toward him with the other hand. Due to the shift of weight to one leg, resisting the pull by her lover and turning her head towards him with a loving look, the curves of her body have become pronounced. Pulling the lower garment with her free hand to collect herself, as a modest Indian woman does, she further emphasizes the outline of her full round hip and thigh, and has created delicate ripples in the garment. Other carvings of loving couples depict delicate females with body bends in an expression of joy and love.

The interior columns are fluted with vase and foliage motifs on the base and capitals. The *Vimana* appears similar to the *Vimana* of the Galaganatha temple at Aihole. The fully preserved four-sided tower, curving gently inside, is decorated with interlocking *gavaksa* and miniature *amalaka* designs. An enlarged *gavaksa* arch on the *sukanasa* is carved with a dancing Siva. The tower is crowned with an *amalaka* and rod-shape grooved *kalasa*. Many of these features are seen on the dilapidated Galaganatha temple tower at Aihole built in the seventh century. It is possibly that the Alampur temples may have served as models for the Galaganatha and some other temples at Patadkal.

The Padma-Brahma temple is unfinished. It is crowded by other buildings. Possibly it was built in the last years of Vikramaditya's reign (733-744). The next regime, Kirtivarman's (744-755), was not stable and he could not complete the construction; then the dynasty came to an end. Most of the niches are left empty. The grill of the lattice window on the façade is lost. The entrance door is flanked by door guards and a garuda on the lintel of the door. The ceiling is carved with lotus. The sanctum is enshrined with the Lingam, with Nandi sitting in front. The northern-style tower without *sukanasa* and *gavasha*, is well preserved.

Taraka-Brahma, the only southern-style temple at Alampur, may have been built during Vikramaditya's reign (Fig. 2.85). It is located near a Muslim shrine. It has a small entrance porch with one of the pillars of the façade missing, a very small vestibule with Ganesha carved on the entrance lintel and an empty shrine. There are three empty niches on the outer walls. The square tower with two tiers is dilapidated. A large shoe-shaped *sukanasa* on the tower is carved with a sitting Siva in the company of males and females. On this southern-style temple for the first time a *sukanasa* appeared. It was copied on two other southern-style temples at Patadkal.

Fig. 2.85. Alampur. Taraka Brahma temple.

Ca. 733-744. Sandstone.

About 2 kilometers (1.2 miles) from Alampur is a temple locally called the Sangameshvara temple (Fig. 2.86).

This unique and beautiful temple stands on an elegantly carved platform, about 1.5 m (4. 5 ft.) high, reached by a flight of steps. The Nandi mandapa in front of the temple appears to be reconstructed. The plinth of the temple was possibly discovered buried, and restored.

Fig. 2.86. *Kadlur. Sangameshvara temple. Ca. 6th Century. Sandstone.*

Fig. 2. 87. *Kadlur. Sangameshvara temple. Façade of temple. Ca. 6th Century. Sandstone.*

A parapet wall of about 0.7 m (2 ft.) height constructed on the margins of the platform encloses the temple in an outer circumambulatory passage. On the right front corner of the parapet is an oblong shrine with a vault roof decorated with a cornice and *sala*. The platform side walls all around are carved with *kudus*, *sala* above, and divided in bands below. The bands are carved with deities and animals. The façade of the temple is carved intricately. *Kubera* flanks the temple entrance (Fig. 2.87). The sloping roof of the temple is in three tiers. The four-sided, four-tiered tower has gentle curves; it lacks a *sukanasa*. The *amalaka* is almost round with a *kalasa* similar to that of the Svarga-Brahma temple. The interior of the mandapa bears decorated pillars. The pilasters flanking the sanctum entrance are carved with doorkeepers. The sanctum with Nandi sitting in front and an enshrined Lingam is similar to the sanctums in the other Alampur temples.

The windows on the exterior walls are carved in geometric designs and enclosed in beautifully decorated niches between short pilasters. A niche with a window bearing a swastika design is carved above with elephant heads holding round pots in their trunks, giving a bath to Lakshmi sitting

below (Fig. 2.88). The bodies of the elephants are carved in a beautiful foliated pattern. A band of dancers is carved above.

Fig. 2.88. *Kadlur. Sangameshvara temple. Temple wall. Window. Ca. 6th Century. Sandstone.*

Another window with a fish circle is decorated with peacocks with beautiful foliated tails drinking water from a fountain. There are many such attractive niches carved around the temple. Most other niches are carved with deities. The carving of Siva as Aghora-Bhairava (Angry Siva) is dramatic. Ten-armed Siva with fangs protruding from his mouth and a skull on his headdress is standing, feet set apart, holding a trident with a human impaled on it (Fig. 2.89). Most of Siva's hands are broken, but in one hand he holds a snake.

Multi-armed Siva as naked Nataraja is carved in one niche. All his hands are broken. He appears calm and unaware of his surroundings, absorbed in the dancing (Fig. 2.90).

A band of dancers is carved above. Ardhanari has three heads and four arms, and short legs. The large tilted hip of Parvati, also on short legs, does not look natural. Her upper body is no different from Siva's except the breast and large earring. The side head of Ardhanari is not distinct. Siva is standing with his hand resting on Nandi.

Siva as Lakulisa with stout body and short legs is standing with erect phallus, holding his hand in a protection gesture. Durga and other deities are also carved in the niches.

A group of interesting shrines called the Papanasanama is located across the riverbed two kilometers (1.2 miles) from Sangameshvara temple (Fig. 2.91).

Fig. 2.89. Kadlur. Sangameshvara temple. Temple wall. Siva impaling demon. Ca. 6th Century. Sandstone.

Fig. 2.90. Kadlur. Sangameshvara temple. Temple wall. Nataraja. Ca. 6th Century. Sandstone.

One may be bewildered by the sight of some 20 small and medium shrines of various shapes and designs intermingled in a small area. Some shrines are one-celled, some have a mandapa and some have a mandapa and tower. Some cells have a partition inside. Some are double shrines and some are

triple shrines sharing a mandapa. There are northern, southern, *kadamba, visra, gopura* (or oblong-shaped) towers, their height varying from four to six flat steps or four tiers. The shape, size and thickness of the crowning elements vary immensely. Some shrines have Nandi sitting on the mandapa roof corners and some have Nandi in front of the sanctum. Some shrines have door guardians standing in front. All the shrines are installed with deities and are currently in use. The majority are dedicated to Siva as Lingam. Other shrines are dedicated to Ganesha, Seven Mothers, Vishnu, Lakshmi, Hanuman, Naga Raja and Durga.

Fig. 2.91. Kadlur. Papanasanama Temples. Ca. 7-8th Century CE. Sandstone.

In one shrine Durga is carved killing the buffalo demon (Fig. 2.92). Her trident has pierced the back of a human hip and Durga is apparently holding the severed buffalo head by a horn. Her Vahana, the lion, is standing behind.

It is hard to understand the reason for constructing such a diverse group of shrines in a confined area. It cannot have been experimental, as most of the shapes and sizes of these shrines were already in existence. One probable factor could be that the spot is popular with families, devotees of various gods, who come to bathe in the small stream, picnic, worship their gods, and spend some leisurely time together enjoying the company and the cool shade of the shrines and trees while the children play. Still, that does not seem sufficient explanation.

A little distance from this group a shrine was reconstructed from stones collected from rubble. The sanctum is empty.

After the open mandapa of the early temples was enclosed in walls, as in Lad Khan temple, the development of the basic internal units of temple took place inside the shell of the mandapa at Aihole. Some efforts to arrange the basic units of the temple in linear fashion outside the mandapa were made at Aihole, Badami. This divergent development took distinct separate lead at Alampur and Patadkal.

At Alampur all the units of the temple except the entrance porch were enclosed in the shell of the mandapa. The need for circumambulation of the sanctum was accomplished by the addition of two rows of pillars forming a nave and aisles and extending the mandapa with additional pillars on the back of the sanctum, where the aisles served as a circumambulatory passage. Additional subsidiary shrines were added in the mandapa of some temples.

Fig. 2.92. Kadlur. Durga in a Papanasanama shrine. Ca. 7-8ᵗʰ Century. Sandstone.

This design had architectural and aesthetic limitations. Large temples could not be built without the addition of more pillars, which makes the interior resemble a maze.

At Patadkal the arrangement of basic units of the temple in linear fashion with the mandapa as a second unit took a firm lead and the complex design of modern Indian temples took shape. This design facilitates development of large, grand temples as the size of the individual unit can be varied to some extent and decorations can be added to each unit to one's heart's content. With different styles of decoration on the exterior wall and a different shape of towers, northern- and southern-style temples came into being. The design developed and perfected at Alampur had reached a dead end.

Fig. 2.93. Patadkal. Temples at Patadkal. Ca. 7-9ᵗʰ Century. Sandstone

Patadkal stands on the banks of the Malaprabha River a few km. down stream from Aihole. Vijayaditya, Vikramaditya and Kirtivarman II built the temples at Patadkal in a short period of about 50 years, from 696 to 745. In the second half of the eighth and the ninth centuries, the Rashtrakuta built a few temples with plain exteriors. The Chandrasekhara temple in the archeology compound and the Jain temple near the village were built by the Rashtrakuta after the collapse of the Chalukya. Patadkal was the Chalukya royal commemorative and coronation site. The evolution of various styles of temple tower and Dravidian decorations on temple walls, started in the sixth century at Aihole, and continued in Badami, Alampur, and Mahakuta, reached a climax at Patadkal in the latter half of the eighth century. Aihole contributed the basic internal design of the temple, with the decoration of south Indian temple walls and the curvilinear northern-style tower. The pyramidal superstructure and the exterior design of the south Indian temple were finalized at Patadkal and the temple was made a complete entity.

The archeology compound near the village of Patadkal has a group of eight medium and large temples surrounded by clusters of small minor shrines on the banks of the Malaprabha River (Fig. 2.93). Of the four large temples at Patadkal, the Papanatha temple in northern style is the largest; it is located outside the archeology compound. The Virupaksha, Mallikarjuna and Sangameshvara, the other three temples, are Southern in the architectural details of base molding, pilasters, corbels and temple tower. The Virupaksha and Mallikarjuna temples were the largest and most decorated temples of the time.

Minor shrines in the northern style were constructed during the seventh and eighth centuries. Some distance away from Patadkal village is a Jain temple.

A brick temple foundation discovered during an archaeological dig in 1960 near the Sangameshvara temple in the compound possibly belongs to the Early Chalukya period. None of the extant temples at Patadkal predate the Western Chalukya dynasty. Western Chalukya architecture reached

its culmination at Patadkal, and the temple building activity continued even after the fall of Early Western Chalukya. All the temples face east and are dedicated to Siva. Fine-grained gray-yellow sandstone from the nearby hills was used for the temples. Some artists at Patadkal have signed their work.

The Sangameshvara temple is possibly one of the earliest temples constructed at Patadkal by Vijayaditya (696-733), and left incomplete after his death (Fig. 2.94). The rectangular temple in Dravidian style has a molded base decorated with elephants. There is a spacious high platform in front of the temple. Possibly, the original spacious mandapa on a platform collapsed and the present mandapa with two rows of four plain pillars were added during the Rashtrakuta reign. The stairway to the mandapa was completed on only one side. The exterior temple walls bear southern-style niches. Some of the niches bear windows with lattice or geometric designs.

Fig. 2.94. Patadkal. Sangameshvara Temple. Ca. 696-733. Sandstone.

The niches on the antechamber walls are empty, but the niches on the sanctum wall are carved with deities. The cornice above the walls and a small parapet wall above the cornice bears *sala, kuta* and *kudu kaputa* projections. The vestibule has two empty minor shrines, possibly meant for Ganesha and Durga. Two doorkeepers guard the sanctum with clubs. The sanctum is enshrined with a square Lingam and is surrounded on three sides by a passage with windows on each side. The four-sided 16 m (50 ft.) high tower has two stories. The short wall between the stories is decorated with pilasters and sculptured panels. The tower is topped with large *kuta* roof with pot-like *kalasa*. There is no *sukanasa*. A broken stone pillar near the temple bears an inscription giving information about Vijayaditya and Vikramaditya. The plinth of the dilapidated mandapa in front of the temple has a mutilated Nandi.

The Galaganatha temple is similar to temples in Alampur, suggesting it was constructed at the end of the seventh cen-

tury; that would make it the earliest monument constructed in Patadkal (Fig. 2.95).

Fig. 2.95. Patadkal. Galaganatha Temple.

Ca. 7-8th Century. Sandstone.

A broad platform in front of the temple suggests inclusion of a large mandapa in the plan to envelop the sanctum with an ambulatory passage, like the temples in Alampur. As the exterior walls of the hall were not built, the temple now consists of the sanctum with an ambulatory passage on the back and sides with sloping slabs roof. There were three porches on the ambulatory passage's exterior walls. Only one porch on the south has survived. The basement of the platform on the north bears pilasters carved with Lingams and a few spouts in the shape of the *makara* mouth. The Lingams are lost. The entrance door to the sanctuary is decorated with flanking pilasters, Nataraja on the lintel and beautiful river goddesses standing under trees with body bends at the base of doorframe. A black stone Lingam is installed in the sanctum. On one side of the sanctum the broad passage has a porch. The two front columns of the south porch are carved with vase and foliage motifs. On the back wall of the porch, a carving of multi-armed Siva, standing with trident impaling a man, is flanked by windows carved with triangular perforations (Fig. 2.96).

The niches on the outer walls of the sanctum are empty. The well-preserved 15 m (41.5 ft.) high square tower has three projected bands on each side. The damaged portion of the tower façade, showing a hollow interior, was possibly the façade projection representing the *sukanasa*. The central projected bands on the tower have miniature *gavaksa* with human faces in the center, with additional half-*gavaksa* motifs added in the lower tiers. The outer bands are carved with tiers of eave-like moldings decorated with *gavaksa* alternating with *amalaka* pieces. The tower is topped with a big round ribbed *amalaka* standing on a drum base and *kalasa* with a coconut on the mouth of the *kalasa*.

Fig. 2.96. Patadkal. Galaganatha Temple. Porch. Siva impaling demon. Ca. 7-8th Century. Sandstone.

The Kadasiddhesvara temple is possibly one of the early temples built in the first decades of the eighth century during the reign of Vijayaditya. It is the first temple located near the entrance of the archeology compound. The temple stands on a high basement (Fig. 2.97).

Fig. 2.97. Patadkal. Kadasiddhesvara Temple. Ca. 697-734. Sandstone.

The basement of the sanctuary is carved with pilasters flanking carvings of, for the most part, badly worn Lakuli-

sas, recognized by the locks of hair. The exterior walls of the sanctum are decorated niches with full and interlocking half *gavaksa* in a northern-style niche carved with Harihara holding an axe and conch, and a beautifully decorated Ardhanari standing with tilted, voluptuous hips (Fig. 2.98). She is holding a flower in her hand. Siva is resting his hand on Nandi standing beside her. This may be one of the best carvings of Ardhanari. The decorated façade of the sanctum entrance with obliterated carvings on the doorframe is guarded with two doorkeepers holding clubs. The *sikara* has ten tiers of diminishing size. *Amalaka* pieces at the corners alternate with two tiers carved with *gavaksa*. Each tier bears a projection in the center, with badly worn sculpture. The façade of the tower on the east is carved with a large *gavaksa* arch on the bottom two tiers, with a dancing Siva in the center. The top three tiers are flat squares. The *amalaka* and finial are missing.

Fig. 2.98. Patadkal. Kadasiddhesvara Temple. Ardhanari. Ca. 697-734. Sandstone.

Jambulinga temple, constructed in the first decade of the eighth century, is located behind the Galaganatha temple (Fig. 1.99). It appears similar to Kadasiddhesvara. The basement of a dilapidated pavilion in front of the temple has a statue of Nandi. The basement molding is carved with dwarfs, birds and few Lingams on the topmost mold.

The exterior walls of the sanctuary are carved on the south with Siva holding an axe in his left hand, Vishnu with a disc and conch on the north and a faded Surya on the west. The doorframe of the sanctuary is flanked with round pilasters; the sculpture on the doorframe has been obliterated. A black stone Lingam is enshrined in the sanctum, which lacks a circumambulatory passage. The tower, similar to the tower of Kadasiddhesvara temple, has a pronounced horseshoe-shaped arched projection on the east façade carved with the image of Nataraja, accompanied by Parvati and Nandi.

Fig. 2.99. Patadkal. Jambulinga Temple. Ca. 8th Century. Sandstone.

Papanatha, the largest temple in northern style, incorporates some southern-style elements. It is situated adjacent to the Archeology compound (Fig. 2.100). It was possibly constructed in the early eighth century during the reign of Kirtivarman II (745-757).

Fig. 2.100. Patadkal. Papanatha Temple. Ca. 745-757. Sandstone.

The original temple probably consisted of small rectangular mandapa with four sixteen-sided columns, a sanctum with northern-style tower and Nandi mandapa in front. Later the mandapa was dismantled and a larger mandapa was constructed to include a circumambulatory passage around the sanctum, similar to Galaganatha temple, in the complex. Shortly thereafter another larger outer mandapa was constructed, enclosing the Nandi, and the two mandapas were joined making the combined mandapa disproportionately long compared to the height of the tower.

As the temple stands on the bank of the river, it was raised on a 2 m (6 ft.) high platform of stone blocks, facing the river, with opposing steps climbing to the temple. The entrance porch with opposite balcony seats is supported on two intricately decorated pillars bearing loving couples, a horse-headed female and two pilasters (Fig. 2.101).

Fig. 2.101. Patadkal. Papanatha Temple. Entrance porch. Ca. 745-757. Sandstone.

Only one doorkeeper leaning on his club has survived beside the lavishly carved mandapa entrance. The southern-style multi-faceted basement is decorated with foliage in the recesses and lions attacking elephants on the front entrance porch basement. The exterior walls have thirty-four niches projecting slightly from the walls and reaching the *kaputa* cornice. The niches have pilasters on either sides, carrying part *gavaksa* in complex designs above, flanked by flying figures. Some of the niches have beautifully carved windows and intricate floral designs and deities, interposed by beautiful females standing in three body bends. An exterior porch is carved with deities in the niches and on the column (Fig. 2.102).

Fig. 2.102. Patadkal. Papanatha Temple. Exterior. Porch. Ca. 745-757. Sandstone.

A large number of panels are carved with scenes from the Ramayana and the Mahabharata, narrating the episodes of the conquest of Lanka by Rama and the boar hunt by Arjuna and Siva, and the handing over of the magic axe by Siva to Arjuna. Other wall sculptures depict Yama on the buffalo, Brahma, Varuna and Indra on an elephant, Krishna holding Mount Govardhana in hand, Ganesha and Durga, Trivikrama and Vishnu riding Garuda. The exterior walls of the ambulatory passage has three porches.

The outer large mandapa has four rows of four massive columns. A finely polished Nandi, facing the sanctum, is sitting in the passage at the entrance of the mandapa. The central two rows of pillars are sixteen-sided, with females carved on the base. The capitals of the columns bear foliage motifs and brackets with *yalis* and monster masks. Beams carrying the sloping slabs of the roof are carved with dwarfs, garlands, and images of Siva and Parvati. The beams of the passage near the sanctum are carved with figures emerging from the open mouth of the *makara* (Fig. 2.103) and intricate decorations. Amorous couples are carved on the pilasters on the interior walls. The mandapa ceiling is carved with a number of reliefs including Siva dancing in the company of Parvati, and musicians, and Siva dancing with a trident. Parvati, carved in ideal feminine beauty, is standing with three body bends (Fig. 2.104).

Fig. 2.103. Patadkal. Papanatha Temple. Decorated beams. Ca. 745-757. Sandstone.

Fig. 2.104. Patadkal. Papanatha Temple. Nataraja on ceiling. Ca. 745-757. Sandstone.

Decorated niches on the middle of the mandapa interior walls are carved with Ganesha and Durga killing the human-shaped buffalo demon. A Man-Garuda is carved on the door lintel of the second mandapa. Doorkeepers are carved on the pilasters flanking the entrance, holding clubs. The four decorated columns of the second mandapa are similar to the aisle columns of the first mandapa. The decorated façade of the sanctum is carved with a Garuda on the lintel, round pilasters on each side, and Ganga and Jamuna accompanied by females in body bends. A black stone Lingam on a pedestal is enshrined in the sanctum. The tower resembles the towers of Kadasiddhesvara and Jambulinga temples and may have been constructed around the same time.

Lokamahadevi, the queen of Vikramaditya II (696-745), constructed the Virupaksha temple to commemorate her husband's victory over the Pallava. The military campaign with Pallava ended in 745, so that this temple must have been constructed in the second half of the eighth century. The name of the master architect, Gunda, is carved on the mandapa and many artists have signed their creation. This is the best preserved, largest and (originally) the most ornate temple of its time in India. The floor plan of the temple is similar to the Kailas temple at Ellora. The similarity ends with there, as the two structures are fundamentally different. All the units of the temple are aligned on an east-west axis. The rectangular temple stands in a paved court enclosed in a wall with two entrances, one opening to the Malaprabha River on the east (Fig. 2.105) and other, smaller gate on the west.

Fig. 2.105. Patadkal. Virupaksha Temple. East entrance gate. Ca. 8th Century. Sandstone.

The entrance porch with high balcony seats is supported on two pillars and two pilasters. A large weathered Nandi is located in front of the east entrance porch. It appears to be a later addition. The side walls of the porch are decorated with shallow niches with eaves above, with carvings that are now faded. Above the eave the walls are carved with temple models flanked by seated worshippers and a band of dwarfs. Below the deep eave, on top of the wall, friezes are filled with garlands and the parapet wall above is decorated with *kuta* and *sala*. The compound wall around the temple has small, dilapidated built-in sub-shrines facing the temple. The enclosure wall interlocks with the enclosure wall of the Mallikarjuna temple; part of the wall is missing, leaving a gap on the north. The entrance porch leads to an open yard with a large, open, square Nandi Pavilion (Fig. 2.106).

Fig. 2.106 Patadkal. Virupaksha Temple. Nandi mandapa. Ca. 8th Century. Sandstone.

Fig. 2.107. Patadkal. Virupaksha Temple. Apsara. on Nandi mandapa pillar. Ca. 8th Century. Sandstone.

The pavilion stands on a 2.5 m (8 feet) high basement with a flat roof supported on four circular pillars. It is lavishly decorated both inside and out, with beautiful females on the walls and pillars, including a graceful female in three body bends feeding a bird from her hand (Fig. 2.107). A 2 m (6 ft.) tall polished black stone Nandi is seated in the pavilion facing the temple.

The temple stands on a high platform surrounded by small shrines (Fig. 2. 108). The entrance porch on the east has decorated the eaves and balcony seats. Doorkeepers guard the entrance to the temple. The exterior walls have pierced windows decorated with attractive floral designs set in niches that admit light and air to the interior. Niches

with huge panels are flanked by slender pilasters. There are some niches above, with short cornices decorated with *kudus* enclosing Nataraja, human heads or group of men. Some niches are carved above with Lakshmi seated on a lotus and elephants pouring water on her, with graceful trailing vines, or flying couples. Some niches are carved below with friezes of animals. Thirty-five niches on the exterior walls bear elaborately dressed images.

Fig. 2.108. Patadkal. Virupaksha Temple. Ca. 8th Century. Sandstone.

Fig. 2.109. Patadkal. Virupaksha Temple. Right façade. Ca. 8th Century. Sandstone.

On the right side of the porch, Vishnu as Trivikrama is carved in a niche decorated with *makaras* bearing foliated tails on one side of the mandapa entrance and Vishnu standing with a conch and wheel interposed is standing between the windows carved with fancy designs (Fig. 2.109). On the other side, Nataraja is dancing on a dwarf and Siva is standing with Parvati, with one leg on Nandi (Fig. 2.110).

On the east wall of the mandapa, Siva is carved emerging from the Lingam. The Lingam, fringed with flames, is flanked by Vishnu at the bottom and a three-headed Brahma near the top (Fig. 2.111). The niches are decorated with peacocks bearing foliated tails, Lakshmi bathed by elephants, and flying males.

Fig. 2.110. Patadkal. Virupaksha Temple. Temple left façade. Ca. 8ᵗʰ Century. Sandstone.

The next niche, decorated above with flying figures, is carved with Siva standing on a dwarf. The niches are flanked with windows with delightful designs installed between. The corresponding mandapa wall on the other side has a carving of Nataraja on a dwarf and Siva and Parvati standing with pierced stone windows interposed (Fig. 2.112).

Fig. 2.111. Patadkal. Virupaksha Temple. Porch side view. Entrance Ca. 8ᵗʰ Century. Sandstone.

Fig. 2.112. Patadkal. Virupaksha Temple. Carvings on exterior wall. Ca. 8ᵗʰ Century. Sandstone.

The side walls of the mandapa are carved with Siva standing with Nandi. Ardhanari, with her tilted hip, carved in a beautifully decorated niche, has physical features not much different from those of Siva except for her breast. In other carvings Siva is standing in a regal pose, as an ascetic standing with matted hair, with one leg on a dwarf, while above beautiful females are riding *makara*. In other niches Vishnu, in regal pose, is standing with his emblems and as a boar he is standing with one leg on the head of Sesha, carrying Mother Earth on one arm. One carving depicts Siva standing with a trident impaling a human. To the side a panel is carved with episodes from the Ramayana, depicting Ravana kidnapping Sita. He is brandishing a sword at Jatayu while Sita stands in the racing chariot. This is followed by an embracing mithuna couple, the female entangling her leg with the male's. Attractive full-bodied highly decorated damsels with body bends are carved in panels around the temple. A full bodied *apsara* stands, looking into a hand-held mirror (Fig. 2.113). A tall, slim female with broad hips and body bends is holding a staff with elephant carved at the top (Fig. 2.115).

Fig. 2.113. Patadkal. Virupaksha Temple. Carvings on exterior wall. Apsara looking in mirror. Ca. 8ᵗʰ Century. Sandstone.

Fig. 2.114. Patadkal. Virupaksha Temple. Carvings on exterior wall. Apsara holding staff. Ca. 8ᵗʰ. Century. Sandstone.

The three side porches on the exterior wall bear decorations on the side walls and on the ceilings, with Nataraja in the center flanked by old sages and females. The side porches, with columns and balcony seats, admit light and air to the interior.

The large square mandapa has four rows of four columns and two more columns at the sanctum entrance. All the columns in the center of mandapa are lavishly decorated with friezes, one below the other, narrating episodes from the Ramayana and the Mahabharata. Columns near the walls are carved with loving and mithuna couples. The interior of the east porch is decorated with celestials. One west porch column is carved with Surya driving a chariot. The south porch column is carved with Ravana with one of his multiple faces on the back, a twisted body and feet sinking into the ground while lifting the Kailas in one of his multiple hands (Fig. 2.115).

Fig. 2.115. Patadkal. Virupaksha Temple. Carvings on exterior wall. Ravana lifting Kailas. Ca. 8ᵗʰ Century. Sandstone.

The twisted body of Ravana and a hotchpotch of figures on the mountain lack expression and drama. An antechamber leads to the square sanctum guarded by Siva. The sanctum door is flanked by profusely decorated pilasters with river goddess at the bottom. Ceiling is decorated with Siva dancing on dwarf. The sanctum is enshrined with a polished black stone Lingam. Two small minor shrines with decorated entrances flank the sanctum entrance. A circumambulatory passage around the sanctum begins at the right of one shrine and ends at the left of the other. The south shrine is dedicated to Ganesha, but the slab carved with Ganesha has been removed. The north shrine contains a majestic sculpture of Durga killing the buffalo demon. Her trident has pierced the neck and the sword has pierced the chest of the demon. In early carvings, the demon killed by Durga were carved as a buffalo, later changed to a human with buffalo head. In this sculpture the demon is carved as human with buffalo horns.

The highly decorated four-sided small tower has three receding tiers. The walls of the lower two stories are carved with projecting pilasters bearing the *kuta-sala-kuta* sequence. The third story has walls with pilasters and eaves decorated

with *kuta* only. The *sukanasa* with a vaulted wagon roof on the façade of the tower is carved with a temple model. A large square *kuta* decorated with *kudus* on all sides adorns the top. Above the square *kuta* a pot-like finial stands at the height of 17.5 m (54 ft) above the ground, making this the tallest Chalukya tower.

The beautiful stone windows on the walls, relief carvings on the columns, and decorated beams are highlights of Chalukya architecture. The sculpture is soft and lyrical compared to that at Ellora. The temple is contemporary to the Kailas temple at Ellora. Patadkal, for a short period, was under the rule of the Rashtrakuta king, Krishna, who built the Kailas temple at Ellora.

The second queen of Vijayaditya (696-733) was a sister of the first queen, who built the Virupaksha temple. This compact temple is similar to Virupaksha but is advanced in style and was left unfinished. The interlocking of the compound wall with the gap between the compound walls of the two temples indicates that this one was possibly built after the Virupaksha temple. The east gateway may never have been constructed. Part of the west gateway has survived. A damaged Nandi mandapa, standing on a raised, molded basement decorated with animal friezes, features two green, unfinished Nandi; it is located in front of the temple (Fig. 2.116).

An extended porch on the front façade rests on two short and robust decorated pillars. The walls are carved with females in various postures. The sculpture at one corner depicts two beautiful *apsaras* in interesting poses (Fig. 2.117). Both decorated females with body bends are standing under a tree. The posture of the female standing in side profile, with her upper body turned to face the front, is unique. Shifting her body weight onto one leg, she has pushed out her torso out of the niche frame.

Fig. 2.116. Patadkal. Mallikarjuna Temple. Nandi mandapa. Ca. 8ᵗʰ Century. Sandstone.

Fig. 2.117. Patadkal. Mallikarjuna Temple. Carvings on Nandi manda-pa wall. Ca. 8th Century. Sandstone.

The style of her hands resting on her thigh is aristocratic, telling everyone, "I am beautiful and I know it." The pose of the tall, delicate, highly decorated soft-bodied female standing with one leg resting on a tree trunk behind her is very attractive and is unique in the placement of a draped garment between her legs. She is holding a bird in her hand.

Fig. 2.118. Patadkal. Mallikarjuna Temple. Ca. 8th Century. Sandstone.

The temple stands on a basement decorated with a molding (Fig. 2.118). Most of the sculpture and its placement on the exterior walls are similar to the sculpture in the Virupaksha temple, as is the entrance porch, which is likewise badly damaged. Many beautifully-designed stone windows are broken.

There are 27 niches on the exterior walls with decorative carvings above and below. Seven of the panels are empty and seven bear incomplete images. There is no sculpture on the east side of the temple. On the exterior walls a standing Siva, with right hand in a protection gesture, and Ardhanari, are carved in the windows. Ardhanari's half body again shows little differentiation from Siva's, as it lacks curves aside from the slightly bulging hips and large, pimple-like breast. An-

other niche is carved with a standing Siva, and robust Parvati with body bends.

A flying couple carved on the exterior wall is more interesting (Fig. 2.119). The flying pair is carved as a ship sailing on water. The legs of the male are carved in the shape of a boat. He is holding a dish in one hand, heaped with sweets. The female is heavily ornamented and is holding a flower bud in her hand. Usually, the females are carved with a small piece of garment or floating hair to indicate the forward movement of the couple. In this case the female is resting on the bent leg of the male, which resembles a spar on a sail boat. The carvings behind the female appear like a sail decorated with flower petals. Her folded hand resting on the shoulder of the flying male in front has dragged one of her breasts to rest on the shoulder of the male. She looks like she is steering the ship.

Fig. 2.119. Patadkal. Mallikarjuna Temple. Flying couple on exterior wall. Ca. 8th Century. Sandstone.

The porches of the temple are similar but smaller than the porches of Virupaksha. The columns of the east porch are carved with an eight-armed Nrsimha killing two victims at a time and Siva holding a trident and snake. The south porch is badly damage. The better-preserved north porch columns are carved with images of Vishnu on Garuda, lovers, and mithuna couples. Siva with his trident and clubs is carved on the pilasters flanking the entrance.

The interior of the mandapa is similar to but smaller than the mandapa of Virupaksha. Most of the carvings on the pillars are similar to the carvings on the Virupaksha temple. The story of the seduction of Ahalya by Indra, from the Panchtantra, can be seen on the columns. Ahalya was turned into stone after Indra seduced her and made love to her. Vishnu brought her back to life, eons latter. The carving of Durga advancing on a lion to kill the demon is a copy of the carving at Mamalapurum.

Nataraja with Parvati and Nandi, a naga with a coiled tail and elephants giving a bath to Lakshmi are carved on the ceiling. Mithuna couples are carved on columns near the walls. Minor shrines flanking the sanctum door, now empty, were possibly dedicated to Ganesha and Durga killing the demon. The ceiling of the antechamber is carved with Siva and Parvati, with other celestials. Doorkeepers flank the sanctum. The entrance is carved with decorations and man-Garuda in the center of the lintel. A black stone Lingam is enshrined in the sanctum. The ceiling of the sanctum is carved with lotus. The highly decorated pyramidal tower is similar to the Virupaksha temple tower.

The design and layout of the South Indian temple was now complete. By the addition of repetitive units, height was achieved (within certain limits in various regions). The addition of local decoration gives a regional flavor to various examples. Most of the decorative designs of these temples were evolved at Mamalapurum.

Near the end of their reign the Chalukya concentrated again on the construction of northern-style temples.

Fig. 2.120. Patadkal. Kashivishvanatha Temple.

Ca. 8th Century. Sandstone.

The Kashivishvanatha temple was probably constructed near the end of the eighth century. It is situated very close to the Mallikarjuna temple. The enclosure wall stops short of the Mallikarjuna temple façade. A dilapidated Nandi mandapa with plinth and worn down, squatting Nandi stands in front of the temple. The high molded plinth of the temple is decorated at the top with vine decorations. The exterior surface of the temple has a varying number of projection running from thte plinth to the top on the sanctum, vestibule and mandapa. The projections from the sanctum wall continue

on each side of the tower. The highly decorated curvilinear tower ends in a frieze carved with miniature pilasters under the flat top. The *amalaka* is missing. The square tower has five bands of decorations on each side; the central broad band is flanked two narrow bands on each side. All the bands are carved with interlocking *gavaksa*, giving a mesh appearance to the tower.

The bands at the corners of the tower are decorated with small *amalaka* pieces, cornices, and *gavaksa* arches. On the façade of the tower the broad central band composed of four bands of *gavaska* arches and large chaitya window above is carved with Nataraja accompanied by Parvati. The chaitya window is beautifully decorated with beaded garlands and flying figures on the side and above. The flanking chaitya windows with images of gods are not complete.

The entrance façade of the shrine is decorated with three bands of foliations on the jamb and a beautiful Ganga and Jamuna accompanied by mithuna couples at the jamb base. The lintel of the door is carved with man-Garuda. Flanking the entrance are decorated niches carved between sets of pilasters, with eaves above. The carvings in both niches are broken. There is a band of sculpture above the eave. The small rectangular ornate mandapa has four pillars with sixteen sides. The pillars are carved with stories from the life of Krishna and various incarnations of Siva. Siva and Parvati with Kattrikeya in her arms are carved in the center of the ceiling. The entrance to the sanctum, flanked by doorkeepers, is decorated like the temple entrance. Beautiful Ganga and Jamuna, with delicate bodies in three body bends, at the jamb base, are accompanied by two equally beautiful females. One of the females is holding a parasol above the goddess. A black Lingam on a pedestal is enshrined in the sanctum. Miniature Dravidian-style temples are carved on the east wall of the sanctum and a lotus is carved on the ceiling.

Chandrasekhara, a small temple, was constructed during the Rashtrakuta period in the late eighth or the ninth century (Fig. 2.121). It is located between the Galaganatha and Sangameshvara temples. This is the only temple inside the archeology compound constructed by Rashtrakuta. The characteristic feature of the Rashtrakuta temples are the few carving of figures on the walls, the decoration of the temple façade with slender pilasters carrying modeled capitals and brackets, and a porch with squat circular columns and brackets. The plain entrance to the shrine is flanked by pilasters. An antechamber with niches on the side walls is carved with a relief of *sala*.

On the sanctum walls, a pair of *makara* is carved on the brackets of the central pilasters. The sanctum is enshrined with a Lingam. There is no superstructure on the shrine.

Fig. 2.121. Patadkal. Chandrasekhara Temple.

Ca. 8-9ᵗʰ Century. Sandstone.

The Jain temple, constructed in typical Rashtrakuta style in the ninth century, is located some distance away from Patadkal village. The temple stands on a modeled basement with no decoration at all on the exterior walls except between the closely-set pilasters (Fig. 2.123).

Fig. 2.122. Patadkal. Jain Temple. Ca. 9ᵗʰ Century. Sandstone (Photo taken from Album of the Archeological Survey of India on site).

Fig. 2.123. Patadkal. Jain Temple. Dismantled porch. Sanctum in the rear. Ca. 9ᵗʰ Century. Sandstone

The front porch has been dismantled for reconstruction. The spacious porch had twelve circular squat columns, and a life-size front half of an elephant with riders flanking the door to the vestibule. The plain entrance to vestibule of the dismantled temple is carved with *makaras* with exaggerated foliated tails (2.123). There was no figurative carving any-

where in the temple, except a Jain figure in the *kuta* of the *kaputa* cornice on the north side. The one-chambered tower with *kuta* roof decorated with *kudus* on four sides and plain pilasters on the exterior walls has been dismantled for renovation. The outer circumambulation passage around the detached sanctum is not enclosed. Roof slabs from the sanctum project over the passage. The elephants and columns have been removed for renovation of porch and are kept in front of the temple for latter installation (Fig. 2.124).

Fig. 2.124. Patadkal. Jain Temple. Dismantled Elephant. Ca. 9ᵗʰ Century. Sandstone.

The temple building activity of the early Chalukya ended at Patadkal, where the finest of the Chalukya temples were constructed.

12. THE CAVES AT ELLORA
(550 –950)

The Ellora caves were excavated from 550 to 950. They are located 28 km (17 miles) from Aurangabad in central India. There are no lodging and boarding facilities at Ellora but Aurangabad is a convenient base, offering boarding and lodging and convenient public transportation to the site. UNESCO declared the monuments at Ellora World Heritage Monuments in 1983. At Ellora there are Hindu, Buddhist and Jain caves; they reached the climax of development as well as the demise of the cave-carving trend altogether.

The Buddhists had adopted many Hindu temple features at Aurangabad and refined them at Ellora. Many of the changes Buddhism was undergoing under the Mahayana influence are seen at Ellora. Tantrism and the carving of sensual females became prominent, and female deities like Tara and others similar to the Siva Shakti were more often seen. New groups of Buddha and additional shrines were added to existing caves. The stupa lost its original form. The façade of the stupa was occupied by an arch with Buddha seated below. The superstructure appeared like a round pot above the arch. The shrine, under Hindu influence, was detached from the rear wall with a well-defined circumambulatory passage at Aurangabad, but multi-armed goddesses appeared for the first time at Ellora.

The Buddhist excavated grandiose three-storied caves. Though Buddhism did not die out at this time, it appears to have been suppressed by the Hindu Rashtrakuta dynasty in the south. The political and social control of Indian society by Buddhism came to an end in the seventh-eighth century.

Cave 12 is the last and most elaborate vertical cave excavated at Ellora, and with it the era of cave excavation in India by Buddhists came to an end. Each storey of the cave is larger than any single cave at Ajanta. The Moslems' burning of libraries and monasteries, and the prosecution of monks — the nucleus of the Buddhist organization and guardians of Buddhist beliefs — drove them to other lands where Buddhism was flourishing.

The Hindus modified the cave designs evolved by the Buddhists to meet their needs. By this time the freestanding stone structural temple had evolved. The Hindus radically changed the cave, but at first were unable to shake off the cave design altogether. The cave was started as a monolithic structure; the roof was torn open and the fully developed temple was liberated from the dark constraints and exposed to sunlight. The process of liberation of the temple from confinement was started with the three entrances of the Siva cave at Elephanta, the open courtyard of the Buddhist Cave 12, the open courtyard with a monolithic hall in Cave 15 and finally the roofless Cave 16. Cave 16 appears more like an open pit with a monolithic temple sitting in it. In place of residential cells on the side walls, colonnades with galleries were excavated. The Hindus did not excavate important caves after that, although some small minor caves were still carved during the next couple of centuries.

The Chalukya had developed freestanding stone structural temples that could withstand centuries of nature's destructive forces outside the caves, so that it was no longer necessary to confine the temples to caves in hilly regions. In addition, providing residence for monks was not a major function of the Hindu cave.

Hindu royalty began to act as patrons sponsoring the construction of religious monuments, and temples flourished. The caves lost importance and the era of cave excavation by Hindus, Buddhist and Jains was over by the end of the eleventh-twelfth century.

But before then, craftsmen well experienced in cave excavation at Ajanta, and their descendants, created 34 caves at Ellora in the basaltic volcanic outcrops of the Sahyadri hills. The excavation of caves at Ajanta had practically ceased by this time. The technique for excavating the Ellora caves was similar to the technique used at Ajanta. The first 16 caves are in a row and the remaining caves are spread in small groups over an area of about 2.2 km (1 mile) to the north. The caves are given numbers in standing sequence rather than according to the date of excavation. The first twelve caves, located at the south end, are Buddhist Mahayana viharas except Cave 10, which is a chaitya cave. The remaining caves, numbers 13, 14, 15 and 16 of the south row, are Hindu caves. At the north end, in small groups, there are 13 Hindu caves. The last caves, a group of 5, are Jain caves.

It was earlier believed that Buddhists excavated Caves 1 to 5 in the first phase in the fifth century during the Vakataka regime. Some of the early caves excavated at the south end have unfinished sculpture, possibly indicating that the patronage abruptly came to a halt, as in Ajanta, due to the abrupt end of the Vakataka regime.

During the sixth century the Chalukya seized control of the southwestern Deccan, with Badami as their capital, and during their regime in the seventh and possibly the first part of the eighth century the rest of the eight Buddhist Mahayana caves were excavated, in line with the previous caves. Hindus excavated caves starting in the latter part of the seventh and the eighth century. M.K. Dhavalikar states that recent research suggests Buddhists excavated Caves 6, 5, 2, 3 and 1 in the right wing of the south end starting in 600, and after a century of work, in around 700, excavation stopped with numbers 4, 7, 8, 10, 9, 11 and 12 at the south end. The Chalukya ruled this region during the sixth and seventh century CE.

Hindus started the excavation of Caves 28, 27, and 19, followed by 29, 20, 26 and 21, in 550, earlier than the second set of Buddhist caves in the left wing of the south end. The style and volume of the figures in Caves 29 and 21 show the influence of Kalacuri art. Cave 21 has possibly the best sculpture in Ellora and Cave 29 resembles the Siva cave at Elephanta in both the style of sculpture and the layout. All these Hindu caves are scattered north of the Buddhist caves in small groups in an area of about 2.2 km (1 mile).

The Rashtrakuta, feudatories of the Chalukya, seized power from them in 752; they moved the capital to Ellora and then to Paithan, near Ellora, and remained in power till 973. Staunchly Hindu, the Rashtrakuta dynasty excavated the re-

maining Hindu caves (13, 14, 15, and 16) in line with the Buddhist caves at the south end. The order of excavation of the Hindu caves was possibly 28, 27, 19, 29, 21, 20, 26, 17, 19, 18, 14 and 16 (Kailas). Kailas, the last cave, was excavated during 750-800.

Both the Hindus and the Buddhists were busy excavating caves in the seventh century. The Buddhists stopped this work by the start of the eighth century; the Hindus worked vigorously in the eighth century and stopped after the excavation of Cave 16 in 783. A couple of minor groups of cave temples were excavated in the eleventh and twelfth century. In the ninth century, during the reign of Rashtrakuta ruler Amoghavarsha (819-881), a great patron of Jains, the Jain excavated five caves at some distance from the Hindu caves, in a group at the north end. The Jains ceased excavating in the early tenth century. It is interesting to note that Jain caves are located in association with Hindu caves in all the religious centers, indicating the cardinal relationship between Jains and Hindus. Possibly in the twelfth century the Ganesha Lena caves, located 100m above Cave 29, were excavated, with images of Ganesha, Siva, Vishnu and Brahma. Yageshvari, the last group of small cave shrines, is located further up. Siva as Trimurti is carved in one shrine. None of these shrines have sculpture of much artistic value.

Lay Buddhist worshippers sponsored the Buddhist caves. The Kalacuri, Rashtrakuta and possibly Chalukya were the patrons of the Hindu caves. The Rashtrakuta king Amoghavarsha was a probable patron of the Jain caves. Jains by their religious beliefs are restricted to professions in trade and they are a rich community; they may also have contributed to the finances. All the Buddhist caves, and some of the Hindu and Jain caves, were decorated with paintings but these have faded. A few faded murals on the ceiling of Cave ceiling and patches of paintings in Hindu Cave 16 have survived.

Fig. 2.125. Ellora. Caves 1-5.

Ca. Early 7th Century. Basalt.

Fig. 2.126. Ellora. Cave 2. Façade.

Ca. Early 7th Century. Basalt.

The early Buddhist caves, 6, 5, 2, 3, 1, were excavated during 600. Caves 1-5 are located at the start of the south group (Fig. 2. 125). Cave 1, a monastery with a dilapidated verandah and eight residential cells on the side walls, was possibly an experimental cave.

Fig. 2.127. Ellora. Cave 2. Tara. Ca. Early 7th Century. Basalt.

Cave 2, a large cave with verandah, is reached by a flight of steps (Fig. 2.126). In a small shrine at one end of Cave 2, in the verandah, pot-bellied Jambhala, the guardian of treasure, is seated, possibly holding a lotus in one hand, attended by a *chamara* bearer. A bag of money is lying near his other hand. He is wearing a decorated headdress. The façade of the cave is decorated with small figures of Buddha and others. Two huge guardians, possibly Avalokiteshvara and Vijarapani, wearing jewelry and with halos behind their elaborate headdress, flank the entrance door. On the other side of the verandah there may have been another shrine, which has collapsed. The square hall inside has twelve massive pillars and galleries on the opposite side. There is a carving of a sensual Tara holding a lotus in one hand and the other hand in a protection gesture, with two female attendants flanking her and flying figures in the corners (Fig. 2.127). A highly decorated Vijarapani stands in similar niche. Each cell in the side wall is decorated with a seated Buddha flanked by *chamara* bearers. Some of the carvings are unfinished.

On both ends of the back wall is a double cell aligned with the side aisles, with several figures of Buddha. The shrine guarded by Avalokiteshvara and Vijarapani has a colossal image of a seated Buddha on a lion throne with hands in preaching gesture, flanked by Tara and possibly Avalokiteshvara holding a *chamara*, and flying Vidyadharas. There are no residential cells in the cave and possibly it served as shrine for meditation.

Fig. 2.128. Ellora. Cave 3. Verandah chapel. Buddha. Ca. Early 7th Century. Basalt.

Cave 3 is a Vahara with residential cells in the side walls. The cave has a verandah with a chapel on the left side with an image of Buddha seated cross-legged in the witness-calling position, on a lotus flanked by *chamara* bearers (Fig. 2.128). Nagas holding the stalk in their hands support the flower above by their hoods. The chapel on the right side of the verandah has collapsed. Near the cave entrance Avalokiteshvara is carved. He is the protector of travelers. He is surrounded by eight small carvings depicting travelers facing the perils of the journey (Fig. 2.129). He is holding a lotus bud with a long stalk. The carving is similar to carvings in Cave 8 at Aurangabad, but not as sophisticated. The square hall of the cave has twelve square pillars with square shafts. There are five residential cells on the left side wall and four on the right; a fifth cell was destroyed when the chapel on the right collapsed on the verandah. There are two cells in the back wall flanking a shrine with an unfinished image of seated Buddha.

Fig. 2.129. Ellora. Cave 3. Avalokiteshvara. Ca. Early 7th Century. Basalt.

Cave 4, a vihara, is smaller than Cave 3 but has two stories. The façade pillars carved with pot-and-foliage motifs and the façade are badly damaged. The square hall has unfinished cells. On the left Avalokiteshvara is seated, a halo behind his head, on a throne, with a small image of Buddha in his crown. He is holding a rosary and lotus in his hands and is flanked with by female attendants. One of the attendants, holding a lotus in hand, is possibly his spouse Tara. Above, to the left, Buddha is standing with his hands held in a protection granting gesture. Two pillars are in front of the vestibule. The shrine on the rear wall flanked by guards has a seated Buddha with his hands in a teaching gesture. Tall attendants and a female *chamara* bearer flank Buddha. To the west of the cell door Avalokiteshvara is standing. On both ends of the back wall is a cell. A small shrine in the cave houses Avalokiteshvara. Four small carvings on one side depict devotees praying to him for protection from assault, a man holding a sword, imprisonment, and shipwreck. The upper storey has no direct passage, but it connected with Cave 5 on the south. It is depilated. Only a few cells have survived. The shrine on the back wall has an image of a seated Buddha with attendants, and a circumambulatory passage. Sensual Tara, with her ideal feminine body posed in body bends, is standing with a lotus in her hand, flanked by female attendants and Vidyadharas (Fig. 2.130).

Fig. 2.130. Ellora. Cave 4. Tara. Ca. Early 7th Century. Basalt.

Fig. 2.131. Ellora. Cave 5. Hall. Ca. Early 7th Century. Basalt.

Cave 5 is a large vihara with a rectangular hall 35m (109 ft.) deep (Fig. 2.131). The façade of the cave was destroyed, possibly by landslide. Two rows of eight massive square pillars near the side walls and two rows of four pillars near the front and back end surround a deep rectangular hall in the center. The pillars have square shafts and cushion capitals. Two long rows of low stone benches are carved in the center of the hall. Monks possibly used the benches to sit and chant Tantric ritual recitations. On the rear wall Buddha is seated on a throne, his hands in a teaching gesture and legs resting on a lotus in the main shrine. A highly ornamented Avalokiteshvara and Vijarapani with crowns and halo behind their heads guard the entrance. Small residential cells are cut into the side walls along with two spacious and better-planned additional shrines in the center of the side walls. The side walls are carved with highly decorated niches, some of them featuring images of Vijarapani and Avalokiteshvara holding a lotus attended by females with body bends.

All the remaining Buddhist Caves were excavated during 630-700 (Fig. 2.132).

Fig. 2.132. Ellora. Caves 6, 7 and 8. Ca. 630-700. Basalt.

Cave 6 is reached by descending a few steps. The façade is totally destroyed. Only a square hall with three cells on the back wall has survived. The vestibule is decorated with the Buddhist goddess of learning, Mahamayuri (Fig. 2.133). She is very dignified and beautiful, but not as beautiful as in Cave 6. She is carved with an idealized feminine body without body bends. She is attended by a female on one side. On the other side a pupil sitting below the spread tail of a peacock with a writing tablet in front. There are flying Vidyadharas in the upper corner. The Vidyadharas are mostly carved single, not as pairs. There is another image, possibly of Bodhisattva Manjusri, carved on the wall. He wears a deerskin on his left shoulder. In the main shrine a seated Buddha is flanked by attendants and devotees. Small images of Buddha flanked by attendants and devotees are carved on the side walls.

Fig. 2.133. El-
lora. Caves 6.
Mahamayuri.

Ca. 630-70. Basalt.

Fig. 2.135. Ellora. Cave 8. Façade. Ca. 630-700. Basalt.

Cave 7, a dilapidated vihara, has a hall with four pillars decorated with bracket figures.

Fig. 2.134. Ellora. Cave 7. Maitreya Buddha.

Ca. 630-700. Basalt.

Two of the five cells in the cave are incomplete. The future Buddha, Maitreya, is standing in royal pose with folded hands and slightly flexed body, guarding the shrine (Fig. 2.134). There is a halo behind his beautiful headdress.

Cave 8, with two stories, was possibly excavated around 700 (Fig. 2.135). The façade of the ground storey bears incomplete carvings on one side. The ground storey is incomplete and the cave resemble Hindu Cave 14. The entry to the first storey is through a tunnel from Cave 7. The two pillars and pilasters are decorated with carvings. The façade of the first storey is carved with a row of seated Buddha and above with chaitya windows occupied by seated Buddhas in three rows and other standing figures. There are three cells on the left wall of the hall. Carvings of Buddha figures adorn the walls of the hall. Side wall has an image of a seated Tara. The vestibule is pillared. The main shrine, surrounded by circumambulatory passage, has the image of Buddha detached from the rear wall and is guarded by Avalokiteshvara holding a lotus, and Vijarapani.

The southern end of the ambulatory passage is carved with an image of Mahamayuri (Fig. 2.136). Her carving is not as attractive as the one in Cave 6. She is attended on one side by a beautiful *chamara* bearer and on the other side by a peacock carved in profile and a pupil seated on the ground with a writing tablet.

Fig. 2.136. El-
lora. Cave 8.
Mahamayuri.

Ca. 630-700.
Basalt.

Cave 9, tentatively dated to 700, is dilapidated. A band on the façade is carved with small figures of Buddha and the Bodhisattvas, above which are chaitya windows carved with Buddha figures. The façade has an unusual carving of the Goddess Tara rescuing devotees from the perils of a journey. This is the only depiction of the Tara litany in India. A chapel on the back wall is carved with Buddha, seated, with hands in a teaching gesture, on a throne, with Vidyadharas in the corners (Fig. 2.137).

Vijarapani and Avalokiteshvara, in the company of male and female attendants, flank Buddha, standing in niches with pillars with cushion capitals.

Fig. 2.137. Ellora. Caves 9. Side chapel. Ca. 630-70. Basalt.

Fig. 2.138. Ellora. Cave 10. Façade. Ca. 630-700. Basalt.

trance on the ground floor leads to a high, spacious, apsidal chaitya hall divided into central nave and side aisles, supported by pillars carved with hunting scenes and Buddha, with his hands in a preaching gesture, flanked by attendants and dwarfs. The roof is carved with rafters imitating the wooden beams of south Indian huts. The stupa at the far end has a huge carving of Maitreya Buddha, seated on a throne, his hands in a teaching gesture, under an arch covering the front face of the stupa (Fig. 2.139).

Fig. 2.139. Ellora. Cave 10. Stupa. Ca. 630-70. Basalt.

Cave 10, excavated in the early eighth century, is the only chaitya at Ellora (Fig. 2.138). It is the last chaitya excavated in central India.

The entrance to the cave was through a gateway in the front rock screen wall, now broken. The gateway with a few steps leads to a spacious, open courtyard and pillared verandah on either side. The back walls of the verandah on both sides have unfinished chambers, possibly intended as subsidiary shrines. At the far ends of the verandah, on the back walls, a single cell and another cell on the right of the first cell were possibly intended as shrines. The pillars of the corridors have massive square shafts with vases and foliage carved on the capitals. A flight of steps from the verandah leads to the upper storey, which is similar to the chorus gallery of a modern church. The parapet wall of the gallery at the base is carved with herds of various animals. Above the animals a band is carved with seated figures.

It has the smallest chaitya window known. The window is flanked by flying *apsaras*, small figures and sculptural decorations. At one corner of the gallery Avalokiteshvara is carved, standing in a decorated niche with attendants. At the other end a similar niche has a carving of Vijarapani. The en-

He is flanked by two attendants, possibly Avalokiteshvara and Vijarapani. A Bodhi tree and *Vidyadharas* are carved on the arch. The umbrella on the top of the stupa has been replaced with a structure resembling a round pot.

Fig. 2.140. Ellora. Cave 11. Shrine in verandah. Broken statue of Buddha. Ca. 630-700. Basalt.

Caves 11 and 12 are the largest Buddhist vihara caves, excavated with three stories, in the seventh century. The entrance to both caves is through a gateway cut through a rock screen in the front leading to a spacious rock-cut court. The floor level of Cave 11, buried in debris accumulated over the centuries, was exposed during 1876-1877 cleanups. Several sculptures, in caves used by all the three religions while Aurangzeb was Mughal viceroy of Deccan at Aurangabad, were mutilated and broken by Muslims. A statue of Buddha, with a broken head and damaged arm, is located in a verandah shrine (Fig. 2.140).

Cave 16 (Kailas) was the most damaged. To the left of the court in a shrine near the near entrance is a shrine with Avalokiteshvara seated cross-legged. Tara and four-armed Bhrikuti are seated on either side (Fig. 2.141).

Fig. 2.141. Ellora. Cave 11. Shrine in verandah. Goddess with four arms. Ca. 630-700. Basalt.

Another four-armed goddess, Chunda, is carved on the left wall. Another shrine had a statue of Buddha flanked by the Bodhisattvas. The Rashtrakuta carved the Hindu gods Ganesha and Durga on this wall. The ground floor has a long, pillared verandah and a shrine in the back wall with a Buddha figure flanked by Padmapani and Vijarapani. To the left of the shrine is another cell. In the left hand corner, a cell with a staircase leads to the first floor.

The first floor has a long, pillared hall with five cells on the side wall. The first cell is incomplete. The last cell has a rock-cut bed. The remaining three cells house Buddha, attended by the Bodhisattvas. There are three shrines on back wall. The first cell is unfinished. The next cell has a small shrine with a huge image of a seated Buddha with hands in a gesture of calling the earth to witness, flanked by Padmapani and Vijarapani. A devotee is prostrated before Buddha. A female figure facing Buddha and holding a pot in her hand may represent Sujata. Buddha practiced extreme austerity and

self-mortification, eating only roots and fruits for six years. Sujata offered him his first solid food when he decided to give up self-mortification. On the left wall of the shrine, seated Bodhisattvas are carved. Maitreya Buddha with a miniature stupa in his crown, the Bodhisattvas Sthirachakra, holding a flag, and Jnanaketu, with a pennant, can be recognized among the group. Above the carving are Buddha figures. To the left of the entrance are Jambhala and a man holding a pot full of gold coins. To the right is goddess the Tara, holding a lotus. The central shrine has a colossal image of Buddha with hands in a witness-calling gesture flanked by Bodhisattvas.

The next shrine is similar to the main shrine. A small cell next to the shrine, at the end of the verandah, has a rock-cut bench and a small shrine with a seated Buddha flanked by three females on one side and three male Bodhisattvas on the other side. At the left end of the verandah a staircase leads to the top floor with a pillared verandah and a shrine in the center of the back wall, similar to the shrine on the first floor. A shrine in the northeastern corner has an image of Buddha with attendants. Another shrine in the southern half is left unfinished. On the walls are many figures of Buddha, and Avalokiteshvara attended by a female with four hands.

Fig. 2.142. Ellora. Cave 12. Ca. 630-700. Basalt.

Cave 12, the last Buddhist vihara with three stories, excavated under a single unified plan, is dated to 700 (Fig. 2.142). It is largest cave at Ellora, with each floor larger than any cave at Ajanta. It accommodated forty monks. A gateway cut through a rock screen (now broken) leads to a spacious open court at a slightly higher level. The austere, 15.2m (46 ft.) high façade belies the wealth of sculpture and decoration inside (Fig. 2.143).

The few ground floor façade pillars are carved with decorative sculpture featuring a pot motif. Some façade pillars of the upper storey are carved with beautiful females with three-body bends (Fig. 2.144).

Fig. 143. Ellora. Cave 12. Façade.
Ca. 630-700. Basalt.

Fig. 2.144. Ellora. Cave 12. Sculpture on 3rd floor façade pillar. Ca. 630-700. Basalt.

Fig. 2.145. Ellora. Cave 11. Ground floor. Shrine wall. Buddha surrounded by Bodhisattvas. Ca. 630-700. Basalt.

The ground floor is 35m (107 ft.) wide and 13m (40 ft.) deep, with three rows of eight pillars each on the horizontal axis of the hall. The central two rows of pillars continue in the antechamber, which is almost as long as the hall. There are nine panels representing the magic diagram of the cosmos. Eight seated Bodhisattvas are carved in separate squares, arranged around Buddha in the center, accompanied by a *chamara* bearer (Fig. 2.145). Bodhisattvas that can be recognized include Avalokiteshvara, Vijarapani, and Sthirachakra holding a flag, Jnanaketu with a flower stalk in the left hand, and possibly Manjusri. The attributes held in the hands are not clear. A corresponding space on the other side is carved with a seated Buddha, now mutilated. Buddha seated on a lion throne is carved on the left and right sides of vestibule, each accompanied by a female on his left, holding a lotus. Pilasters on the side walls are carved with Buddha, the four-armed goddess Chunda holding her hands in a protection-giving gesture, a bowl, rosary and lotus stalk. Another similar carving shows Chunda holding a ladle in place of the lotus stalk, along with another goddess. The shrine doors are carved with Maitreya holding a flower and Manjusri holding a flower on a book. In the shrine, a colossal image of a seated Buddha is enshrined. The shrine walls are carved with several seated meditating Buddhas and Bodhisattvas covering most of the walls. There are twelve cells in the hall. The first cell in the south wall has a staircase leading to another chamber near the first floor. The chamber is carved with several sculptures including a seated Buddha with attendants, Avalokiteshvara with a male and female attendant, and some small carvings along with a four armed-goddess, possibly Bhrikuti.

Fig. 2.146. Ellora. Cave 12. First floor. Padmapani with Tara and Jambhala. Ca. 630-700. Basalt.

A further climb leads to the first floor with a long verandah with entrances to the hall near each end and a large entrance in the center with two massive pillars. The central hall is 35m (107 ft) wide and 21.3m (65 ft.) deep, with two rows of eight pillars on the horizontal axis dividing the hall into three aisles. Small cells are cut on the back and side walls of the hall. The aisle in the center of the hall leads to the antechamber and shrine. The wall facing the shrine has two cells. The shrine in the rear wall has a small antechamber housing an image of Buddha flanked by three Bodhisattvas on each side. The walls of the vestibule are carved with Avalokiteshvara with female attendants, a stupa, four-armed Bhrikuti, and Avalokiteshvara with Tara and Jambhala (Fig. 2.146).

Avalokiteshvara holding a lotus, and Vijarapani, holding a thunderbolt and wearing elaborate jewelry, flank the shrine door. Inside a seated Buddha is flanked by Avalokiteshvara, Vijarapani, and Sujata holding a pot. An attendant is standing over a prostrate figure. Above, on the wall, seven seated Buddhas are carved.

Fig. 2.147. Ellora. Cave 12. Top floor. Manusi Buddha. Ca. 630-700. Basalt.

The long verandah outside at both ends provides access to the ground floor. In the north end of the verandah a staircase leads to the top floor, which is fully finished. It consists of a spacious hall, a vestibule and a shrine in the back wall. The spacious hall is divided into five bays, by five rows of eight massive square pillars. Two pillars and two pilasters separate the vestibule from the hall. The sidewalls of the hall have large sculptured panels of a seated Buddha with attendants. On the south end of the back aisle a large panel is carved with Buddha in a preaching gesture. The corresponding position on the opposite aisle is carved with Buddha going to heaven to preach the Law to the gods and entering Nirvana. The back wall of the hall on the left side has six manusi Buddha (Buddhas re-incarnated in a cosmic period) and Buddha seated under the particular sacred tree under which they achieved enlightenment (Fig. 2.147). On the right side sit seven Bodhisattvas, their hands in a teaching gesture and a parasol over their heads (Fig. 2.148). They are Vairochana, Akshobhya, Ratnasambhava, Amitabha, Amoghasiddhi, Vijarasattva and Vajraraja. In the vestibule side walls are

twelve goddesses seated on lotus wearing halo behind their heads, including various representations of Tara on one side and Bhrikuti, Pandara and Tara on the other. On the right side of the back wall is a goddess wearing snakes around her waist, and a headdress. Next to her Mahamayuri, with peacock feather in hand, is followed by a goddess holding a water vessel. The image of Buddha in the shrine was adopted for worship as a Hindu god after obliterating the facial features. This was restored in plaster in the eighteenth century. Buddha is flanked by Padmapani holding a lotus and on the other side a male holding a sword, one holding a *Chamara*, and a devotee. Above on each side are seated Buddhas. On the inner side of the front wall is the donor couple holding a sack of money. A human-sized image of Buddha and a Bodhisattva in the antechamber and the shrine surrounding a devotee possibly make him feel more humble than if he were standing surrounded by the paintings.

Fig. 2.148. Ellora. Cave 12. Top floor. Seated Bodhisattvas with parasol over head. Ca. 630-700. Basalt

The next four caves in line with the Buddhist caves are Hindu caves. These are the last Hindu caves excavated, although the date of excavation of Cave 13 is not certain. It is a small, plain hall, almost totally dilapidated.

Fig. 2.149. Ellora. Cave 14. Durga standing with leg on lion. Ca. 550-750. Basalt.

Cave 14, excavated in the seventh century, is the first cave that introduces Hindu gods. The Hindu gods, active and energetic forces of creation, destruction and preservation, contrast starkly with the calm and peaceful atmosphere of the Buddhist caves.

Cave 14 has a square hall with sixteen pillars with four pillars in row. The pillars and pilasters are lavishly decorated with demon heads, human figures, chaitya arches, floral bands, and peacocks surmounted with humans. At the back is an oblong shrine with circumambulatory passage. The walls of the hall are carved with large, powerful and dramatic carvings, as though in a gallery, in similarly decorated niches. Most of the carvings are damaged or worn, but they still radiate power and energy of the gods. Starting on the left Durga, with a delicate, well-proportioned body, stands with one leg resting on a lion, holding a trident in one hand; all other hands are broken (Fig. 2.149). She has a decorated headdress and a halo.

Beautiful Gajalakshmi, in another niche, is seated on a lotus in a lotus pond flanked by attendants. Two elephants standing in the corners are bathing her, pouring water from pots held in their trunks (Fig. 2.150). One of her attendants has four arms and is holding a conch in one hand.

A damaged panel depicts Vishnu in his boar incarnation. He is standing with one leg on the coil of Sesha. An attendant and possibly the spouse of Sesha, with a cobra hood, are standing alongside. The goddess Earth, with her delicate body, rescued from the cosmic ocean, is standing crossed legged with three-bends on the palm of Vishnu.

Lakshmi, flanked by attendants and seven dwarfs in a panel below. The shrine is located on the back wall guarded by doorkeepers and decorated with Ganga standing on crocodile and Yamuna standing on a tortoise. There is an altar and a broken image of Durga inside. In the north side of the circumambulatory passage are seven mothers, each holding an infant in her lap, followed by Ganesha eating sweets, Kali, and Kala. Beyond are seven mother goddesses with halos behind their heads. Parvati is carved on a pedestal with Nandi (Fig. 2.151), and Lakshmi is shown being carried by Garuda (Fig. 2.152).

Fig. 2.151. Ellora. Cave 14. Parvati.

Ca. 550-750. Basalt.

Fig. 2.152. Ellora. Cave 14. Lakshmi.

Ca. 550-750. Basalt.

Fig. 2.150. Ellora. Cave 14. Lakshmi. Ca. 550-750. Basalt

The next two panels are carved with Vishnu seated with his consorts Sridevi and Bhudevi, with six human figures carved below. In another panel he is sitting with beautiful

Fig. 2.153. Ellora. Cave 14. Nataraja.

Ca. 550-750. Basalt.

Saivite sculpture includes Siva killing the demon Andhaka. When Siva wanted to kill Andhaka, his friend Gajasura attacked Siva in the form of elephant. Siva had to kill Gajasura first. In the carving Siva has spread the skin of Gajasura over his head, stretched by four hands, while with the other hands he is attacking Andhaka. Parvati, Ganesha and a dwarf accompany him. The next panel depicts an enraged Ravana with his multitude of hands shaking Mount Kailas. There is no panic. Everybody is calm, giving a sense that Siva is in control of the situation. The carving is not as dramatic as the one that was to come in Cave 16.

Fig. 2.154. Ellora. Cave 14. Siva and Parvati playing chess. Ca. 550-750. Basalt.

With one hand Siva is holding Parvati's hand; his second hand is resting on his seat, a third is holding the dice and a fourth hand is partially broken. Spectators include Ganesha with his elephant head, two females holding *chamara*, and two males. Below, dwarfs are playing with the Bull, the mount of Siva. Another panel depicts a four-armed Durga killing a demon. She holds a sword, a trident, and the head of the demon Mahishasura in her hands. The fourth hand is broken. The gods created Durga to slay the demon Mahishasura, son of Rambha, who had obtained a boon from Brahma that no man would kill him; that sounded good, but left him vulnerable to being killed by a woman. He was killed by Durga when he became a potent force and started harassing the gods.

Fig. 2.155. Ellora. Cave 15. Monolithic hall in verandah. Ca. 550-750. Basalt.

Cave 15 with two stories is located at a higher elevation. A long flight of steps leads to the spacious open courtyard cut in the rock with the first monolithic pavilion carved at Ellora standing in the center of the courtyard (Fig. 2.155). It may have served as a Nandi pavilion. It has windows cut in a geometric design. A small porch in front of the pavilion was supported on two pillars. The entrance is guarded by a beautiful Ganga on a crocodile and Yamuna on a tortoise. The exterior walls are carved with sculpture and statues. Seated and reclining lions and dwarfs on the roof are broken. The two-storey cave behind the pavilion was started as a Buddhist monastery in the early eighth century. The Rashtrakuta king Dantidurga made a donation while the excavation of the cave was in progress but later the cave excavation continued as a Hindu temple. The modification of the Buddhist cave design by Hindus is evident in the layout. The spacious ground floor of the double-storied cave behind the monolithic hall has fourteen square pillars in two rows of six and two pillars in the vestibule. The interior of the cave has a few sculptures in low relief. The walls surrounding the hall have a few cells indicating the origin of the cave as Buddhist monastery.

Fig. 2.156. Ellora. Cave 15. Carving on pillar. Ca. 550-750. Basalt.

A flight of steps in the southeast corner of the front aisle leads to the upper floor with a spacious hall with forty-four pillars in seven rows of six pillars each and two pillars in vestibule. In the center of the hall are a few pits, which were possibly used to light fires. The front pillars are carved with attractive designs with floral patterns, snakes and dwarfs (Fig. 2.156).

The spaces between the pilasters on the side walls are carved with huge sculptures in bold relief. Large panels on the surrounding walls depict various incarnations of Vishnu and Siva. Siva as Andhakasura is slaying the demon. He has stretched the skin of the elephant over his head with four hands and is thrusting the trident in the neck of the demon. He wears a garland of skulls and sharp teeth are protruding from his mouth. The skeletal Kali is holding a bowl in her hand to collect the blood of the demon. Parvati is standing on one side of Siva. The next panel depicts Nataraja accompanied by musicians, Parvati, and his infant son. In another panel Siva and Parvati are playing chess, watched by Ganesha and other gods. Other panels display the marriage of Siva and Parvati, where Parvati is standing on the left of Siva, three-headed Brahma is conducting the marriage and other gods are witnessing the marriage; Ravana is shaking Kailas. Sculpture on back wall depicts Siva pushing Yama, the god of death, with his leg (Fig. 2.157). A storey in the Puranas states that Markandeya, son of a sage, was great devotee of Siva. At the age of 14 the god of death came to take his soul. But Markandeya clutched the Lingam and did not let it go. Siva emerged from the Lingam and saved his devotee. In the carving the devotee is carved praying to the Lingam, and one leg of the emerging Siva is still inside the Lingam.

Fig. 2.157. Ellora. Cave 15. Siva emerging from Lingam to save his disciple from Yama. Ca. 550-750. Basalt.

The next panel depicts Siva as the bearer of Ganga. In the carving Siva is standing with Parvati on the left and Nandi on the right. Above, an elephant is supporting a lotus with a sage sitting on it. Five human heads are near the feet of Siva. A storey in the Purana narrates that King Sagara had a wicked son, Asamanjasa. He was a bad influence on the other children. The gods complained to Indra. When Sagara was to perform a horse-sacrifice, Indra kidnapped the horse and hid it in the hermitage of Kapila in the netherworld. When the Sagara's sons rushed to kill Kapila, the sage reduced them to ashes. They could be brought back to life only by the waters of Ganga. Bhagiratha, born in the Sagara family, by severe austerities brought Ganga down on the matted hair of Siva's head, and to the earth. When Ganga's water was sprinkled on the ashes of Sagara's sons, they came back to life. Sculpture on the back wall of antechamber depicts the myth that Siva is greater than Vishnu and Brahma. While Siva is emerging out of the Lingam, Vishnu and a three-headed Brahma are searching the bottom and top of the Lingam but both fail to locate the ends. Brahma is carved flying near the upper end of the Lingam and Vishnu is diving below. In another panel Siva is killing the demon Tripurasura. He holds a bow, an arrow, a sword and shield in his hands and is driven in a chariot by Brahma.

The Vaishnava sculpture on the right wall includes Krishna lifting Mount Govardhana to protect the people and cattle in a village of Mathura region from the deluge of rain

sent by Indra. In another carving Vishnu is reclining on the serpent Sesha while a lotus has emerged from Vishnu's navel, bearing a seated Brahma on a lotus flower. Vishnu is also carved riding his mount Garuda in human form. Vishnu as the Boar is shown rescuing the goddess Earth from the cosmic ocean in one panel. The goddess Earth is sitting on one of his arms. Vishnu as Trivikrama follows. King Bali, according to a storey in the Puranas, was a great devotee of Vishnu. Vishnu as a dwarf went to him and asked Bali to give him as much land as he could measure in three steps. Bali granted him his request. Vishnu turned into a giant and covered the earth, heaven and nether world in three steps. In the carving Vishnu is holding his emblem and various weapons in his hands. One of his legs is resting in the heavens. In a man-lion incarnation Vishnu is holding a battle-ax and conch and has caught the demon Hiranyakashipu with his three hands, to destroy him. The carving is vibrant with the forceful action of Vishnu. In the vestibule Ganesha and Parvati, seated on a lotus and holding a rosary, are carved along with musicians. On the opposite wall stands Kattrikeya, son of Siva, holding a bowl, a trident and a lotus beside a peacock. Amorous couples are carved on the pillars. Four-armed guards holding a club, snake and thunderbolt guard the shrine. A Lingam is enshrined in the sanctum. On the side wall Gajalakshmi, seated on lotus, holding fruit and a lotus in her hand, is carved. Elephants are bathing her. Two male attendants hold water pitchers. The one holding a conch, discus and lotus is Vishnu.

Dantidurga, the first Rashtrakuta king (who ended Chalukya rule) made Ellora his capital. He may have started the excavation of Cave 16 (popularly called Kailas) in the middle of the eighth century. It is the largest and most splendid monolithic rock cut Dravidian temple in India.

It stands in a roofless cave. King Krishna I, uncle of Dantidurga, completed the construction in six years from 757-783. A number of subsidiary shrines were added later. Kailas temple appears to be an attempt by the Hindus to surpass the largest Buddhist rock-cut cave in Ellora. They succeeded splendidly. Virupaksha, a structural temple at Patadkal, constructed in 740, superficially resembles Kailas in layout and Jain Cave 32 is a miniature replica of the Kailas temple. The rock cut city of Petra in Jordan is a large enterprise of similar nature.

After excavation of this extraordinary monument, the Hindus apparently lost interest in caves, possibly because there was nothing more to achieve and caves had lost their utility. Freestanding stone structural temples had been evolved that did not require the protection of caves in any part of India. The need to provide a residence for Hindu monks was not as important as it was for Buddhists. After reaching this climax, the Hindus basically stopped excavating caves, although some small cave shrines were excavated later.

Fig. 2.158. Ellora. Kailas Cave 16. Gateway connected on back to Bull pavilion by bridge, seen from mountainside. Ca. 750-800. Basalt.

The caves cut deep into the rock do not provide much exterior surface for carvings. Verandahs added in front would provide limited additional space for decoration. By an imaginative, bold attempt the architects at Ellora isolated an enormous piece of rock near the center of hill, which had gentle slope on one side. Two longitudinal deep trenches cut towards the center of the hill and two horizontal trenches cut to join the ends of the longitudinal trenches isolated what is almost a small hillock in the part sloping towards the front margin. All the trenches were cut to the depth of the surrounding terrain. The floor of the temple courtyard at the rear is 30m (93 ft.) deep and 51m (154 ft.) wide. A comparatively small mass of rock was left outside the front horizontal trench to carve a gateway. The temple and other associated structures were carved out of the large mass of rock commencing from the top and developing into a three-storey high temple, Bull pavilion, two freestanding columns 20m (61 ft.) high, a flanking bull pavilion and two life-size elephants all attached to the mother rock. The rock was cut into small units and both exterior and interior surfaces of these units were decorated with sculpture. The temple is rock sculpture rock on a grand scale, innovative in design.

The mass of rock left outside the front trench was carved into a monolithic gatehouse (Fig. 2.158). The 15m (45 ft.) high façade of the gatehouse is two-storied. The graceful monolithic entrance of the cave is carved with Saivite deities on the left façade and Vaisnavite deities on the right façade of the lower storey. In niches between the pilasters along with a few Vedic gods, episodes from the Mahabharata are carved (Fig. 2.159). Most of the carvings are mutilated.

Fig. 2.159 Ellora Kailas, Cave 16. Façade. Gateway. Ca 750-800. Basalt.

The façade of the upper storey bears a wide balcony window in the center flanked by blank niches. The entrance to the cave in the center of the lower storey is flanked by Ganga and Yamuna and embellished with decorative sculpture. The square chamber in the first storey has raised platforms along the side walls with a passage in between. The margins of the platform bear square pillars with capitals carved with vases and foliage. The back walls are carved with Ganesha and Durga. At the end of the entrance on either side are guardians holding pots of money. The upper storey of the gatehouse is not connected to the lower storey from the chamber. The passage opens to the temple complex surrounded by high walls and colonnades on left right and back of the temple.

Not all the units of the temple are at the same level. The front part of the courtyard is cut deeper, necessitating a few steps to get down into the courtyard from the gateway, possibly because the sloping rock mass remaining was not high enough in front. Inside, the elephants stand at the lowest level, the bull pavilion on a slightly higher level and the main temple stands on the second higher level with a couple of steps leading to the two levels.

In front of the gatehouse is a Bull pavilion (Fig. 2.160). It is 15m (46 ft.) high single-storey flat roof structure resting on a 7.5m (23 ft.) high solid rock plinth. Steps cut through the plinth on the side walls access the pavilion from the courtyard. The solid rock plinth of the pavilion has elevated the pavilions to the height of the upper floor of the gatehouse and is connected by a bridge to the gatehouse upper floor. This bridge provides the only access to the upper storey of the gatehouse. Nandi, the vehicle of Siva, rests on the floor of the pavilion facing the temple. Twenty meters (61 ft.) high. two freestanding columns and monolithic life-size elephants are carved to flank the pavilion. the freestanding columns and elephants are possibly artistic, more than symbolic, motifs. The elephant on the south is mutilated. The pavilion and the huge pillars are profusely carved with images of deities and structural decorations.

Fig. 2.160. Ellora. Kailas Cave 16. Bull pavilion connected to Gateway and Temple by bridges. Monolithic pillar seen from mountainside.Ca. 750-800. Basalt.

Fig. 2.161. Ellora. Kailas Cave 16. Mandapa connected to Bull pavilion in front. Ca. 750-800. Basalt.

Behind the bull pavilion stands the temple, consisting of entrance porch, flat roofed *mandapa*, sanctum and three-storey-high tower (Fig. 2.161). The rock mass left behind the bull pavilion was not wide enough to carve a tower to reach the top of the cave with a proportionally wide sanctum. To push the tower higher and achieve proportional units, the temple was built on 7.5m (23 ft.) high solid rock plinth. The floor of the temple and the bull pavilion in front are at the same level and are connected by stone bridge. The bull pavilion is connected to second storey of the gatehouse in the back and to the entrance porch of the temple in front by stone bridges providing passage from the temple porch to upper storey of the gatehouse. Steps cut through the solid plinth of the entrance porch on both sides provide direct access to the temple from courtyard. Thus from sloping rock mass surrounded by trenches proportional height of the units was maintained between entrance gate and bull pavilion by lowering the floor of the temple behind entrance gate, constructing the bull pavilion on a high plinth and constructing the temple on a high plinth to push the temple tower out of the pit.

Facing the gatehouse entrance on the bull pavilion plinth under the bridge joining the gatehouse is a huge panel carved with Lakshmi seated on lotus flower in a lotus pond covered with leaves (Fig. 2.162).

Fig. 2.162. Ellora. Kailas Cave 16. Lakshmi facing entrance. Ca. 750-800. Basalt.

Two elephants standing in the corners are pouring water on Lakshmi from round pots held in their trunks. Two small elephants are carved beside Lakshmi, holding round pots in their trunks to fill with water from the pond. The panel is flanked by two smiling guardians.

Fig. 2.163. Ellora. Kailas Cave 16. Siva killing Elephant demon. Ca. 750-800. Basalt.

The east face of the bull pavilion plinth is carved with a large panel depicting ten-armed Rudra, an early form of Siva (Fig. 2.163). As Andhakasura, the vector of the elephant demon, he is dancing holding a slain elephant's skin in his hands over his head. He is wearing a garland of skulls like a sacred thread. On one side is the head of the slain elephant and on the other side Parvati is seated. A small carving at the lower left of the panel depicts seven mothers send by gods to suck up blood drop of Andhaka to stop multiplication of the demon. Bhringi is carved near the legs of Siva and Vidyadharas are flying in the upper corners.

Fig. 2.164. Ellora. Kailas Cave 16. Durga fighting buffalo demon. Ca. 750-800. Basalt.

The rear of the front entrance gate wall as seen from courtyard is carved with an eight-armed Durga riding a lion and shooting arrows at the demon (Fig. 2.164). Her graceful and delicate body is more beautiful than the body of Durga carved in Mamalapurum. Riding her fierce lion amidst fallen demons she looks majestic, fearless, dashing and all-powerful. The brute demon with human body and buffalo horns is standing close to her, in front. She is aiming an arrow at the heart of the demon. The lion also appears to be attacking the demon. The gods above are watching the combat. The next series of panels depicts Krishna lifting mount Govardhana, Vishnu and Lakshmi followed by Lakshmi. Kama (Cupid) holding a sugarcane like a flag stands with his consort Rati, followed by Vishnu flying on Garuda (Fig. 2.165). The rear of the screen wall on the other side is carved with Siva impaling a demon, and various avatars.

Fig. 2.165. Ellora. Kailas Cave 16. Gods. Rear wall of Gateway. Ca. 750-800. Basalt.

The last carving of these panels depicts Siva ridding a chariot to kill the demon Tripurasura (Fig. 2.166). Brahma is driving the chariot, which is drawn by four horses. Five more carvings on this side are damaged and are not clear.

Fig. 2.166. Ellora. Kailas Cave 16. Gods. Rear wall of Gateway. Ca. 750-800. Basalt.

The temple consists of an entrance porch, *mandapa* with two side porches, vestibule, a flat-roofed sanctum (Fig. 2.167) and a three-storey high tower (Fig. 2.168).

Fig. 2.167. Ellora. Kailas Cave 16. Decorations on flat roof of all the temple units. Ca. 750-800. Basalt.

Fig. 2.168. Ellora. Kailas Cave 16. Mandapa and Tower on sanctum seen from mountainside. Ca. 750-800. Basalt.

The flat roof the entrance porch supported by two thick square pillars and two pilasters is decorated with lotuses in receding tiers (Fig. 2.161). The plinth of the entrance porch is carved in bands with episodes from Ramayana and Mahabharata and the life of Krishna. On the front of the plinth

Brahma with three faces sits in meditation. The façade of the plinth under the bridge has a gigantic panel depicting Siva as a Yogi, eyes closed, deep in meditation, seated on a lotus throne supported by lions. Many Vedic gods surround him.

The massive plinth of the temple is carved with elephants and lions, some in combat. It appears as though the temple is being carried by the elephants. A sculpture on the front exterior wall of the mandapa depicts Ganga falling from heaven (Fig. 2.169).

Fig. 2.169. Ellora. Kailas Cave 16. Mandapa wall. Siva receiving Ganga on his matted hair. Ca. 750-800. Basalt.

The composition narrates the complete myth with all the characters involved. Ganga is carved as a beautiful female on the top of the panel above Siva, flanked by flying figures and deities. One figure in the upper left corner appears to be standing on one leg, carrying a Lingam on his head. The lower body of Ganga, shaped like the body of a serpent, is falling on the matted locks of Siva and flowing away from the head without wetting him. From the lock of hair she widens and falls in torrents beside the head of a sage, and flows down over the five heads of Sagara's sons to bring them back to life. Bhagiratha, whose penance succeeded in bringing down Ganga from heaven, is carved kneeling before Siva. Beautiful Parvati is standing cross-legged beside Siva.

The exterior walls of the temple are carved with many huge panels. One of the masterpieces of sculpture at Kailas, with exceptional dramatic quality, is the legend of Ravana carved on the temple plinth under the south porch of the temple (Fig. 2.170).

The Demon king Ravana with 10 heads and 12 hands is trying to uproot Mount Kailas, the abode of Siva, to throw it like a missile in his battle against Rama (the hero of epic Ramayana). The body of Ravana is detached from the mother rock behind. Only the hands of Ravana, his flat foot and the knee of a folded leg are anchored to the floor to provide the power to uproot and throw Kailas. His twelve hands attached to the walls like the spokes of a wheel exert enormous pressure to shake Kailas off its foundations, making the whole mountain quake. The small platform with seated Siva, Parvati and attendants above Ravana's cage does not appear strong enough to withstand this vigorous shaking by Ravana. Parvati has clutched Siva's arm in alarm and her attendants are fleeing in panic. Siva is seated, calm. With the effortless pressure of his big toe on the top of the cage, he has kept the cage closed and Ravana imprisoned. The carving is exceptionally dramatic. On the northern side Siva is protecting his devotee, who is clutching the Lingam, from the god of death. When Yama wanted to take the soul of this devotee, Siva emerged from the Lingam and here he is shown as he is about to thrust his trident into the body of Yama.

Fig. 2.170. Ellora. Kailas Cave 16. Ravana shaking Kailas. Ca. 750-800. Basalt.

The northern exterior of the temple is extensively carved with deities and structural decorations. One panel depicts Durga killing Buffalo demon (Fig. 2. 172).

The carving depicts Durga with an exceptionally energetic, twisted body. She is thrusting a trident into the chest of a demonic soldier squatting beside the head of the Buffalo. Another panel depicts Nrsimha killing demon Hiranyakashipu. The rarely depicted episode of Sita's abduction shows Ravana carrying her away in a chariot and the bird Jatayu attacking him. Ravana is about to injure the bird. A series of carvings depict the fight between monkey chiefs Sugriva and Vali, Rama killing Vali and Rama and Lakshmana consoling Tara, wife of Vali. Other carvings depict a Buddha-like figure, possibly a Vishnu incarnation, seated under a naga hood, and loving couples. The temple was once embellished with painting, now seen only in traces.

Fig. 2.172. Ellora. Kailas Cave 16. Durga killing buffalo demon. Ca. 750-800. Basalt.

The interior of the *mandapa* is free of figurative sculpture. The ceiling was once painted but the only picture remaining is one near a beam in the south balcony; it depicts a dancing Siva. Groups of four pillars arranged in a square stand near each corner of the *mandapa* hall. The hall has side porches and is connected to the colonnade cut on the left side of the hill by the stone bridge. The vestibule is carved with Somaskanda, Siva and Parvati playing chess, Vishnu, Brahma and the goddess Annapurna on the ceiling. Ganga and Yamuna with three-body bends guard the small sanctum. Their heads are broken. The sanctum with the Lingam is surrounded by extremely thick walls. The Lingam in the shrine is badly mutilated. The shrine is surrounded by a semi-circular open ambulatory passage, lined on the outer margin with five small shrines designed as replicas of the main shrine. The entrance and exit door to the passage flank the entrance of the main shrine.

The flat roof the *mandapa* is carved at the margins with larger elevated *sala* and small square *sikaras*. The flat roof is carved with lotus and four lions facing the cardinal directions. The pyramidal southern-style tower, capped with a

square *sikara*, is 29m (87.3 ft.) above the floor of the courtyard, reaching almost to the top of the rear wall of the pit. The square tiers on the tower, diminishing in size, are decorated with barrel-shaped structures, chaitya windows and various deities.

Six small caves were added to the complex at various times. The Rashtrakuta king Govind III (794-814) commissioned the shrine of the River Goddess at the northwest corner of the court. A huge doorkeeper guards the shrine. Three exceptionally beautiful statues of river goddesses Ganga, Yamuna and Sarasvati stand in a row in the shrine. Ganga, standing between arched pilasters, is particularly beautiful (Fig. 2.173). To her left is Yamuna. The goddess Sarasvati (Fig. 2.174), rarely carved in temples, is seen twice at Ellora. She is also carved as a door guardian in Cave 21.

Fig. 2.173. Ellora. Kailas Cave 16. River Goddess Ganga. Ca. 794-814. Basalt.

Fig. 2.174. Ellora. Kailas Cave 16. Goddess Sarasvati. Ca. 794-814. Basalt.

The Hall of Sacrifice is located in the colonnade excavated in the side escarpment opposite to the carving of Ravana shaking Kailas. It is reached by a flight of steps. The front two pillars of the hall are carved with elegant female figures. In the hall starting on the right wall, the first carving is of Durga seated on a lion (Fig. 2.175). The next, Goddess Chamundi, has lost one left hand. In one of her right hands she holds a trident and in a left hand holds a bowl of sweets, and a snake. In the corner is a horrific scene that sends chills up the spine. Skeletal Kali is sitting with the head of a naked male corpse in her lap and another naked corpse lays her legs. On the back wall Ganesha is sitting, eating sweets from the bowl in his hand.

Fig. 2.175. Ellora. Kailas Cave 16. Hall of sacrifice. Ca. 750-800 CE. Basalt.

The seven mother goddesses follows him. Most of the statues are broken but by their mounts carved below the statue the broken figures can be identified.

At the eastern end are three elegant statues of seated females (Fig 2.176). The female in the center with broken hands and legs appears to be queen of Rashtrakuta king Govind III (794-814). She is flanked by two females bearing *chamara*.

Fig. 2.176. Ellora. Kailas Cave 16. Hall of sacrifice. Rashtrakuta Queen. Ca. 794-814. Basalt.

The Yajana-Shala Cave on the southern escarpment features sculpture in the round with firm, slender bodies. It may have been excavated in about 800. The Paralanka Cave, in the middle of the southern escarpment, is an unfinished four-storey structure. It was joined to the temple by a bridge which is broken now. The Lankeshvara Cave in the northern escarpment on a level with the main temple is reached by a flight of steps located near the Gajalakshmi panel on the Bull Pavilion. It was probably carved in the early ninth

century. It consists of a Nandi *mandapa* with a male deity attended by two females near the *mandapa* and a sanctuary with ambulatory passage. The hall bears short and stumpy pillars, richly carved. The walls of the hall are carved with Nrsimha pulling out the entrails of the demon and the Hindu trinity along with Surya, Ganesha and other gods and goddess, including Siva and Parvati playing chess. The sanctum door is enshrined with the Lingam with Ganga and Yamuna. On the back wall is the Hindu is carved. On the right wall we see Ravana shaking Kailas. On the left wall, a dancing six-armed Siva is carved in bold relief, holding a small drum and a snake in hands that are almost free from the background. With matted hair and a third eye on his forehead, he is wearing a little jewelry and trampling a dwarf. Pillars on the south side are carved with Gangadhara, Siva and Parvati, Ardhanari and Durga — all mutilated. On the faces of the trenches surrounding the rear and the sides of the temple deep incisions were cut to construct multi-level colonnades in the ninth and tenth century. Huge panels are carved in the colonnades with reliefs, mostly depicting Siva, alone or with Parvati or with his vehicle Nandi and other gods. The carvings are not very artistic. This additional space for carving, in addition to all the external and internal surface of the various structures, was a bonus of the innovative design of the complex.

After witnessing the grandeur and beauty of Kailas a visit to other caves comes as an anticlimax — except for Caves 21 and 29. The Hindus lost any interest in caves after excavating Kailas, the grandest of all temples. Caves 17 to 29 were excavated before that. Starting from the middle of the sixth century, Caves 28, 27, and 19 were excavated. These are modest caves without many artistic attributes. Cave 29 and 21 followed along with the other caves. But Cave 29 is a copy of the Elephanta Siva cave; and Cave 21 has the most exquisite sculpture at Ellora. The recent understanding is that the Kalacuri of Aurangabad excavated these caves. This theory is supported by the characteristic bulky females of Kalacuri sculpture in a few caves. The previous view that the Chalukya of Badami excavated the caves at Ellora needs to be re-evaluated.

The porch of Cave 17, situated some distance from Cave 16 (Kailas), was possibly excavated in the seventh century. The porch of the cave is ruined, leaving twelve massive pillars of the hall with carvings of human heads and with female figures on brackets. The porch retains a carving of Vishnu and Brahma. There are carvings of Ganesha, and Durga slaying demon in the hall. The sanctum is enshrined with the Lingam. Cave 18, excavated in the seventh century, retains its porch, and a hall with two square pillars and two pilasters. The pillared vestibule is followed by the sanctum, enshrined with the Lingam. Cave 19 is damaged and incomplete, with pillared hall, square shrine with Lingam and ambulatory passage.

Some distance away in the next group are three caves (Fig. 2.177).

Fig. 2.177. Ellora. Caves 20 and 21. Ca. 6-7ᵗʰ Century. Basalt.

The incomplete Cave 20A has a court. On one side of the cave façade, a carving resembling the Jain yaksa Matanga can be seen. There is a halo behind his head and two flying figures in the corner. It may have been added later, or else the cave is a Jain cave. The verandah has four pillars with an unrecognizable shallow carving on the capitals and empty cells at either end. The main door, flanked by two additional doors, leads into the hall. Some believe that the hall was added later when the Jains were actively excavating caves at the north end.

The almost-destroyed Cave 20B is situated on a higher elevation with steps to reach it. It has a ruined pedestal in front, behind which is a small verandah with two huge, thick pillars, square at the base and with bulbous capitals. Possibly these are pillars from a hall which is completely destroyed. The carvings of Ganesha and Durga on the side walls are in poor condition. The cell entrance is flanked by two huge guardians who are reminiscent of the Buddhist Vijarapani and Avalokiteshvara. Both hands of the statue on the right are broken. The statue on the left holds an unrecognizable object in his right hand. Two curvaceous females holding unrecognizable objects in their right hands accompany them. The highly decorated cell entrance door bears another small pair of figures at the bottom. The pedestal in the cell with ambulatory passage around it is empty.

Cave 21, one of the early caves, possibly excavated in the late sixth century, bears the finest sculpture, reflecting the beauty of the golden age of Indian sculpture with the volume typical of Kalacuri sculpture figures. A pedestal in the court-yard bears a monolithic Bull on the plinth. In the northern corner of the court is a small Ganesha shrine.

The right end corner of the cave is carved with a graceful Goddess Ganga with her hips slightly thrown to the side, standing with a dwarf attendant and a female *chamara* bearer (Fig. 2.178). Flying figures are carved on the upper cor-

ners. Yamuna is standing on a tortoise on the other side.

Fig. 2.178. Ellora. Cave 21. Ca. 6-7ᵗʰ Century. Basalt.

A low parapet wall on the façade of the cave is carved with structural decorations, elephants and *mithuna* couples. The parapet wall is carved above with four massive, richly decorated pillars and a pilaster at each end. The capitals of the pillars are carved with foliage decorations. Charming damsels with slight bends and body curves decorate the pillars as bracket figures. Above the capitals of the pillars, mythological creatures and a frieze of a floral scroll and a dwarf are carved. Behind the parapet is a hall. The hall has a chapel on each end separated from the hall by two pillars with square shafts and cushion capitals. In the left chapel on the west wall, Kattrikeya is standing with his mount, the peacock, on one side and flanked by goat-headed gods and flying figures in the upper corner. On the back wall of the chapel is a large panel depicting the marriage of Siva and Parvati. On the left is Brahma, negotiating with the father of Parvati, who is standing beside her. Next Siva is holding Parvati's hand with Ganesha in between and Bhringi behind Parvati, followed by Brahma officiating at the marriage near a sacred fire, and Parvati's father standing between Siva and Parvati. Vishnu with conch is one of the spectators. Other carvings show Parvati standing as an ascetic holding a rosary to perform penance to gain Siva as her husband. Siva is shown approaching her to test her loyalty. To the right is a tall female, in front of whom a youth is coming out of a crocodile's mouth. He is Siva, saved by Parvati. In one end of the chapel Durga is carved slaying the buffalo demon. She is holding a sword, a trident, a shield and a buffalo head in her hands. On one side of the shrine large panels are carved. One panel shows Ravana shaking Kailas. Ravana has five heads, one of which appears like that of boar. The chapel on the other side has horrific carvings of Kala and Kali. Kala holds, in two of his remaining hands, a curved knife, and a man in another hand. He is dancing with joy. Kali has a human head in her hand and a Vidyadhara is holding a cup to collect the blood.

A child and a man are standing by. On the back wall is Ganesha. In his hands he holds a battle-ax, sweets, a rosary and a broken tooth. Next to him are the seven mother goddesses. They can be recognized with the mounts carved under them. The last one is Virabhadra. A panel on the next wall shows eight-armed Nataraja accompanied by Parvati, musicians and Bhringi near Siva's leg. Above are the guardians of the directions, on their mounts. Three hands of Siva are broken, yet the figure displays vigor and energy. With his attractive and dramatic pose he captivates the audience.

Fig. 2.179. Ellora. Cave 21. Chamara bearer.

Ca. 6-7ᵗʰ Century. Basalt.

The shrine in the center of the rear wall is separated from the hall by two pillars with cushion capitals and square abaci. Two lovely *chamara* bearers are carved in front of the pillars (Fig. 2.179). The doorway of the shrine is profusely decorated with *mithuna* couples, auspicious symbols, mythological creatures and chaitya windows. The sanctum is enshrined with the Lingam, with a circumambulatory passage. On the other side of the shrine, the carving depicts Siva and Parvati playing chess in the company of female and male attendants. Parvati looks irritated because Siva is cheating in the game.

Cave 22 has a ruined Nandi pavilion in the court. A shrine in the southern wall of the court has the seven mothers, Ganesha, and Kala. The pillared hall has chambers on the walls, a vestibule and then a shrine. Among other sculptures in the shrine is an image of Ganga. Caves 23 and 24 are small shrines without any special features.

Cave 25, a short distance away from Cave 24, has a large court in front with a shrine in the right wall. The front portion of the hall has been destroyed. The hall has massive pillars decorated with *mithuna* couples, peacocks, and lotus, and capitals decorated with vases and foliage. The ceiling of the antechamber is carved with an image of Surya. The shrine is square. Cave 26 is similar to Cave 25. The sanctum with ambulatory passage is enshrined with the Lingam. Cave 27, similar to Cave 26, is in poor condition, as is Cave 28. It has a hall and a shrine. The shrine door is decorated with guardians and Vidyadharas. The outer wall has an image of Am-

bika, attendant of the Jain Tirthankara. It is possibly a later addition. Beside the cave is a waterfall and picnic ground.

Cave 29, a short distance away from Cave 28, was built in 580-642. It resembles the Siva Cave at Elephanta with its cross-shaped layout. The same craftsmen moved to Ellora to excavate this and certain other caves after their work at Elephanta was done. The façade of the cave has two pillars and two pilasters (Fig. 2.180).

Fig. 2.180. Ellora. Cave 29. Ca. 6-7ᵗʰ Century. Basalt.

A short flight of steps flanked by roaring lions pouncing on elephants leads to the cave. One elephant is missing. The central hall has four vertical rows of pillars and the arms of the cross have two horizontal rows of pillars. At the widest part, the cave is 45.7m (140 ft.) wide. The sanctum is placed at the far end of the two central rows of the pillars, near the back wall, with four entrances like the sanctum at Elephanta cave. Huge, tall doorkeepers in the company of females guard the shrine entrances. The sanctum is enshrined with the Lingam. The walls of the hall are covered with large panels carved with gigantic figures similar to those at Elephanta but most are artistically inferior. One side of the entrance is carved with an eight-armed Ravana shaking Mount Kailas while Siva is cuddling Parvati, seated next to him. All the attendants with Siva and Parvati appear unaware of the shaking (Fig. 2.181).

Fig. 2.181. Ellora. Cave 29. Ravana shaking Kailas. Ca. 6-7ᵗʰ. Century. Basalt.

On the other side Siva is shown killing Andhaka. He has stretched the elephant skin over his head with four hands, and has sword, bowl and snake and in other hands. He looks furious, with bulging eyes. Parvati is standing to his left. On the left Siva, looking ferocious with bulging eyes, is slaying the elephant demon. On the south the verandah has a circular sacrificial pit. There is a colossal image of a goddess, possibly Ganga. In the south verandah is a carving of Lakulisa sitting on a lotus supported by two serpents. He is holding a club in hand. On the other side Siva is dancing his destructive dance while the gods are watching (Fig. 2.182). Parvati with her attendants is sitting alongside. Other carvings in huge panels in the hall include the marriage of Siva and Parvati, where Siva is standing holding the hand of a beautiful and attractive Parvati; and Siva and Parvati playing chess, watched by many spectators. Below a majestic bull is carved. The exits at the end of the arm of the cross on one side lead to a waterfall and on the other side to a few minor shrines, and ultimately to the outside of the cave.

Fig. 2.182. Ellora. Cave 29. Nataraja. Ca. 6-7ᵗʰ Century. Basalt.

Ganesha Lena, a group of five small shrines, is located 100m (300 yards) above Cave 29. They are carved with images of Ganesha, Siva, Vishnu and Brahma. Still higher up is the Yageshvari group of small shrines, possibly carved in the eleventh and twelfth centuries; they bear no artistic carvings.

At the north end of the Hindu caves are five Jain caves in a group. Excavated in the ninth and early tenth centuries, the caves contain beautiful, detailed and finely polished sculpture. Most of the sculpture is repeated again and again with slight variations. Possibly all the caves were excavated during the regime of Rashtrakuta king Amoghavarsha (819-881), a great patron of Jainism. Although the Jains believe in twenty-four Tirthankaras, they have carved images of only a few of them, chiefly Adhinatha, the first Tirthankara, Santinatha, the sixteenth Tirthankara, Parshvanath (who preceded Mahavir) and Gommateshvara (Bahubali), who represents Mahavir in all the carvings. A Jain Yaksa Matanga carved in

some caves with his vehicle Tirthankaras elephant was earlier misidentified as Indra, and his consort Yakshi Sidhiaka as Indrani. Yakshi Chakreshvari, attendant of Tirthankara Adhinatha is rarely carved.

Caves 30, 31, 32 and 33 are a complex of interconnected caves with only two entrances (Fig. 2.183). The complex is entered through Cave 30 and exited through Cave 33. The whole complex, created during the regime of Rashtrakuta king Amoghavarsha (819-881), was possibly intended as a huge complex with many side excavations and shrines, as in Kailas. It is so interconnected and complex that arbitrarily it is classified into four caves.

Cave 30 is the first cave of the series, also called Chotta (small) Kailas. The entrance gateway to the cave is a simple, solid extension bearing a curved eave. The interior wall surface of the gateway is carved with Tirthankara and a twelve-armed Chakreshvari, attendant of Adhinatha. She is holding a lotus, discus, mace, conch, and sword, and wearing elaborate jewelry. Her mount, the eagle, is carved below. There are small figures of Yaksa and Mahavir. The temple in the center of courtyard is a monolithic miniature copy of Kailas temple (Fig. 2.184).

Fig. 2.183. Ellora. Complex of Jain Caves 30, 31, 32 and 33. Ca. 9ᵗʰ Century. Basalt.

Fig. 2.184. Jain Caves 30. Temple. Ca. 9ᵗʰ Century. Basalt.

The façade of the hill surrounding the shrine is excavated with galleries at two levels. Near the entrance gate, due insufficient height, there is only one storey. The first gallery façade is decorated with elephants in front profile. The second gallery façade on the rear is decorated with Jain figures.

The square temple bears square extension porches on all sides with two circular pillars with bulbous cushion tops. Only the front and rear porches have stairs to reach the temple. The façade is without decoration. A huge stone slab carved with a seated Tirthankara is visible from outside. The Dravidian-style pyramidal tower with square tiers is carved with chaitya windows and *sala* on the front façade. It is capped with an octagonal *sikara* (Fig. 2.185). As in Kailas there is a life-size elephant on one side of temple and on the other side a 9.14m (32 ft.) decorated column with four devotees sitting back to back, facing the four directions on the top.

Fig. 2.185. *Jain Caves 30. Temple. Rear view of the tower. Ca. 9th Century. Basalt.*

On one side of the temple a small, unfinished excavation in the lower storey of the mountain sidewall is Cave 31. It has a hall with four pillars. Mahavir is enshrined in the shrine in the back wall.

Fig. 2.186. *Ellora. Cave 31. Mahavir in shrine guarded by Parshvanath and Bahubali. Ca. 9th Century. Basalt.*

Walls flanking the entrance door are carved on one side with Tirthankara Parshvanath standing under seven hoods of a cobra and an attendant holding a parasol above. He is surrounded by a rider on a buffalo, a rider on a tiger and some flying figures. The other side is pictures Bahubali, with vines

growing on his limbs, attended by females, a pair of worshippers and flying figures in the corners (Fig. 2.186).

The flying figures in most of the carvings appear to be hanging awkwardly in the air. On the side wall is a carving of Yakshi Sidhiaka, attendant of Mahavir (Fig. 2.187). There are many carvings of Sidhiaka in these caves, but possibly this is one of the most beautiful. She is sitting under a mango tree on her carrier, the lion, surrounded by attendants and peacocks on both sides. Yaksa Matanga, attendant of Mahavir and the consort of Sidhiaka, is riding an elephant, flanked by attendants.

Fig. 2.187. *Ellora. Cave 31. Yakshi Sidhiaka. Ca. 9th Century. Basalt.*

There are two more small excavations with pillars at the entrance. One excavation has a carving of Bahubali and the other has a carving of Parshvanath (Fig. 2.187). Attempts have been made to carve an erect phallus on him. His attendant Yakshi, with a child on her lap, is seated on a lion (Fig. 2.188).

Fig. 2.188. *Ellora. Cave 30. Tirthankara Parshvanath. Ca. 9th Century. Basalt.*

Fig. 2.189. Ellora. Cave 30. Sidhiaka. Ca. 9th Century. Basalt.

Fig. 2.190. Ellora. Cave 32. Tirthankara Parshvanath. Ca. 9th Century. Basalt.

Cave 32 lies on the back of Cave 31. As the height of the hill at this point had increased considerably, Cave 32 is excavated with two stories. A climb of a few steps leads to the entrance of the ground storey of Cave 32. It is a large square hall with eight square pillars near the periphery. There are a few unfinished cells in the side walls and the pilasters of the front verandahs are carved with two huge images of the sixteenth Tirthankara, Santinatha. On the back wall Mahavir is seated on a lion throne in the shrine. From the entrance

of the ground storey, a stair on the left leads to a verandah with two pillars. Each end of the verandah has a shrine with Tirthankara. The back wall of one shrine is carved with Parshvanath surrounded by worshippers and riders on lions and Buffalo (Fig. 2.190). A tall, lean and beautiful attendant is holding parasol above the head of the Tirthankara (Fig. 2.191). The other shrine is carved with Bahubali with female attendants, worshippers and flying figures.

Fig. 2.191. Ellora. Cave 32. Attendant of Tirthankara Parshvanath. Ca. 9th Century. Basalt.

A further climb of a few steps leads to a large square court with twelve pillars with an aisle around the court. It is fully furnished with beautifully decorated pillars with a molded base, sixteen-sided shaft, cushion capitals and bands of flowers. In the aisles on one side a huge figure of Yakshi Sidhiaka is seated on her carrier lion, a under mango tree with attendants standing beside. The lump on her thigh appears to be the body of a broken child statue. Facing Sidhiaka is huge figure of Yaksa Matanga sitting on a small squatted elephant. In the center of each wall is a shrine. In one side Mahavir is seated on lion throne and is guarded by Matanga and Sidhiaka shrine. In another shrine Mahavir is seated with a Jina on lion throne with triple umbrella over head. The sidewalls are also carved with Bahubali with female attendants and others. The ceiling bears fragment of paintings. In the corner of the hall is a small excavation with four pillars and a shrine in the back wall with Mahavir. At the right ends of the verandah Chakreshvari is carved holding a manuscript and wheel. Opposite to her Sidhiaka is carved riding a lion. At the left a passage is cut leading to the upper floor of Cave 33.

Cave 33 is also two-storied cave. At the southwest corner of the cave steps descend to the ground floor. Mahavir is enshrined in the main shrine with Parshvanath and Bahubali flanking the shrine. There are carvings of Matanga and Sidhiaka in the verandah. The upper floor is huge pillared hall similar to the upper floor of cave 32 with numerous carvings of Mahavir and Parshvanath. Shrines are excavated in the center of each wall. One is carved with Mahavir with triple umbrella above and halo behind head and a Tirthankara with halo behind head (Fig. 2.192).

Fig. 2.192. Ellora. Cave 32. Mahavir with Jina. Ca. 9ᵗʰ Century. Basalt.

Another beautifully decorated shrine guarded by Bahu-bali and Parshvanath is enshrined with Mahavir (Fig. 2.193).

Fig. 2.193. Ellora. Cave 32. Mahavir with Jina. Ca. 9ᵗʰ Century. Basalt.

Fig. 2.194. Ellora. Cave 33. Sidhiaka seated on lion. Ca. 9ᵗʰ Century. Basalt.

There are many carvings of Bahubali and Parshvanath. Sidhiaka seated on lion is holding a child with a broken head on her lap (Fig. 2.194). There are fragments of many faded original paintings on the ceiling. One such painting shows two sensual *apsaras* entertaining a royal (Fig. 2.195).

Fig. 2.195. Ellora. Cave 33. Painting on ceiling. Ca. 9ᵗʰ Century. Basalt.

Cave 34 is located a short distance from Cave 33. It is small, with incomplete carvings on the front pillars. The verandah and the entrance door are carved with small figures. Mahavir is enshrined in the cell, with Matanga and Sidhiaka flanking the cell. On the side wall Parshvanath and Gom-mateshvara are carved.

With the excavation of Jain caves in the ninth and tenth century at Ellora, the excavation of caves by Hindus came to an end in India, although some minor shrines were excavated in eleventh and twelfth century. They seem to have lost interest in caves. The challenge of building monumental, tall, freestanding stone structural temples by Hindu monarchs was by then in full swing.

The Buddhists lost control of the society and were confined to west India. They were driven away by destruction of their libraries and monasteries and by the slaughter of Buddhist monks by Muslim invaders into their home-lands, Bengal, Bihar and Orissa.

After carving the world's largest freestanding monolithic statue in Karnataka, in the tenth century, and constructing temples at Mount Abu, Rajasthan in the eleventh century, the Jains virtually ceased temple-building activity till twentieth century, when they constructed the Digambara marble temple in Delhi.

Printed in the United States
By Bookmasters